Diagnosing management training
and development needs

Concepts and techniques

CONTENTS

INTRODUCTION

How to cope with change, and how to prepare the enterprise for adjusting to environmental changes, is an issue faced by managers in any enterprise. That managers must be able to understand what is happening in their environment is a truism. Changes occur in technology, products, competition, consumer taste, financial markets, audio-visual communication, basic and technical education, labour markets, government regulations, prices of raw materials and energy, international business relations, and in many other areas. From country to country and from sector to sector, these changes take different shapes and their significance and pace are also different. There are "high-tech" industries and "smokestack" industries. There are booming areas and depressed areas. There are highly industrialised countries and underdeveloped countries. Despite these differences, at the present time managers everywhere in the world have to cope, in their own way and within their own environment, with an unprecedented amount of, and an accelerated pace of, change. Many of them are overwhelmed by this change. Old recipes are no longer helpful, foreign models are difficult to imitate and past experience fails to provide answers to new questions such as how to prepare the company for future developments in telecommunications, or what collaborative deal with a number of foreign partners will give the company the most interesting long-term competitive advantage.

When a manager realises that routine job experience no longer provides answers to new questions, he or she may start looking around for information, advice and training. The manager may find an answer or a useful idea, or be bitterly disappointed. Indeed, information, advice and training can be relevant or irrelevant, useful or useless, effective or ineffective, in helping managers to cope with their specific problems of organisational change.

The purpose of this publication is to assist in preparing relevant, useful and effective management training and development through professionally designed and executed diagnosis of the managers' and the organisations' real needs. There is no shortage of courses and other training and development programmes for managers in training centres, universities and consulting firms, and within companies. However, many of these programmes are too general and abstract, try to serve too many different clients, fail to address issues of business practice in a way that could guide managers in solving their particular problems, or describe business and management practices as they were 10-20 years ago.

This does not mean that there would be no identification of needs whatsoever when a course or seminar is first introduced. In most cases some needs assessment has taken place. But this needs assessment is often superficial and incomplete, biased and methodologically poor, and is carried out by inexperienced trainers and assistants, without any involvement of the managers concerned. "Pinpointing precise training and development needs in the management ranks may never be as clear-cut as it is in the technical area. But it is a process that can be more rigorous – much more rigorous – than it has been in the past."[1]

In other cases, the view taken is static in that it tries to react to current difficulties, and little attempt is made to assess the importance of future business trends and prospects for the training and development of managers. "Preparing managers for the future" is a challenging goal to which everyone adheres with enthusiasm, but which is being translated into specific programmes and actions with considerable difficulty. One of the issues is that no one can say exactly what the future will hold, yet there is a consensus that despite this uncertainty it is now that managers must start preparing themselves for the future. Growing emphasis has to be placed on flexibility, mobility, adaptability, quick identification of emerging new needs, an increased capability to detect and understand significant environmental changes, and an ability to speed up processes of individual and collective learning. "From all indications, people entering the workforce will switch jobs, if not occupations and industries, several times in the course of their working lives".[2] Thus, needs assessment faces a wide range of new demands and challenges.

There is another matter of serious concern, however. A considerable amount of management training is done in developing countries, which have great expectations of the development of human resources. An improvement of their management capabilities in all economic and social sectors is generally regarded as one of the main ways of combating underdevelopment. Developing countries need more properly educated and trained managers to take over from the expatriate managers and advisers who are still in post, to apply management styles that are compatible with local cultures, and to accept full responsibility for running the business and the public affairs of the country. Yet in the developing countries current diagnoses of training needs leave much to be desired, as the Economic Development Institute of the World Bank pointed out in a workshop on training needs in Africa: "Poor and inadequate assessment of training needs leads to incredible waste of scarce resources that Africa can ill afford. Training is applied to problems that do not require training as the solution. Managers are subjected to programmes that are irrelevant to their need because of lack of skills in assessing trainability. Most training materials are inappropriate since they are not based on clearly identified training needs."[3]

Therefore the benefits from more professional needs assessment can be quite considerable in the developing countries.

All in all, a needs analysis that is properly done can have a profound impact on the organisation and its performance in any economic setting. It influences managers by increasing the relevance of training to their jobs. It improves the quality of training programmes, as well as the effectiveness of the training function. Finally, good needs assessment improves organisational performance by discovering training and non-training problems and areas of influence.

Outline

In this publication we have tried to tackle a wide range of issues involved in the concepts and practices of needs diagnosis in the field of management training and development.

Part I is a short introduction to the concept of training and development needs. It explains why and in what context needs assessment is necessary, how it relates to organisational change and problem-solving, and what principle dimensions of needs ought to be kept in mind in diagnosing needs.

Part II is a compendium of approaches, techniques and tools suitable for identifying and diagnosing needs. It starts by presenting a few widely used generic approaches to needs assessment (chapter 3). Particular techniques are then grouped in three chapters depending on whether they are generally applied to assess the needs of the individual manager (chapter 4), of management teams and groups (chapter 5) or of whole organisations (chapter 6). It is emphasised that in practice these techniques are always combined and interrelated and can complement each other in many different ways.

Part III was designed as a practical guide for applying and improving needs diagnosis in various contexts. Experience shows that four contextual situations are most common in practice, and therefore each of them is covered in one chapter: needs assessment practices of enterprises (chapter 7), special surveys and studies of needs at sectoral, national and international levels (chapter 8), needs assessment by management institutes and centres for their own programme design and development aimed at improving the quality of services to business and public sector clients (chapter 9), and specific problems faced in diagnosing the needs of new entrepreneurs and small enterprise owners and managers (chapter 10).

Some useful appendices are enclosed as an aid in using rating techniques and in choosing among the many diagnostic techniques that are currently available.

The audience

This book should be of interest to all those who are keen to increase the effectiveness of management training and development. In the text we often refer to "the analyst" and we mean by it any person who wants to gain a deeper insight into management training and development needs with a practical purpose in mind. Among them will be:

o   management teachers and trainers, working with business schools, management institutes, public administration institutes, productivity centres, small enterprise development organisations and similar institutions;

o   personnel, training and human resource development managers and professional trainers in companies, both private and public, and in governmental agencies and social organisations;

o   management and business consultants and organisation development (OD) specialists, who use training as one of their intervention techniques;

o   specialists in organisation and methods, management services and systems analysis and design;

o   general and functional managers who are keen to get a deeper insight into training, improve their own training, and increase the standards of management training and development in their organisations.

How to use the book

First, the book can be read and studied for a better understanding of the concepts and techniques involved in assessing the training and development needs of managers. In this case, the reader will probably read part I, skim through part II and read that chapter in part III which is closest to his or her work situation and professional interest.

Second, the book can be used for more detailed study of the topic by trainers and consultants. It may serve as reading or course material for trainers' or consultants' training, or it may be used by individuals in self-development. In this case, part II should receive considerable attention. Some of the techniques can be practised, and simulation exercises in needs assessment can be mounted and carried out among the trainers participating in a course, or with managers who will agree to participate in this sort of action learning.

Third, and most importantly, the book can help to improve needs assessment practices in the four contexts described by the four chapters in part III: in public and private enterprises and other organisations; in management institutions and consulting firms; in assisting new entrepreneurs and small enterprises; and in designing and running special surveys. For this purpose, a detailed study is required. In addition to the various conceptual approaches discussed in part III, in this instance the book will provide the reader, in part II and the appendices, with a great deal of detailed information on a wide range of techniques, as well as on criteria for their choice and guide-lines for their use.

As regards terminology, the terms "analysing", "assessing", "determining", "diagnosing" and "identifying" training and development needs are used interchangeably in this book in accordance with prevailing current practice.

On opening this book, the reader should keep in mind that our objective is not to provide specific answers to the *what* (content) of management training and development needs. Different managers and organisations have different needs. The same person will have different needs at different points of his or her career and in facing new sorts of management problems. Our book focuses on the *how* (methodology) of effective needs assessment. We have tried to suggest approaches and provide methodological tools based on sound experience, but not to provide a blueprint for exactly what to do in every situation. The reader will have to choose among these approaches and tools, combining and adapting them with imagination to fit the given context.

---

[1] R. Mirabile, D. Caldwell and C. O'Reilley: "Soft skills, hard numbers", in *Training* (Minneapolis), Aug. 1987, p. 53.

[2] D. Feuer: "The skill gap", in *Training*, Dec. 1987, p. 35.

[3] *EDI Review* (Washington, DC), Oct. 1986, p. 5.

CONCEPTS, PRINCIPLES, APPROACHES

NATURE AND SCOPE OF NEEDS ASSESSMENT

1

1.1 Some basic concepts

In this publication we are concerned with concepts and techniques of diagnosing management training and development needs. Management training and development are defined as a set of activities whereby practitioners – managers or would-be managers – are assisted in improving their individual competence and performance as well as the organisational environment, with the ultimate goal of raising the standards of organisational performance. The purpose of needs diagnosis and assessment is therefore to find out what training and development managers actually need and want to receive, and what conditions ought to be created in order to make sure that this training and development will have a practical impact.

Competence or performance?

The two above-mentioned terms – "competence" and "performance" – are concepts that are both equally significant in the context of this publication. The purpose of management training and development is to increase competence for doing certain jobs. However, the development of the manager's competence cannot be an aim in itself and the relevance and usefulness of this competence can be demonstrated only in a work situation, by achieving certain practical results, or a certain level of performance. "Effectiveness in management or administrative jobs requires the assessment of performance of an organisational unit " ... and ... "an individual's competencies are necessary but not sufficient for effective performance in a job."[1]

If competence is low, performance is likely to be low. If competence is high but performance remains low, something is wrong in the organisational and management system, or in the definition and profile of competence. When the competence profile does not fit the job profile, the result is the same as if competence is low. Therefore, competence cannot be viewed as an isolated and abstract phenomenon, outside any organisational or job profile context. In management training and development we are concerned both with competence and with the results that are being, and should be, obtained by applying this competence in a particular business, managerial and human work environment. These results must be reflected in better performance. It is for this reason that businesses and governments are prepared to finance management training and development, whose cost is steadily growing.

In practice, this basic relationship between competence and performance can be rather complex. Experience has provided ample evidence that every improvement in competence is not necessarily followed by a commensurate change in performance. There can be first-class training that produces no practical results. Management and business reality is infinitely more complex, and some determinants of performance may be much stronger than the quality of a training and development programme. They can even annul all results of training. Many readers could tell stories of training programmes and investments whose impact on the organisation was nil.

In addition, there is a more or less important time-lag between training and the use of its results. This time-lag is small in training aimed at immediate results. It can be even reduced to zero in on-the-job training and action learning, where practical results are being achieved directly as an outcome of the training process. However, in preparing for the future, managers need to develop competencies (in forecasting, planning, analysis and understanding of future prospects) that broaden their horizons, acquaint them with new trends in technology and society and prepare them for facing new realities. These competencies may not lead to any immediate improvement of performance but will be critical for future performance. Thus the relationship between competence and performance ought to be viewed (in particular in training for higher-level and more complex managerial jobs) in the proper time perspective.

Factors affecting performance

Let us, therefore, take a closer look at those factors that jointly determine, together with the competence of the individual persons concerned, managerial and organisational performance. The range of these factors can be wide. Typically, many of them can be observed in organisations where managers have had enough training and their competence is judged as normal and satisfactory, but organisational performance is substandard. For example, in the public enterprises of many countries these fairly common impeding forces include low managerial authority, vague definition of responsibility, red tape, distorted criteria for the selection and promotion of managers, poor motivation, and arbitrary interference in the operational matters of the enterprise by political and governmental authorities. In any organisation, including those reputed for their progressive management methods and high standards of performance, thorough analysis may reveal some impeding factors that hamper managerial performance.

Does this imply that management and organisational performance could never be improved by training and developing people? In certain cases, performance problems can be solved by training. This tends to be possible in the case of rather straightforward, mainly technical, problems. For example, training in a new market research technique, or a new system for monitoring clients' orders, may bring about an immediate visible and measurable improvement. In dealing with complex and open-ended organisational problems (which prevail in management practice), however, one usually encounters the presence of some factors and influences that cannot be changed by training alone. An alteration in organisational structure, an enlarged authority, a salary increase, a transfer of a manager to another unit, or some other intervention may be necessary.

Training and non-training interventions

Put in more general terms, there are training problems and non-training problems. Accordingly, there are training interventions and solutions, and non-training interventions and solutions. Their relative importance and "chemistry" differs from case to case and has to be assessed on its own merits. No universal recipe can help. This is what most management and diagnostic surveys conclude if asked to recommend a plan of action for achieving higher performance and better business results. Increasingly, professional consultants and trainers warn against programmes that would ignore one of these two basic dimensions of business and management problems.

For example, several years ago the municipal water supply companies in some Caribbean countries took a decision to improve their bookkeeping standards through better training of accountants. A trainer in accounting was recruited. Before starting any training, however, the trainer insisted on studying the bookkeeping systems used, to determine whether these systems fitted the companies' needs. Management agreed. The accountant found that each company had a different system, mostly following government accounting procedures rather than the commercial accounting functions of a properly managed water supply agency. The needs analysis also indicated that the bookkeepers already knew how to do their work – there was no knowledge or skill gap. The accountant redesigned the accounting system of two water supply agencies and designed a new accounting manual which would also double as a training manual. The bookkeepers in these two companies were then trained to use the new systems. This training was different from that originally envisaged. Once the new system was running properly in two companies, it was transferred to other companies, and their bookkeepers were trained as well. There was general satisfaction with the results obtained by this combination of "non-training" and "training" solutions of a distinct financial management problem.

The distinction between training and non-training interventions can be very subtle. Often a "non-training" solution (e.g. merging two organisational units and abolishing one management position) also has its own training dimension and creates new training needs. More importantly, training and development events can serve as entry points for identifying and developing non-training solutions and getting them accepted by the decision-makers. One often hears that unless salaries are increased, decisions decentralised and certain managers transferred or sacked, any training would be useless. However, such statements may ignore the fact that some of these "non-training" solutions can be prepared and promoted by the training of those decision-makers who can consider, negotiate or approve such changes. Training may even be the only way of explaining the need for an important policy or systems change to the decision-makers, and getting it recognised by them.

Thus, a non-training problem may be defined as such only within certain limits and from a certain point of view. A supervisor cannot change the company's wage system; the supervisor's low salary or distorted bonus scheme may be a "non-training" factor affecting his or her performance. However, there are decision-makers in the company who can be made aware, through training, of this problem and of alternative solutions that are available to them. Of course there must be a will to make changes and the courage to take decisions. If some non-training solutions have been identified as necessary but there is reluctance to adopt them, it may be that no training will help. Maybe it will take a serious crisis within the organisation to open the decision-makers' eyes and make them receptive to changes that can no longer be delayed.

These points are demonstrated in a diagram (figure 1.1) where the main types of interventions (or solutions) in developing managers and improving organisational performance are related to each other, while a distinction is made between training and non-training interventions. This diagram indicates only approximate relationships and not exact proportions. It includes seven types of interventions for increasing competence and improving performance. Each of these interventions is somehow related to the issue of training and non-training needs, as discussed below.

The seven types of intervention for improving performance

Management education provides students of management or practising managers with basic or advanced management knowledge and skills required for a wide range of managerial jobs in unknown organisational contexts. It is a pre-employment activity in most cases. But it also includes post-experience or further education, which prepares managers for widening or changing the scope of their competence and responsibilities at various points in their career. Therefore management education is not concerned with solving the problems (including training needs) of a specific job or organisational unit. However, the

Figure 1.1.   Interventions for improving performance

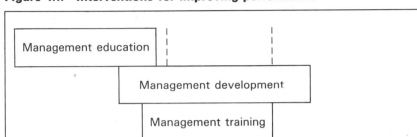

knowledge and skills acquired in a specific programme of management education can be directly applicable to specific jobs. For this reason management education programmes are also used in certain cases as a response to quite specific training and development needs.

Management development is a complex and continuous process providing a wide range of activities and learning opportunities for improving managerial competence and performance. It is job and organisation related, but uses a variety of measures and techniques to develop the manager's total personality and ability to handle both present and future tasks. In addition to training interventions and programmes, management development makes use of managerial career planning, job rotation and planned promotion, coaching and counselling, working on new projects, action learning, motivation for personal growth, self-development, improvement of leadership and communication styles, working with and learning from consultants, participation in organisation development programmes and exercises, and so on.

Management development is an essentially open concept: it would make use of any suitable tool or method likely to increase the manager's effectiveness and efficiency. That is why it is impossible to give an exhaustive definition of what management development includes and what it does not. For example, transferring a manager to a new job may be a distinct contribution to personal development or simply a transfer with no developmental impact. It may even have a negative effect if the manager's personal development opportunities are thus reduced.

Management training is sometimes seen in a narrow way, involving only the acquisition and improvement of practical skills in the use of job-related management techniques and methods. More often, however, this term is used in a broader sense and embraces other developmental activities as well. Training can take place either off the job (in courses and seminars) or on the job (by practising certain methods and techniques in real work situations).

In making these comments we have intentionally refrained from defining the exact difference between, and limits of, management development and management training. Indeed, this would be difficult and probably artificial. Also, many people speak about management training when in fact they mean management development. To avoid semantic and definitional problems, it is often better to use the combined term "management training and development". To be brief, when we refer in this book to "training" or "management training", we also mean "management development".

Experiential learning is the process of drawing lessons from practical work experience in order to improve work methods and effectiveness. Experiential learning occurs on the job, on condition that the work content and objectives provide opportunities for learning. There may be no more learning if the same tasks are repeated many times over a long period of time. Experiential learning depends, as discussed later in more detail, on the individual person's ability and keenness to learn from experience: two persons may draw different lessons from the same experience.

A great deal of experiential learning occurs at work normally and naturally, without any special planning for management development. However, an important technique of management development is the engineering of practical situations in which managers will learn better, more and faster than in other situations. Experiential learning then becomes a tool of management development. Action learning (see section 4.9 for more details) provides an example of a management development approach based on these principles.

Techniques such as action learning combine training and non-training solutions. The managers involved work on practical tasks chosen because of their distinct learning implications. At the same time, these tasks aim at specific practical measures (non-training solutions) required for improving the performance of an organisation.

Organisation development (OD) is normally defined as a set of activities directed to increasing overall organisational effectiveness and health, based on the concepts and approaches of behavioural science. OD focuses on issues such as organisational climate, information sharing, communication, team building, collaborative relationships between units, and so on. Special attention is paid to the identification and change of values, attitudes, interpersonal relations and organisational processes.

The non-training needs and solutions identified as essential in connection with training needs assessment are often in areas that can be handled by OD. Conversely, in examining and improving organisational climate and processes, OD often uncovers training needs and suggests training as an intervention for improving performance. OD is therefore also used as a needs assessment technique (see section 6.8).

Improvements in organisational systems and practices are typical non-training interventions for improving effectiveness and performance. They can be introduced by higher management decisions, or by the initiative of individuals or teams responsible for particular organisational tasks. Examples are changes in organisational structures and procedures, new computer hardware and software, new planning and control techniques, new systems of records and management information, changed wage schemes and systems, and so on. Necessary personnel changes, such as transfers, promotions, demotions, terminations, and redefinition of authority and responsibility, also belong to this group. Improvements in systems and practices are "hard" and tangible measures as distinct from OD which focuses on the "soft" and not so easily identifiable aspects of organisational behaviour and interpersonal relations (e.g. improved communication and sharing of information). However, the relationship between these two groups of interventions is very close and they usually complement each other.

We have seen that, on the one hand, improvements in organisational systems and practices are often identified as non-training needs, those which ought to be examined in greater depth and met if the training envisaged is to have any sense and impact. On the other hand, changes in systems and practices are a major source of training needs (people need training to be able to work with new systems and techniques).

Management consulting is mentioned in our review of training and non-training interventions for several reasons. First, a consultant can (but does not have to) be brought in by management to assist with the interventions described above. For example, an in-plant training programme for supervisors (including the relevant training needs assessment) can be developed and implemented:

Figure 1.2. Key characteristics of the seven types of interventions

Concept structure	Management education	Management development	Management training	Experiential learning	Organisation development	Improvement in organisation systems and practice	Management consulting
1	2	3	4	5	6	7	8
DEFINITION	Formal learning process which helps managers to acquire and develop mainly basic or advanced knowledge and to a lesser degree skills for a wide range of managerial jobs	Planned integral, comprehensive and ongoing process of developing managers' abilities and organisation environment at all levels in order to improve organisational performance	Formal learning process which helps managers to acquire and develop mainly practical skills and abilities to manage, and to a lesser degree knowledge and attitudes under well-defined training needs	Process of learning by solving open-ended problems in organisations with emphasis on acquiring skills for analysing and solving future problems	Process of planned and purpose-oriented development of the human side of organisations as well as their norms, culture and psychological climate using behavioural science to improve the general organisational performance	Process of planned introduction of new organisation structures and systems, including management techniques and procedures	Process of providing professional and independent assistance to help in problem identification and solving and to improve general management competence
OBJECTIVES	To enable people to enter the managerial profession and to cope with a large number of broadly defined tasks in different and organisational contexts	Improve managers' performance and potential for promotion. Management team building within the organisation. Improving organisational climate and opportunities	Improve skills in accordance with well-defined jobs and tasks and for immediate application. The nature and volume of new knowledge is defined by practical tasks	Improve managerial competence through identification and solving real organisational problems	Improve organisational performance, integrate organisational and individual objectives, introduce positive organisational changes to achieve organisational goals	Improve organisation systems and practices, better management technology, information systems, procedures and communication	Improve organisational performance through consultants' intervention, assist in practical implementation, suggest solutions, upgrade managerial abilities
ORIENTATION	People oriented, aimed to improve the manager's system of knowledge covering the broad range of managerial disciplines	People and task oriented, aimed to develop performance of all managers in accordance with organisational objectives	Task oriented, aimed at specific, well-defined jobs or functions	People and action oriented, aimed at improving practical abilities to identify and solve real organisational problems	Aimed to improve organisation system and behaviour rather than individuals, and to introduce changes	Aimed to improve organisation system and structure, opportunities to use advanced managerial skills and talent	Aimed to solve specific organisational problems or improve specific parts of the organisation, to introduce changes and to develop problem-solving capabilities
EVALUATION	Impact on organisation effectiveness can be logically traced, but not proved	Certain results can be immediate and easily measured if component of management education in the development process is not essential. Otherwise, results should be considered in the long term	Results can be immediate and can be easily traced and evaluated	Results can be immediate and can be easily traced and measured	Results can be immediate and easily traced and measured	Results can be both immediate and long term, and are easily traced and measured	Results can be immediate and can be easily traced and measured in the whole organisation
CLIENTS	Students, as a rule without or with little management experience, often too young. In some cases also, experienced managers	All managers, and would-be managers, within the organisation	Mostly practising individual managers or those who are being prepared to enter management	Managers, sometimes technical, non-managerial personnel	Organisation and its human components, management teams	Organisation structures, systems ('hardware'), managers	Managers and non-managerial personnel, organisation or its parts

○ with the firm's own resources;

○ by a management consulting firm or training institution; or

○ by combining these two approaches.

Second, the process of management consulting, if carried out in a participative manner involving the managers concerned, is not only a problem-solving but simultaneously a learning intervention and a contribution to developing managers. Third, it is quite typical for consulting assignments dealing with specific organisational problems to address both non-training and training aspects of each problem. A proper use of consultants thus helps to bring to light the relationship between non-training and training interventions and to solve this relationship case by case, in order to implement practical im-provements and make them long-lasting.[2]

These brief comments show that the relationships between the seven types of interventions are quite complex and that there is some overlapping. Comprehensive programmes of organisational performance improvement or restructuring may use all these interventions. Also, the terms concerned tend to be used in various ways, sometimes with little care for precision. This should be kept in mind in reading this book. We will frequently refer to training and non-training needs, interventions or solutions. In practice these needs, interventions or solutions can be tackled in many different ways, through various combinations of the types of intervention technique described above (and some others).

The key characteristics of the seven types of intervention are summarised in figure 1.2.

1.2 A general model for diagnosing needs

We can now try to present training and development needs in the form of a simple model. The idea of such a model is not new: various models have been used and some will be known to the readers. However, although the model shows only the very basic relationships, it provides a useful framework for understanding the concept of needs and dealing with the whole range of practical issues involved in needs diagnosis.

Five different situations

Our basic model (figure 1.3) shows that in defining training needs we have to start by identifying and comparing two levels of performance: the standard (desired, optimum, future, planned) level (Ps) and the current (existing, real) level (Pc). The difference between these two levels is the performance gap (Pg). This relationship is shown in case X.

Figure 1.3. Basic model of the training and development needs concept

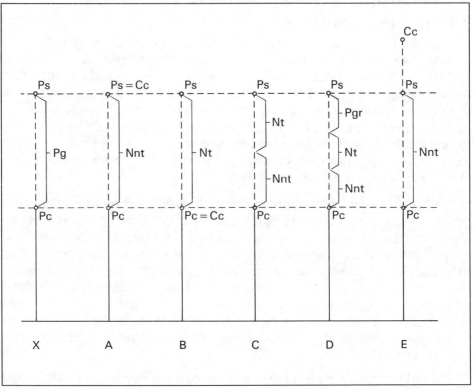

As discussed in section 1.1, to improve performance we normally have to deal with certain non-training needs in addition to training needs. There are two extreme cases, however.

The first extreme is shown in case A. To fill the performance gap, no training is necessary to attain the performance standard since the manager's current competence (Cc) is sufficiently high. Only non-training needs (Nnt) have been identified and corresponding non-training interventions or measures are required, such as changing the work environment, organisation, incentives and so on.

The second extreme is represented by case B, which is the opposite of case A. Here the current competence (Cc) is not high enough. The performance gap is equal to training needs (Nt) and can be closed by training. This means that the organisational environment and climate, as well as the conditions of the manager's work, are fully satisfactory and what is required is some specific training, nothing else.

In management and business practice cases A and B are rather the exception. The situation encountered most frequently is that shown in case C.

Here to fill the performance gap it is necessary to apply a package of both training and non-training interventions, as already explained. The safest way to approach needs diagnosis is to assume that we are facing case C.

Case D is one that managers and trainers hope to avoid. In this case a package of training and non-training interventions was devised, but this package does not fill the whole performance gap. There will be a residual performance gap (Pgr), which can be due to various factors. For example, the organisation may conclude that even by applying a set of training and non-training measures, it would not be in a position to achieve a performance standard that is already being achieved by its competitors. Such a finding may concern an individual job and its holder, a unit or a whole organisation. The reasons may be objective (e.g. geographic location and high transport costs) or subjective (e.g. the competence of the owner/manager of the business can no longer be increased, but there is no possibility of removing him or her from this position in the short run).

As a matter of interest, we also show case E. Here the job holder is already more competent than necessary, but performance can be improved. The performance gap can be filled by applying a set of non-training measures. However, even when all these measures are successfully introduced and the performance standard is reached, there will still be some difference between the incumbent's individual competence and the standard performance requirements of the job or the organisation. This gap may continue to exist unless a new higher performance standard can be established, or another more challenging position found for the current job holder.

Defining current competence and performance

The identification of current performance and competence starts by fact-finding, which consists in collecting information indicative of performance or competence, describing it and, if possible, measuring it in quantitative terms.

For example, the plant utilisation may be chosen and measured as a global indicator of performance. The related competence problems of production managers may be in areas of production scheduling and control, maintenance management, quality improvement and purchasing. Factors other than the production managers' competence (calling for non-training solutions) may include cumbersome procedures for import licensing, a shortage of foreign exchange, the absence of any bonus systems for stimulating quality improvement and better utilisation of plant, company management's failure to recruit a technically competent maintenance manager, and so on.

We need, of course, some assessment of the present state of affairs – of current competence and/or performance. Without this, we would have no starting-point, no base from which any training and other needs could be

---

identified and any improvements could emerge. In the above-mentioned case, is the utilisation of plant substandard or satisfactory? Are equipment breakdowns or stoppages within acceptable limits? Are there excessive or insufficient stocks of raw materials and parts? The only way in which this assessment can be done is by comparing our findings on the current state of affairs (absolute data) with some standard.

Defining standard (desirable) competence and performance

The definition of the standards to be achieved in enhancing competence and improving performance is the most responsible and difficult part of any needs assessment exercise. The data indicative of the organisational and individual work characteristics and results have provided a starting-point. But how are we to judge these data? How are we to define the desired standard, thus determining how important the performance and competence gap is now? What is the trend, and what should be the future targets of performance improvement and management development efforts?

In many situations, no appropriate standard will be readily available, and even if there is a technical standard (of output, raw materials or energy consumption, etc.) there will certainly be differences in the environmental factors and conditions of operation. The definition and proper use of the standard thus becomes essentially a matter of *expert judgement*. This judgement will be required in order to fix a standard that is high and challenging enough, but remains within realistic limits, to be achievable and to stimulate both learning and practical efforts for improving performance. Two basic types of standards will be used: current and future standards.

The first type includes standards used for judging *current competence and performance*:

o   standards achieved by some other organisations, serving as models ("excellent" companies, industry leaders, organisations representing a "solid" standard without being the top performers, etc.);

o   sectoral or national standards, reflecting agreed levels of "good practice" in particular industries, services, etc. (e.g. standards recommended by trade associations, centres for interfirm comparison, or consulting firms);

o   standards established as performance targets or quotas (planned standards), to which actual performance in the current period of time can be compared;

o   standards used and achieved by the same organisation in the past (in order to show trends in performance improvement or deterioration).

The second type of standard is used to determine *what might or should be achieved in the future*. Here again, standards achieved by organisations that can serve as models, or sectoral standards reflecting good practice, will be used whenever available and appropriate. However, the analytical and conceptual work on needs assessment and objectives setting will have to go beyond these models to produce a particular tailor-made standard for the given organisation, the unit or even the individual. If this is not done, it will be impossible to arrive at any meaningful, action-oriented definition of needs to be met in the future. In the absence of such future standards, both trainers and managers have recourse to platitudes and generalities ("our people need more training in marketing and public relations") without being able to establish any relationship between current performance, the specific training to be undertaken and the performance to be achieved in the future.

1.3 Various dimensions of needs

For the practical purposes of needs assessment and remedial action, management competence and training and development needs are broken down into more detailed and specific elements and looked at from various perspectives.

Content and structure of managerial competence

A manager's competence is his or her ability to perform a certain job, or a range of jobs, and to attain certain performance levels. This is how the term "competence" has been used in the previous paragraphs. For needs assessment, as indeed for other purposes (job descriptions, selection of managers, education), total competence has to be broken down into a number of elements to throw more light on its structure and dynamics and focus on assessing and changing those elements of competence that ought to be improved. Global statements on management training and development needs (e.g. "this manager's competence will remain substandard if you don't send him on a course") provide summary judgements on the desirability of doing something, but hardly any indication of what the actual problems are and what to do to increase competence and performance. The most common ways of describing and structuring managerial competence will be mentioned below.[3]

The first (and most common) way is one that lists and describes the manager's *knowledge, traits and attitudes, and skills*:

Knowledge is retained information concerning facts, concepts and relationships. For our purpose, knowledge covers the following elements:

o   knowledge of the economic, business and management environment;

o   sector-, product- and technology-related knowledge;

o   knowledge of a particular organisation (firm, enterprise, public agency, etc.);

---

o	knowledge of management concepts, systems, principles and methods;

o	knowledge of social, psychological, cultural and political factors and issues.

To define the specialised knowledge required by the job and assess the manager's actual knowledge is not difficult, although it may not be easy to draw precise limits in defining "necessary", "desirable" and "irrelevant" knowledge in changing environments.

Traits and attitudes constitute a complex and often tricky area. Much ink has been used to define an ideal personality of manager, and to provide checklists of characteristics or attributes that a manager should possess. These efforts have been inconclusive. While certain characteristics are clearly needed for certain types of job, it has been impossible to develop universal personality models and prove that a person fitting the model will have guaranteed success in a given managerial position. Nevertheless, in practice it is often found useful to consider selected personality traits, aptitudes and attitudes particularly relevant to the job in question.

For example, a general manager who is permanently in contact with other managers and employees and has to do a great deal of negotiation, task explanation and persuasion, cannot be someone who is timid and shy, resents dealing with unpopular issues and dislikes frequent social contacts with other people. A financial manager, in addition to a positive attitude to working with great amounts of data, must have a great deal of perseverance and patience, and be able to think and work systematically without, however, becoming a hair-splitter and someone for whom figures have become more important than people and the enterprise.

Personality traits are defined by Richard Boyatzis as "dispositional or characteristic ways in which the person responds to equivalent sets of stimuli". Such traits determine how a person will react "to any general set of events which allow the trait to be expressed".[4] Thus, traits define a typical thought pattern and resultant behaviour characteristic of a person in a variety of situations. The overall probability that any event will arouse the thought pattern, and resultant behaviour, is high. Examples of personality traits are: propensity to take initiative, flexibility, adaptability, self-confidence, shyness, aggressiveness, tolerance, perseverance, patience, and the like.

Attitudes "consist of feelings or statements for or against certain issues".[5] In business and management, attitudes are the individuals' predispositions to view their jobs, other people, and the work and business environment in a certain way. The managers' attitudes are reflected in their behaviour. For example, a manager who does not believe in the usefulness of teamwork and the necessity of consulting his staff will tend to decide by himself even in dealing with problems which clearly require collective wisdom and a participative approach. A manager who believes that Anglo-Saxons are more pragmatic and efficient than Latin Americans is likely to be influenced by this attitude when making personnel decisions. Attitudes reflect *values* that a person holds. Values, and the resulting attitudes, are moulded by the person's total life experience and socialisation in a particular family, school, social, ethnic, cultural and work environment. Values are concerned with matters of human preference and result from choices between competing interests. Often they are irrational and emotionally rooted.

The basic question concerning attitudes is whether it is possible to influence them by training and development. Indeed, if attitudes could not be changed, they should be considered in describing the requirements of a particular job and in choosing a manager but could be ignored in determining training needs. There is no single and unique answer to this question. Experience shows that attitudes do not change easily but may change under certain circumstances on the basis of one's own experience and feedback from other people, if the individual concerned has enough will, talent and interest to understand and modify his attitudes. That is why the assessment of training and development needs also tries to deal with those attitudes that are related to the manager's job and influence managerial behaviour and effectiveness.

Skills are the abilities to do things, to effectively apply knowledge and personal aptitudes and attitudes in work situations. If managerial competence can be defined by describing skills, this may overcome some difficult problems involved in describing and discussing attitudes or values. For example, if a manager "can organise teamwork and motivate people for working with him on difficult new tasks under time pressure" (skill), there are underlying assumptions concerning both his or her knowledge and attitudes needed for work planning, communicating with people and motivating and organising teams, while respecting strict time schedules. Generally speaking, the skills involved in managerial jobs include technical subject skills; general management and organisational skills; analytical and conceptual skills; social and cultural skills; management of people, communication and leadership skills; and political skills.

Experience (defined by its nature, level and length) is sometimes also used as an indicator of competence, the widely held assumption being that competence increases with the length of experience. This assumption cannot be accepted without scrutiny as the actual result depends very much both on the learning opportunities provided by a particular sort of practical experience, and on the manager's ability and will to learn from this experience (the classic question is: Does this manager have 20 years of experience, or 20 times one year of experience?).

The second way of describing managerial competence groups the above-mentioned attributes in *two broad areas: technical and behavioural*. The technical area includes knowledge, skills, aptitudes and attitudes concerning technological, economic, financial, structural and procedural aspects of the job. The behavioural area includes all people-related aspects affecting the manager's communication and dealings with people within and outside the organisation. This grouping is meaningful because it reflects the two fundamental sides of every management job: the technical side and the human side. It is helpful in needs assessment since the techniques used can be chosen to fit the side being explored. Also, different management development approaches and techniques can be chosen for developing technical and people-related skills.

The third way describes *managerial behaviour* rather than characteristics that the holder of the job must possess. In this way we are also getting closer to performance, in particular if the description of a behavioural pattern can also refer to the results to be achieved. For example, a marketing manager "makes sure that all customers' complaints are handled, or at least acknowledged, within one week of reception, and that no more than 5 per cent of customer complaints remain unresolved after one month". However, despite its advantages, this way of describing applied competence may be impractical and difficult to use for complex tasks and positions, and in rapidly changing situations.

The fourth way is that of *competency models*. A competency model – a variant of the previous approaches – defines a set of individual characteristics required for effective or superior performance in a job, or a class of jobs. These characteristics are derived from observation of actual managerial behaviour in particular jobs, and from the identification of capabilities exhibited by those individuals who achieve superior job performance.

According to Richard Boyatzis, a competency model should have two dimensions: it should describe the various types of competencies (first dimension) and the required level of each competency (second dimension). Boyatzis defines a job competency as "an underlying characteristic of a person in that it may be a motive, trait, skill, aspect of one's self-image or social role, or a body of knowledge which he or she uses".[6] These underlying competencies can manifest themselves in various types of activities in various environments or tasks. The implications of this definition are fairly obvious. An individual who possesses a broad range of competencies defined in such a model should be able to deal with various tasks and jobs which cannot be described in advance on conventional lines. Therefore competency models appear to be an interesting form of describing competencies for jobs requiring solid theoretical background, analytical and conceptual skills, flexibility, quick reaction to new conditions, imagination, creativity, leadership ability, and so on. In the past ten years competency modelling has become increasingly popular and has been used in various ways, including applications to more routine management jobs.

An example of the competency model approach is provided by the so-called "management competency clock"[7], which defines 12 *generic performance competencies* whose "hourly position on the clock" is determined by their association with the higher-level *learning competencies*. These learning competencies are needed for more complex organisational structures. They include behavioural competence in taking initiative and responsibility under conditions of risk and uncertainty, perceptual competence in gathering and organising information, affective competence in empathising with others and resolving conflicts, and symbolic competence in conceptualising the organisation as a system (figure 1.4). The 12 generic performance competencies are then extended downwards by one or two levels to analyse managerial competencies in a specific organisational setting and to identify the specific training and development needs required. This specialised training needs analysis is complemented by an integrative needs analysis focused on the integrative competence required to cope with the complexity and uncertainty inherent in higher-level jobs and complex environmental relationships. While specialised competencies become increasingly simple, behavioural and focused on content as one moves down the hierarchy, the integrative learning competencies are more complex, internalised and focused on processes.

Other examples will be found in sections 4.1 and 8.1 describing the practical use of competency modelling in assessing and meeting training and development needs.

The fifth way takes a reversed approach: rather than defining managerial competence, it tries to detect evidence of incompetence or *the absence of specific competencies*. George Odiorne has compiled the following list of reasons why managers were fired in several organisations he observed[8]:

o   Could not control emotions

o   Behaved immaturely

o   Lacked a sense of urgency

o   Was stopped by trivial obstacles

o   Could not respond to change quickly enough

o   Hung on to obsolete ideas

o   Hung on to obsolete ways of doing things

o   Persistently tore up employer-employee relations

o   Did not know when to stick with policy (when to enforce company rules rigidly and when to be soft)

o   Could not delegate

o   Could not communicate

o   Was not tough enough

Figure 1.4. A hierarchical map of managerial competence

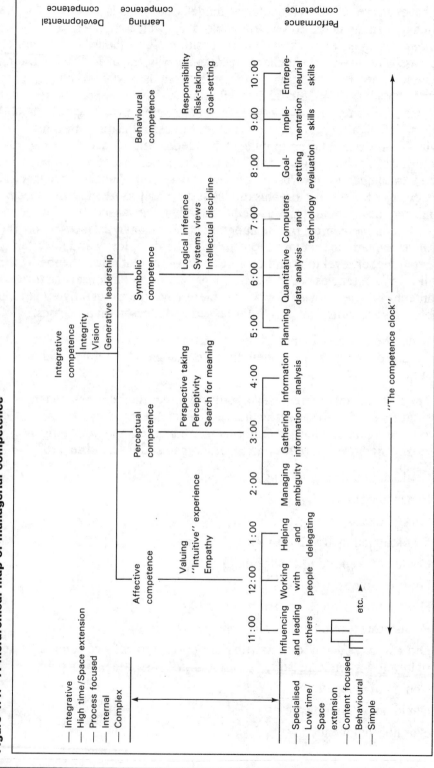

Source: D. Kolb et al.: "Strategic management development: Using experiential learning theory to assess and develop managerial competencies", in *Journal of Management Development* (Bradford, West Yorkshire), Vol. 5, No. 3, 1986, pp. 18-20.

o   Lacked a sense of humour

o   Did not anticipate.

These reasons can be analysed with a view to identifying training needs and developing tailor-made training programmes. Clearly, such analysis can be useful if it is made before it is too late for redressing the situation through training.

The sixth way describes management competence and training needs indirectly, in terms of certain training programmes that should be provided to meet the needs. It would be impractical to describe all knowledge required for a managerial position in detail. Such a description is often replaced by a reference to a certain type and level of educational programme whereby that knowledge is normally acquired (e.g. an MBA, a diploma in management, a university degree or an advanced 6-9 month programme in marketing). Many companies have developed induction or training programmes for new recruits, or for staff promoted to a particular level or function of management. This approach is based on a sort of "packaging" and "standardisation" of training needs. Strictly speaking, all individuals concerned will not need every single item included in the packaged programme. However, it has been established that the target population (new recruits, etc.) will need most of the material provided (say 80-90 per cent), hence the training need is described as the need to attend the programme. It is deemed more effective to provide the total programme to all individuals in the target population than to redesign it for every individual. Another example is a standard rule whereby in some international companies a manager, on reaching mid-career, should have worked for at least 3-5 years abroad, in a foreign subsidiary or office. Here again, a training and development need regarded as common (acquiring international experience and perspective) is described in terms of activity whereby it will be met.

The management system perspective

Individual managerial jobs do not exist in isolation. They are part of a management system in a particular organisation and are related to other jobs, managerial and non-managerial, within this system. It is important to keep this perspective in mind in using any of the above-mentioned approaches to describing competence, performance and training needs of individual managers.

To begin with, we need to get a complete picture of the structuring of the given management system. There are, of course, many alternative structures, but in most medium-sized to large business organisations we could normally find three basic echelons of the management hierarchy: lower, middle and higher management. The number of echelons tends to grow with the size and complexity of the organisation and can reach 4-7 levels in large organisations.

Figure 1.5.   Competence structure at various levels of the management hierarchy

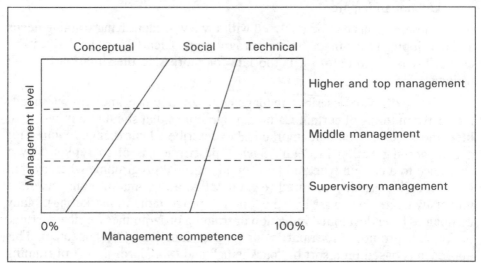

In contrast, in a small enterprise, all functions may be concentrated in the hands of one sole person – the owner/manager.

In addition to this vertical structuring there is normally some horizontal structuring resulting in specialisation by functions, sectors, divisions, products, and the like. While the person at the top level of the organisation would be responsible for total management, i.e. for all functions and aspects, those assisting the top manager in a large enterprise as deputies or vice-presidents would normally specialise in areas such as finance, marketing, research and development, production, human resources, and so on. As we move down the hierarchy, this specialisation of managerial positions tends to be even more pronounced. However, there is also some decentralisation of global functions and responsibilities, in particular towards subsidiaries and divisions specialised geographically or by product.

The scope of competence and the nature of training needs are different at each echelon of the hierarchy, as shown in figure 1.5.

The first echelon (lower or supervisory management) normally operates within a defined range of business objectives and policy guide-lines; its principal task is to ensure smooth execution while respecting efficiency criteria. The time-horizon is short term and technical specialisation is important though relatively narrow. Management of people is important and requires a broad range of communication, motivation, team-building and organisation skills.

The second echelon (middle management) embraces a broad range of managerial positions at diverse degrees of specialisation. The focus is on tactical management and plan execution, however, with some participation in company-level strategic planning and management. The time-horizon can be both medium and long term. People management skills continue to be important, but the importance of organisational, co-ordination and conceptual skills is larger than at the lower level of management.

The third echelon (higher and top management) is characterised primarily by the need for de-specialisation as regards individual functions, services and technologies, without however, losing contact with the current state of the art and development trends of the industry in question. The focus is on conceptual and strategic management and business policy, with considerable demands on skills required for managing the organisation as part of its external environment. The time-horizon is essentially long term, but medium- and short-term concerns may become important in crisis situations and in periods of accelerated change. The critical social skills include leadership, understanding environmental trends, constraints and opportunities, conceptualisation, organisation, co-ordination, negotiation and public relations.

In dealing with training and development needs, one can assume that the above-mentioned characteristics are indicative and very broad. It is therefore necessary to find out how a particular organisation describes the work content, responsibility and competence required for the various positions at each echelon of the hierarchy. Such a description may be available from organisational documentation (statutes, mission statements, organisation manuals and charts, internal instructions, job descriptions), or we may find that it does not exist or is incomplete. In the latter case it may be appropriate to analyse the organisational mission and objectives and bring organisational documentation up to date.

The next step consists in finding out how the management system really works. It is important to find out what managers do, not on paper but in reality. Clearly, competence relates to real situations, tasks and problems, not to descriptions that are no longer used because they have become obsolete, or for any other reason.

The managerial career perspective

In addition to operating within a certain management system, the manager whose training and development needs are being assessed is also at a certain point in his or her managerial career. Thus, the training needs will be related not only to the manager's role in the system and to the problems involved, but also to the specific pattern of his or her managerial career. On the one hand, the manager's background and needs will be affected by past career. On the other hand, the assessment of training needs will keep in mind, as much as possible, the manager's future career prospects. Career planning therefore becomes one of the essential techniques for individual needs assessment, as shown later in section 4.12.

The career perspective is related to the management system perspective. As a rule, the career progression in organisations is in one of two directions:

o   upwards, i.e. moving from lower to higher management echelons (with corresponding changes in job content, responsibilities and training needs, as discussed in the previous section);

o   sideways, i.e. continuing to work at the same rung of the career ladder (in this case the training needs will be affected mainly by environmental and organisational changes, and the need to keep the whole management system, including those individuals who are not promoted to higher-level positions, in line with these changes).

There may be a third direction in an individual career if for any reason the manager leaves the organisation and starts a new career elsewhere. This can be the source of specific training needs such as mid-career retraining of managers who have to change employment, or training of managers (and others) who intend to establish their own enterprises.

Levels of needs

The assessment of management training and development needs can be undertaken at different levels of generalisation. This has many methodological and organisational implications, as will be discussed in detail in parts II and III. Here we will confine ourselves to a short description of each level.

(1) *Individual level.* This is the starting-point and basic building-block of any needs assessment. Every manager has unique needs owing to the particular combination of his or her job profile, educational and cultural background, experience and personality. Emphasis on individual needs assessment makes it possible to have development programmes that are tailored to individual needs and aim at results that are visible and understandable to each individual concerned and for which he or she can feel responsible.

(2) *Group and team level.* To identify and meet needs, we also have to group managers for the following reasons: (i) while some of their needs are individual and unique, other needs are common; and (ii) as mentioned above, managers do not work as isolated individuals, but in groups and teams: this brings out needs that could not be identified in dealing with each individual separately. Also, needs that concern relations and interaction with other managers and workers often have to be treated through collective training and development. Therefore at the second level we would deal with groups and teams of managers within an organisation. The nature of the management system and process will determine the criterion for establishing these groups and teams. As a rule, they will reflect the management reality rather than administrative

criteria and organisational rules. Typically, managers directly associated with an important activity or with a project that cuts across the limits of several organisational units will have common needs and should be treated as a team although they belong to various units. In other cases, the grouping of managers may be by organisational units, e.g. marketing managers and sales supervisors within the marketing department.

(3) *Organisation level.* This level is particularly important for relating management development and training needs to organisational systems, problems, diagnoses, objectives and performance improvement programmes. In practice, most needs assessment exercises take place at organisation level and include the two previous levels as their components. To meet the needs, many organisations design and implement their own management development and training programmes. A key issue faced in these programmes is how to balance the approaches taken and the resources allocated for meeting organisational and individual needs. Typical organisation-level management development needs are those related to organisational (corporate) culture. Organisations that have developed a set of shared values, constituting their specific culture, tend to use management development programmes for strengthening this value system, in particular in training newly recruited and junior managers and staff members.

(4) *Sectoral level.* The definition of sectoral needs may be quite meaningful if a sectoral development policy or plan is being considered, or if a sectoral body (e.g. an employers' or trade association, or a ministry) intends to alert organisations in the sector to their management problems or to inbalances in the managerial manpower supply and demand, and provide a service for dealing with these problems (e.g. a sectoral training institution or special ad hoc programmes).

(5) *Country (national) level.* In a similar vein, we are often interested in common nation-wide characteristics and needs of the management population, in planning or suggesting country-level programmes or in establishing national management institutes, centres, faculties or foundations. Typically, country-level needs are examined by national surveys and studies. Often, these surveys would also use a sectoral breakdown, differentiate between regions (e.g. urban and rural, less or more developed, geographically remote) and consider needs by major occupations or functions (e.g. financial managers, marketing managers) that are found in most enterprises.

(6) *Regional level.* Regional aspects and considerations are of interest if regional programmes, projects or institutions can provide useful guidance and support to governments and private organisations in individual countries of the region. For example, the European Foundation for

Management Development has undertaken several projects looking into the future needs of European managers, and one of the main objectives of the Asian Productivity Organisation has been to meet training and development needs in conjunction with efforts to improve productivity in Asian countries.

(7) *Global level.* This is the highest level of generalisation in respect of training and development needs. A global, world-wide view tends to be taken selectively by associations or institutions involved in exchange of experience, information services or new programme development of the widest international interest. The globalisation of world markets, the current trends in financing business and trade or the progress in information and communication technologies are regarded as factors that will influence management in all regions and countries; hence the existence of global needs, and an opportunity to think of policies, programmes and services that are of global interest.

Present and future needs

Present (short-term, current) needs can be established by comparing the real present performance of managers with a standard that should be attained immediately or in a relatively short time. For example, performance may be substandard and corrective measures are required as soon as possible to redress the situation. In another case, some change in the environment or in the organisation itself may be occurring (e.g. computerised production control is being introduced) that requires virtually immediate training so that managers develop new competencies in parallel and in accordance with this change.

Future (long-term) needs are linked with future projections and long-range objectives. The underlying idea is that the existing managerial population should not only be made more efficient in the short run but should also be prepared to face new situations likely to develop in the future. At the same time, the education of the future generation of managers should not be oriented only to the present state of the science and art of management and the present requirements of the social and business environment but should anticipate future developments and requirements. This can be particularly useful for determining curricula of management faculties and business schools, bearing in mind that their present students will be taking up managerial positions within 5-15 years and may still be in senior positions 15-40 years from now.

As present and future needs may call for different types of training content and methodology and may require action by different types of institutions and at various levels of management, they should be indicated separately in diagnoses of training needs. The relativeness of the concept of present and future needs should not be lost sight of. Needs defined as future today may become present and extremely pressing tomorrow. Needs regarded as long-term in one organisation may be short-term needs and require immediate action in another.

Qualitative and quantitative needs

The final dimension of needs concerns their qualitative and quantitative aspects. *Qualitative needs* reflect the content of managerial jobs and comptence and of the required changes. They define main problem and/or functional areas (accounting, leadership, motivation, maintenance, etc.) and those sorts of additional knowledge and skill that have to be developed, or attitudinal and behavioural changes to be achieved, in identified areas. In other words, qualitative needs help to identify programme subjects or disciplines as well as objectives of qualitative change to be achieved through training and development interventions.

Quantitative needs do not exist independently of qualitative needs. They indicate how many managers have identical or similar qualitative needs, and what volume of developmental effort and what resources will be required to achieve a defined qualitative change. Thus the main indicators of quantitative needs are numbers of managerial posts, numbers of managers to be trained, developed and replaced, time allocated to training, the volume of training and development activities, and the human, material, and financial resources required.

1.4 Needs, demand and objectives

By defining the difference between real and required management competence (and performance), we come close to *objectives* of management training and development. Indeed, objectives are normally established on the basis of needs: in principle, the objective will be to meet the needs that have been identified.

Experienced trainers and managers emphasise that management development can be meaningful only if it is geared to clearly defined and precise objectives. These objectives express the purpose to be achieved, constitute a basis for the planning of programme content as well as for the selection of training and development methods, and permit control and evaluation of results. Determining objectives is a key feature and component of planning and designing management training and development programmes.

However, it is important to understand that *the difference between needs and objectives* is more than semantic.

First, by determining training and development objectives we take an important step towards remedial action: while statements of needs tend to be

---

descriptive of the existing gaps and possible improvements (even if needs are seen in the context of evolving realities of management and business systems), statements of objectives indicate the course of action to be taken and the results to be obtained.

Second, the objectives of training and development programmes and activities are determined not only on the basis of needs, but also on the basis of resources that are available or can be mustered for training (the managers' time, competent trainers, training and development materials and facilities, financial resources, etc.), as well as for improvements in the management systems and methods whose desirability was established.

Third, objectives are defined for the various partners in the total management development process, thus specifying and harmonising their respective roles in meeting the needs (for example, in a sectoral management development programme, the objectives of programmes given at a central training establishment will not be identical with those of line managers engaged in self-development programmes, but can be complementary).

Fourth, the definition of objectives is also affected by *the difference between needs and demand*. There is demand for management development programmes (courses, seminars, materials, packages, action-learning projects, etc.) if needs have been perceived and recognised by the managers and organisations concerned and if there is a will to take action. This demand tends to be expressed in terms of interest in programmes that are offered: some may be overbooked, while others may have to be cancelled because of a shortage of applicants. In many cases there is definitely a need but no demand, or only modest demand, due to lack of information, awareness, resources or motivation. On the other hand, demand for existing programmes does not always reflect actual needs. There may be demand (which can be a passing one) for programmes whose practical value is dubious and impact on the participants' performance negligible.

If needs are important but demand is low, this usually means that some impeding forces inhibit performance improvement and negatively affect the managers' interest in training and self-development. In such situations, looking for "non-training" factors and interventions may be essential in order to enhance motivation and demand for management training and development.

However, low demand for management training and development may be traced to other causes. The institutions and programmes available in the country may enjoy a poor reputation. The training function may be generally misunderstood and understaffed. Or there may be no role models to demonstrate convincingly what a company can achieve through a well-designed performance improvement and management development programme. These and similar factors have to be kept in mind in drawing conclusions on needs, demand, courses of action and objectives to be pursued. A special effort may be needed to stimulate demand of the managers to be served, as well as interest and support of those decision-makers who will have to authorise action and resources.

1.5   Psychology of needs assessment

Some of the factors affecting the managers' interest in training and development are of a psychological nature. They include personality traits such as a person's natural curiosity or eagerness to learn new things, and attitudes such as the readiness to admit ignorance or the recognition of the fact that a senior manager can learn from junior colleagues. Some psychological factors can play a major role in recognising and admitting training needs and taking effective steps to meet them.

Criticism involved in assessing training needs

The purpose of needs assessment is not to criticise the individual or the organisation, but to improve competence and performance in the individual's and the organisation's interest. Yet a certain amount of criticism is inherent in any assessment of training needs. This criticism may concern a knowledge gap, a recurrent behavioural or communication problem, a conflict with other managers or another existing problem. If current or immediate needs are diagnosed, this criticism can become quite pronounced and explicit, in particular if it has been established that a feasible standard is not being achieved and that remedial action is required immediately. There is much less criticism in assessing future needs, since these can be viewed as challenges generated by changes in the environment, and by new emerging opportunities to which even the best managers and organisations will have to adjust.

The criticism involved in training and development needs assessment is similar to that implied in decisions concerning the use of management consultants. Some managers resent using any consultants since, in their opinion, this would be an open recognition of weaknesses that they prefer not to admit.

This may be a psychological problem reflecting individuals' perceptions of themselves and their environment. The fear of criticism, and the tendency to interpret comments on work methods and results as criticism, may indicate that the manager is not sure of himself and his own abilities. In contrast, successful managers with strong and dynamic personalities usually do not see any problem in admitting a gap in knowledge or a behavioural weakness, which, they think, is largely compensated by their good qualities. After all, it is the results that count and these managers are getting results. However, even individuals who are sure of themselves, and are keen to receive constructive feedback from which they can learn, may choose to ignore such feedback if it is coming from people for whom they have little respect.

Furthermore, there may be cultural barriers to admitting the existence of training needs in communities where criticism tends to be regarded as unacceptable because the person being criticised is losing face. In particular at senior levels, it may be difficult to open a discussion on training needs. Training needs may be viewed as something that concern junior managers, not senior ones.

Training and learning needs

At this point we should bring up the subtle difference between training and learning. Consider the following definition: "A manager has learnt something when either or both of the following descriptions apply – he knows something he did not know earlier, and can show it; he is able to do something he was not able to do before."[9] There can be training but no learning if some training has taken place, when for any reason the manager has refused or was unable to learn what he or she was supposed to learn. Conversely, there can be learning without training since training is only one of the processes whereby managers learn. It is not even the most important among these processes. Most of the manager's learning is experiential learning that occurs at work. The work content and environment are the crucial elements that influence that learning, in addition to the manager's ability and will to learn. Generally speaking, since the learning process requires various other influences (OD, teamwork, practical experience, etc.) and incentives, and not only training, learning needs tend to be broader than training needs. Often a wide range of non-training interventions is required to facilitate and stimulate the learning process.

Furthermore, an individual's ability and will to learn cannot be taken for granted when assessing training needs and using this assessment in planning training and development.

First, *the ability to learn* is itself a skill that can be identified, assessed and improved. According to Alan Mumford, the development of managers' learning abilities involves:

o helping managers to know the stages of the learning process and blockages to learning;

o helping them to understand their own preferred approaches to learning;

o assisting managers in making best use of their existing learning preferences or building additional strengths and overcoming blockages;

o helping managers to carry their understanding of learning from off-the-job to on-the-job opportunities.[10]

Second, *the will to learn* will depend on a number of factors of an essentially motivational nature. The manager must be convinced that learning is worth while and necessary and that both he or she as a person and the organisation will draw some benefit from it. It has been demonstrated many times that managers tend to adopt such an attitude if they internalise their training needs and perceive them as learning needs. Put in other terms, it is not the training director or a higher-level boss who has concluded that a manager needs some training, but the manager concerned who has come to this conclusion.

Ownership of training needs

This positive attitude to training and learning is often referred to as "ownership of training needs". It can be achieved by explaining to an individual why he (or she) has a certain training (or learning) need and what will happen if this need is met successfully. Even better, it can be achieved if the manager concerned arrives (alone or with some assistance) at a conclusion that he has a learning need and decides to do something about it. That is why this book consistently emphasises throughout managers' active participation in the assessment of their own training needs, which, case by case, can differ in degree and form.

There is another important aspect of ownership of training needs, however. Training or learning needs are something very personal and are often regarded as a matter of individual rights. At any level of the management hierarchy, as indeed among non-managerial workers, an individual's training needs may be perceived differently by management and the individual. This can turn into a serious issue if an important training opportunity is being considered that would affect the individual's future. A middle-level functional manager may believe that he (or she) should be sent, at company expense, to a course that is normally required in connection with promotion to a higher position. The company may conclude that this is not desirable since the manager concerned is not promotable. The reverse situation may also occur. The company may force a manager to attend a seminar on how to improve management style, although he believes that it is his superiors who should attend such a seminar. Or a manager may feel comfortable in his or her present position and may not be keen to be given more responsibility.

There is no blueprint for handling these situations. A dialogue, a participative approach and the encouragement of self-assessment seem to help in most cases to harmonise the organisation's and the individual's perceptions of his or her training and development needs. No one should feel that he is treated as a passive object whose needs are determined, and participation in training approved or not approved, by someone else without due consideration for the individual's concerns, aspirations and feelings.

There will be cases when such an agreement cannot be reached. Different perceptions of what can really be achieved by training may be the cause. However, more often such a disagreement will be a symptom of divergent views concerning the individual manager's real contribution and future potential. Or there may be no disagreement, but the individual's legitimate aspirations cannot be satisfied by the organisation because of its smallness, limited growth potential, overstaffing or other reasons.

Overcoming psychological and cultural barriers

There are ways of dealing with the psychological and cultural barriers to needs assessment:

o   an atmosphere of full trust has to be created, ensuring confidentiality if necessary, and providing a guarantee that information on training needs will not be used for appraising performance, against the individual manager's interests (e.g. reducing or blocking salary, limiting career prospects);

o   self-assessment assisted by providing information and advice on request may often be more acceptable and productive than assessment by other persons;

o   in certain situations managers may find it easier to discuss their training needs with external experts (consultants, trainers) than with colleagues from within the organisation;

o   demonstrating that non-training issues will receive equal attention with training needs may be an essential condition for dissipating mistrust and creating positive motivation for needs assessment;

o   an example set by senior managers will have a positive influence on junior managers;

o   needs assessment exercises where managers of comparable levels help each other to gain insight into their individual training needs may be effective;

o   the needs assessment process ought to be carefully monitored to prevent blockages caused by the analyst's clumsy or tactless approach;

o   terms such as "performance problems" or "training needs" can be avoided completely if this helps to prevent suspicion and resistance; these terms can be replaced by "providing new information", "creating learning opportunities", "trying out something of interest to top executives", "considering the feasibility of a practical approach that has helped other respectable organisations to become more profitable", and the like.

In summary, training needs are more easily identified and dealt with if they are presented to managers and perceived by them as challenges and opportunities to be taken in the common interest of the individual and the organisation. It may be helpful to emphasise future perspectives, national interests and the societal dimension of increased competence.

---

[1] R.E. Boyatzis: *The competent manager: A model for effective performance* (New York, Wiley, 1982), pp. 11 and 20.

[2] See also chapter 1 in M. Kubr (ed.): *Management consulting: A guide to the profession* (Geneva, ILO, second (revised) edition, 1986).

[3] Useful observations on current practices of British organisations in defining management competencies (for recruitment, appraisal, potential assessment, promotion, etc.) are made in W. Hirsh and S. Bevan: *What makes a manager?* (Brighton, University of Sussex Institute of Manpower Studies, 1988). The study shows that various approaches and definitions are used and that some of the commonest skill items, such as leadership, are used with the most diverse meanings. Personal attributes form the most complex language type of all competencies, spanning *intellectual attributes* (e.g. intellegence), *personality aspects* (e.g. self-confidence) and *motivational aspects* (e.g. ambition), although these three aspects are by no means distinct and overlap strongly.

[4] Boyatzis, op. cit., pp. 28-29.

[5] ibid., p. 34.

[6] ibid., pp. 21 and 25.

[7] D. Kolb et al.: "Strategic management development: Using experiential learning theory to assess and develop managerial competencies", in *Journal of Management Development* (Bradford, West Yorkshire), Vol. 5, No. 3, 1986, pp. 18-20.

[8] G.S. Odiorne: *Strategic management of human resources: A portfolio approach* (San Francisco, California, Jossey-Bass, 1984), pp. 190-193.

[9] A. Mumford: "Learning to learn for managers", in *Journal of European Industrial Training* (Bradford, West Yorkshire), Vol. 10, No. 2, 1986 (special issue), p. 3.

[10] idem: "Helping managers learn to learn", in *Journal of Management Development*, Vol. 6, No. 5, 1987, p. 50.

A SYSTEMS VIEW OF NEEDS ASSESSMENT

2

Chapter 1 explained the concept of management training and development needs and examined various aspects and dimensions of these needs. In chapter 2 we shall look more closely at the activity called "needs assessment", including its integration with other organisational processes. The purpose is to show that needs assessment should not be regarded as an extraordinary diagnostic exercise introduced into the organisation from the outside from time to time, but as one of the normal functions of every organisation that cares for its people and uses training to achieve better organisational results. In keeping with the spirit of part I, the discussion will be confined to basic relationships and principles. Practical applications in various contexts (e.g. in large and small enterprises) will be reviewed later in part III.

Three mutually related perspectives will provide us with a fairly complete systems view of needs assessment:

o   organisational problem-solving and performance improvement (2.1);

o   the management development cycle (2.2);

o   organisational responsibility (2.3).

2.1   Results-oriented needs assessment

The term "results" is particularly important in dealing with conceptual issues of training and development needs. We often hear and read about "results-oriented training", and "results-oriented needs assessment". The underlying idea is simple but powerful: If you are assessing training and development needs, always keep the results in mind and direct your assessment to these results. The results referred to in this connection are results achieved by the organisation or unit whose member (manager, worker, etc.) is to be trained. Therefore application must take place in addition to the acquisition of new knowledge or skill.

For example, a senior manager, a member of the company executive committee, has problems of communication and interpersonal relations that affect the working of the committee. The manager runs easily into conflicts with other members of the committee, and this makes it more and more difficult collectively to examine policy issues and reach a consensus on important investment and financial decisions. Quite often these decisions are unduly delayed, or emergency decisions have to be taken by the chief executive officer (CEO) without having discussed the issue properly in the committee. The CEO and the manager concerned have come to the conclusion that attending a workshop or another form of training in communication, teamwork and interpersonal relations may be helpful to the manager. Such training will be especially valuable if the required practical result is defined and achieved – changing the working practices of the executive committee, and making sure that all important decisions are collectively examined and taken in time. If this is achieved thanks to training, the training has been results oriented. If the manager in question attends seminars and learns about organisational behaviour, communication, management of conflict, and so on, but nothing changes in the working of the executive committee, the training has not been results oriented.

What is the problem?

In our example, an organisational problem was identified first (ineffective executive committee due to the behavioural problems of one of its members) and training was thought of as a possible way of solving this problem. This is the thrust of a systems approach to assessing management training and development needs. Such an approach makes it possible to discriminate between training and non-training interventions and solutions, take a realistic view of what can really be achieved through training, and insist on the necessary non-training measures. In our example, one or more non-training measures may be necessary in addition to training, or instead of training, to solve the problem (e.g. restructuring the executive committee or re-examining its mandate).

Defining the problem to be tackled and focusing needs assessment on results is not too difficult if current performance is regarded as substandard. This can mean that, with perhaps the same resources, a better performance was achieved in the past than is now the case. Alternatively, performance may have stagnated, while competing organisations have made considerable progress. The problem is clearly defined if it is accepted that the restoration of the original condition is what is required, or that it is necessary to achieve a new standard which is already being achieved in some other organisation or unit referred to as a model. This approach has been extensively applied in the so called "performance-based", or "performance-oriented" training.

Focus on future results

Not all problems faced by management can be defined in such a clear-cut, simple way. It has been rightly pointed out that "performance-based training does little to help us prepare people for jobs that are evolving, jobs that demand a lot of different responses to the shifting needs of the organisation or the overall business climate".[1]

This does not mean that the concept of results-oriented training and needs assessment described in this section will have to be abandoned. What is increasingly required is a broader conception of "results". Focus on immediate, short-term and easily measurable results will continue to be necessary in many enterprises, both large and small. The ability to achieve immediate results and demonstrate this achievement may be the most convincing argument for "selling" any needs assessment and training interventions to higher management if the latter has doubts about their usefulness.

However, "results" are being increasingly thought of as embracing both immediate and future results. Future training needs (i.e. those related to future results) are receiving growing attention. They are related to expected or envisaged future changes in technology, new areas of business, new types of customer services, innovative ways of co-operating with foreign partners, and so on. The required management skills and training needs will concern skills and work methods for enhancing creativity, stimulating and implementing innovation, assessing political and financial risk, establishing productive relationships with new business partners, being sensitive to changing social values and preferences, running multinational projects, managing a more educated and sophisticated labour force and so on. The acquisition of these and other new skills may give no immediate results, but will be a *sine qua non* of future results.

Understanding the context and planning needs assessment

In focusing needs assessment on results, both immediate and future, it is necessary to understand the context in which a particular needs assessment exercise is to take place. If the request for needs assessment comes from higher management in a business company, or in a management training centre, it would be good to write down draft terms of reference and look into the sense and the feasibility of the exercise. What should be the purpose of needs assessment? What results are expected? For what reason should it be undertaken just now? Who wants to see it carried out? Was needs assessment triggered by some specific organisational problems? Are these problems clearly defined and understood? Or is there just a vague feeling that "some training might help"?

It may be that the purpose is not clear and possibly not serious enough. Some needs assessment surveys in companies and even sectoral and national surveys are undertaken although there are no resources, and no real intention to mobilise resources, for implementing the measures that may be proposed.

To understand the context better, a quick pre-assessment of the needs and of the environment may be carried out. If a major in-depth diagnostic study is contemplated that would last several months and use up considerable resources, a pre-assessment is not only necessary for focusing and planning the survey but it may even reveal that another survey is not needed, or that formal training needs assessment is not at all what is required. This information may be obtained by interviewing experts knowledgeable of the situation under scrutiny (see section 3.3) or by finding out about past efforts to tackle the same issue (previous needs assessment exercises that remained without follow-up).

When the basic purpose has been clarified, it is useful to draw up a work plan of the particular needs assessment activity. This includes specification of:

o   scope and purposes;

o   time horizon;

o   methods for collecting data and drawing conclusions on needs;

o   form of presenting conclusions;

o   organisation and responsibility;

o   time schedule.

The time and resource constraints will be also considered. For example, in an emergency situation it would hardly be acceptable to propose a lengthy comprehensive diagnosis based on extensive data-gathering schemes. A quick diagnosis followed by some immediate remedial measures would be required and a more thorough diagnosis would be done later. If a major structured needs assessment exercise is planned, such as a company-wide survey, the detailed plan will be stipulated in the terms of reference or the project specification. This will not necessarily be done in less important and less formalised analyses of needs. However, it will always be useful to keep in mind the specifications listed above.

A major needs assessment exercise may require a pilot study (with a small sample of respondents) which will make it possible to test the methodology and finalise the plan.

Model of results-oriented needs assessment

The approach described in this chapter, namely a consistent results orientation of the assessment of training and development needs, is shown in a model form in figure 2.1.

In this model, the starting-point is not the individual managers with their training needs and requirements, but the existing (or potential) organisational problems. Therefore step 1 consists in spotting organisational problems (in productivity, profitability, quality, marketing, etc.) and determining the degree of their urgency and the order of priority in which they will have to be tackled.

Figure 2.1. Model of results-oriented needs assessment

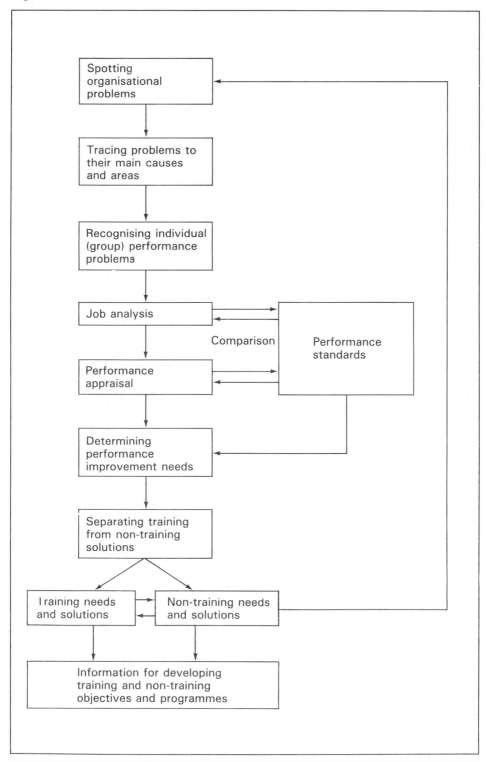

Step 2 is tracing and identifying the main causes and areas of the problems. Here we could identify causes such as lack of communication, discipline and poor morale, wrong or inefficient equipment and facilities, problems with excessively complex organisational design and cumbersome procedures, and so on. At the same time we could identify precisely the main areas (technical, functional, geographic, etc.) where the problems arise. It could be the marketing department, assembly line, financial or planning department or a workshop.

Step 3 is building awareness and recognition of the problems and their causes and the areas affected by them. During this stage it is important to identify precisely those managers at different levels and in different parts of the organisation who "have created" these problems or influenced their existence in some way. This step enables us to avoid total analysis of the training needs of all the management teams in an organisation, and to concentrate only on those units or individuals who are really the sources of the problems and who are working within the areas where problems have arisen.

When the problem areas and the particular managers responsible for them have been identified, step 4 is to analyse each job (including the job requirements and the actual behaviour of the job holder) and compare it with the performance standards and the results of performance appraisals. The results of this comparison will show the gap between performance standards and actual achievements, expressed in terms of missing competence, which in turn will have to be broken down into specific skills, knowledge, attitudes and managerial behaviour, as well as other organisational factors and forces that co-determine managerial behaviour and effectiveness (step 5).

This analytical exercise will be pursued in step 6 by separating non-training needs from training needs and suggesting the required non-training solutions (interventions) in addition to training solutions. However, full attention will be paid to the relationships and mutual influence of these two sorts of solutions, as was stressed in chapter 1.

The assessment of training needs has thus been completed. In step 7, the conclusions reached are translated into specific objectives and programmes for training and action.

2.2 The management development cycle

Needs assessment is only one stage of the management development cycle. Only the completion of the whole cycle will make it possible to verify if the original needs assessment was correct, and if it directed all subsequent activities in the management development process to desired results in a meaningful way.

The following comments illustrate this issue:

Figure 2.2. Global model of the management development cycle

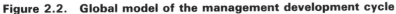

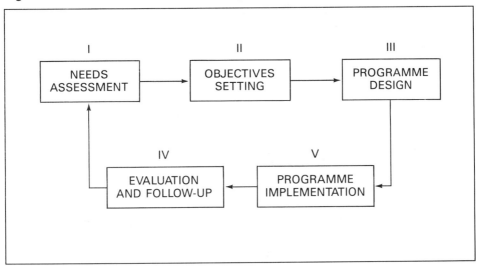

"It really began with training packages. We had been developing training packages and were very pleased with them: with their appearance, and the way they taught, with the test data we were getting. Our clients were also pleased. The trainees were mastering the skills and knowledge taught with our packages, and they passed criterion reference tests at the end. However, we wanted to see if they transferred those skills back on the job. This led us to do the follow-up evaluations which in those days were jokingly called rear-end analysis. Surprisingly, in spite of all our experience in training technology, we found that almost as many times as not the skills were not in fact used back on the job. The trainees were not doing what our training packages had taught them to do."[2]

A study by the Conference Board in the United States concluded that "needs-driven training entails a number of closely linked steps assessing individual and group needs, defining training objectives, selecting participants, designing training courses and instructional methods, providing feedback and evaluation ... Most companies do some of these things well, but few do them all well ... Several recently appointed training directors commented on the poor connection they found between company needs ... and the training programmes in place".[3]

These and similar pitfalls can be prevented by assessing and reassessing needs at a proper point of the management development cycle, and by signalling the necessity of corrective measures before time is lost, resources wasted, the managers discouraged and the trainers declared to be inefficient. A five-stage model is frequently used to decribe the systems approach to the management development cycle (figure 2.2).

The five stages or blocks

Needs assessment is the first stage. The scope of the exercise depends on the envisaged scope and broad orientation of the programme (e.g. marketing managers are to be prepared for coping with new developments on world markets and for using new marketing techniques and distribution networks). This is important, because needs assessment for management training and development never starts in a vacuum, without any underlying assumptions and focus. In principle, and if possible, needs assessment ought to be completed before defining training and development objectives. Training needs should be shown separately from non-training needs, but non-training measures that are conditions of efficient learning and application of results ought to be pointed out at this stage.

The most widespread error in training and development practice is the failure to respect this basic sequence. The needs assessment block may even be completely left out. This inevitably leads to setting the wrong objectives and designing (or purchasing) programmes that miss the target.

Objectives setting is the second stage. As explained in section 1.4, there may be valid reasons for certain differences between the needs that were identified and the training objectives that can be approved. The objective-setting stage starts to shape the programme and course design and provides essential data for choosing both programme content and methods, and deciding on organisation and resources. Objectives set a baseline for comparing the intermediate and final programme results with what was planned to be achieved. Without objectives, evaluation of training results can be only impressionistic. Even if interesting data are collected in evaluating the programme, without comparing results to objectives it will be impossible to assess overall effectiveness and the rational use of resources.

The objectives to be achieved can be defined in qualitative and/or quantitative terms. An objective of improving the organisational climate is qualitative. To determine whether such a result has been achieved will be a rather complex task. An objective of reducing from 20 to 12 the number of consumer complaints received per month is quantitative, very specific and easily controllable.

Programme design is the third block. It determines the technical content, outline, sequence and detailed scheduling of the actual training and develop-ment events that are envisaged. Appropriate methodology and organisation is chosen in harmony with the content to be covered, bearing in mind objectives, resources, and the actual possibilities and working and learning styles of the manager(s) for whom the programme is intended.

Programme implementation is the fourth block. If the design was correct, implementation should be smooth and on schedule. However, the more

Figure 2.3. A multi-level model of programme evaluation

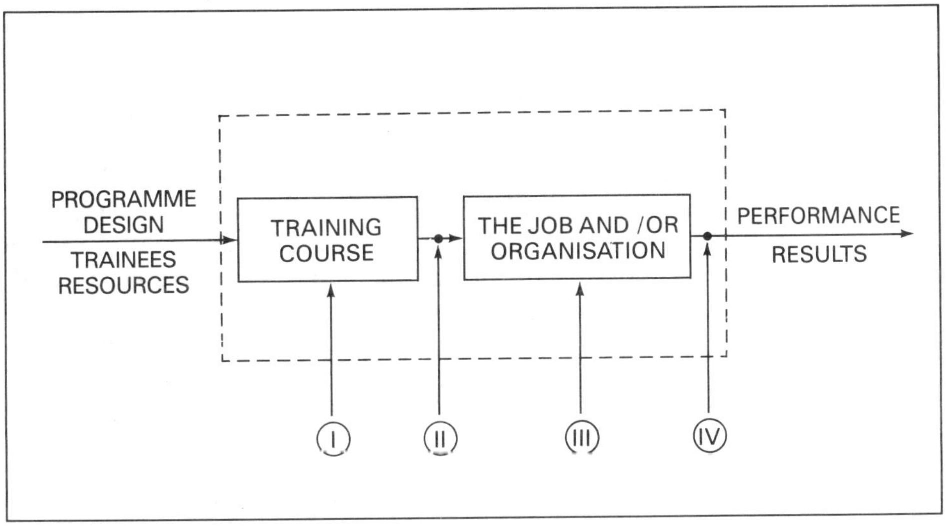

```
┌─────────────────────────────────────────────────────────────────┐
│                                                                   │
│              ┌ ─ ─ ─ ─ ─ ─ ─ ─ ─ ─ ─ ─ ─ ─ ─ ─ ┐                 │
│  PROGRAMME   │                                                    │
│   DESIGN     │  ┌──────────┐     ┌──────────────┐ │ PERFORMANCE   │
│              │  │ TRAINING │◄───►│ THE JOB AND/OR│    ───────────► │
│  TRAINEES    │  │  COURSE  │     │ ORGANISATION  │ │  RESULTS      │
│  RESOURCES   │  └──────────┘     └──────────────┘                 │
│              │        ▲      ▲          ▲        │ ▲               │
│              └ ─ ─ ─ ─│─ ─ ─ │─ ─ ─ ─ ─ │─ ─ ─ ─ ─│─ ┘            │
│                       │      │          │         │               │
│                      (I)    (II)      (III)      (IV)             │
└─────────────────────────────────────────────────────────────────┘
```

complex and longer the programme, the greater the need for adjustment, during implementation, to changed conditions and demands.

Evaluation and follow-up is the fifth and final block. Results achieved are assessed in the light of objectives, and the reasons why objectives were not achieved are thoroughly examined. Evaluation itself is normally also broken down into several levels or steps (figure 2.3).

Levels of evaluation

Level I of evaluation answers the questions: "Are the participants happy with the course? Do they like the learning process and environment, teaching methods and programme content, the trainer and the other trainees?" This feedback is useful for correcting teaching methods, course content and organisation and the learning environment. If carried out during implementation of the programme, it permits immediate correction.

Level II answers the question: "How well did the participants learn the knowledge and skills taught?" At this stage it is too late to correct errors in programme design. However, this information will be useful for the next group of participants and for the design of new programmes.

Level III deals with the question: "Are the new knowledge and skills used back on the job, and if not, why not and what should be done about it?" It provides information for improving the organisational climate and dealing with non-training problems and needs. It helps to evaluate how realistic the development objectives were and to assess the balance between the training and non-training aspects of the programme. Even after the end of the programme it may be possible to intervene to create a better organisational climate and other conditions for using new skills. This activity is sometimes called a follow-up of training.

Finally, level IV of programme evaluation deals with the measurement of performance results of the individuals and/or the organisation. It answers the question: "How did the management development programme contribute to meeting organisational objectives and what was achieved in practice?" This is the most critical and delicate point of programme evaluation. It gives an integrated assessment of overall training and development efforts, as well as of the quality of the other blocks of the management development cycle – needs analysis, objectives setting, programme design and programme implementation. It shows how the needs were met and, at the same time, uncovers new needs. Often it will be impossible to discriminate between results obtained thanks to the training and development of people, and improvements that will be the result of non-training interventions.

In programmes that are oriented to the future rather than aimed at immediate results, it will be difficult to use levels III and IV of programme evaluation in the short-term. The reasons were already explained in section 2.1: in future-oriented staff development programmes there is a time lag between training and learning, on the one hand, and application and results, on the other. Only the future will show whether all currently provided training was actually necessary and geared to results.

The steps of the management development cycle are shown once again in more detail in the model in figure 2.4.

Continuity in needs assessment

To close the whole loop we need to use the information from programme evaluation and feed it back to the first block – to training and development needs assessment. So when management development becomes a permanent process for a company or other organisation, programme evaluation, the final stage in the cycle, already provides information and prepares needs analysis for the next round of the cycle. And the same applies to the development cycle seen from the viewpoint of an individual trainee/manager: an evaluation of the process and the results achieved is a source of information and ideas for planning further training and development.

This, however, does not exhaust the roles and possibilities of needs assessment within the cycle. There can be a useful needs assessment (or reassessment) element in every stage of the cycle. If the definition of objectives is done thoroughly, it helps to discover gaps and correct inaccuracies in needs assessment. Many questions on what is to be achieved, why and how it is to be achieved, and whether the needs have been perceived and defined accurately,

Figure 2.4. Detailed model of the management development cycle

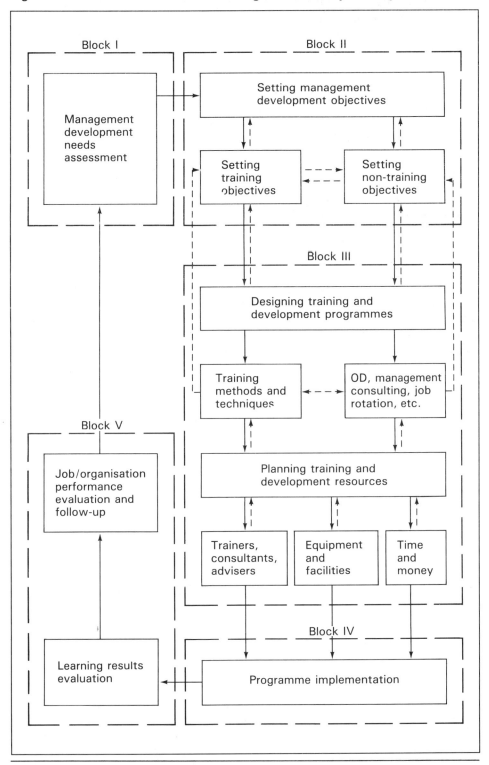

are normally raised when trainers and consultants work on programme design. Programme implementation is the core of the cycle. Here the direct contact with participants provides invaluable additional insights into their needs, possibly including needs that were totally ignored at the stage of needs assessment and in programme planning.

This shows that needs identification cannot be thought of as a one-off exercise and merely one stage in the whole process. It should be pursued during the whole programme and after its completion, using feedback from participants, supervisors and trainers, and examining criticism, new demands and new developments that could not be thought of when the process was started.

The continuity of needs assessment is even more pronounced in various non-conventional management development programmes using problem-solving, action-learning and project-method approaches. In these programmes needs assessment is started but not completed as the first block before commencing any action to meet the needs. The participants work, individually or in groups, on specific organisational problems and projects. During this work, new training needs may be discovered and have to be met immediately so that the project does not come to a halt. Needs are assessed and training provided in little steps. The results orientation of training and development is emphasised since interim results are identified and assessed before starting the next project phase. If final results are not achieved and cannot be verified, the programme cannot be regarded as successfully completed.

2.3 Complementary roles in needs assessment

The results-oriented approach to the assessment of training and development needs has some significant implications of an organisational nature. The needs of each individual manager or worker are viewed as an element of organisational problem-solving. The results to be obtained from training are expected to be of interest both to the individual and the organisation. Therefore the training and development needs of individuals (or their teams) can be best determined by combining, and harmonising, an individual and an organisational perspective in establishing what the needs are and choosing how to meet them.

The individual manager

To begin with, there is the perspective of the individual manager – the person whose needs are to be assessed, and met, in order to solve some specific organisational problems. This perspective is fundamental for reasons already explained in chapter 1. The worst thing that can happen is that managers (and indeed other workers) are regarded as passive objects whose needs can be determined in an authoritarian manner by someone else, e.g. a higher-level manager or a training director.

Therefore a systems approach to needs assessment relies strongly on active participation of those whose needs are being assessed – for example, by interviewing them, identifying their personal attitudes, priorities and goals, establishing the relationship between personal and organisational needs and objectives, using self-assessment techniques and making sure the managers concerned develop a sense of "ownership" of their training needs.

However, managers operate within human and organisational systems. Even the most dedicated and brilliant manager cannot possess the complete systems view of the organisation's problems and cannot be aware of all interpersonal and intergroup relations and related training needs. Some other perspectives are required for achieving a systems view of training and development needs.

Other managers

In our context, "other managers" are defined from the viewpoint of the individual or the team whose needs are to be assessed. The following "other managers" can hold essential information on these needs:

o   higher-level managers: they usually have a distinct opinion as regards the competence, effectiveness and training needs of managers reporting to them;

o   lower-level managers: in a similar vein, lower-level managers tend to have their own opinion on the competence, behaviour and training needs of their superiors;

o   managers of directly co-operating units and services: these managers can provide information on the quality of management and the services provided by other units placed at the same level of the hierarchy – for example, the management of the EDP department, or the management services department, is highly "visible" to all parts of the organisation, and the user units are only too glad if they can comment on their collaboration with these departments;

o   managers in special functional areas: these managers play an important role in developing a balanced interdisciplinary view of training and development needs; for example, if too much emphasis is being placed on problems in current operations and their efficiency, it will be the role of research and development managers, strategic planners, marketing managers, financial managers and others to point to long-term market and business trends in order to anticipate future needs and strike a happy medium between a focus on short-term and long-term training needs.

Individual employees

Not only people in managerial and supervisory positions, but also individual workers, technicians, accountants and other staff specialists, are usually in a position to contribute useful information and views on the effectiveness of organisational processes, on problems of performance and on the potential for improvement of their units, and on the management style and impact of managers with whom they work directly. A systems approach therefore requires to involve them, in a suitable way, in assessing managerial training and development needs despite the fact that they work in non-managerial positions and do not have any direct managerial responsibility.

Human resource development managers

If an organisation has a human resource development manager, or a training manager or director, this function will obviously be very much concerned with training and development needs assessment. Human resource development managers, as indeed the trainers working in this unit, play a number of roles: they help to create awareness as regards the importance of training, suggest useful approaches to needs assessment, provide methodology, help to plan and organise surveys and other needs assessment exercises, and are of personal assistance to all managers in assessing their individual or their units' collective training needs.

External consultants and trainers

In many countries, external management and training consultants, and management development and training institutes and centres, are used by business enterprises and other organisations for assessing training needs and designing and developing in-company training and development programmes.

A methodology or a viewpoint provided by an external professional may be very helpful, and in some cases even critical in viewing needs from various perspectives, and avoiding in-breeding. In more important needs assessment studies and surveys, the use of external professionals may be necessary since the organisation may lack expertise and staff time for such a special project.

The issue of responsibility

The overview given in the previous paragraphs suggests that a systems approach to needs assessment cannot be implemented without active involvement of managers and staff working in various sectors in an organisation and, in some areas, without involving external professionals – consultants and/or trainers. This could create an impression that the responsibility for needs assessment will be utterly diluted – many people will be involved, many views and wishes (sometimes conflicting) will be expressed, but it will be unclear who will make the decisions and see to it that the conclusions reached are implemented.

Once more, the approach whereby training and development needs assessment is directed towards organisational results provides a basic guide-line as regards responsibility. Responsibility for training (and non-training) needs assessment should be seen as part of normal managerial responsibility at all levels of the hierarchy, as well as in all line positions and functional areas of management. This may be self-evident to many readers, but in practice the assessment of training and development needs is often regarded as a responsibility of the training manager. In these situations, training is treated as a separate function, for which line management, and functional managers in other areas than human resources, do not feel fully responsible. There may be a training programme, but this programme risks being irrelevant to the major structural and operational problems and to strategic concerns of the organisation.

As regards the use of external consultants or trainers for assessing management training needs, the basic principles of using external professional experts and consultants apply.[4] Overall responsibility for the conclusions reached and action taken remains with the management of the organisation and cannot be delegated to an external professional who intervenes in an advisory capacity.

---

[1] K.J. Austin and A.A. Titus: "Beyond performance-based training", in *Training* (Minneapolis), Jan. 1988, p. 54.

[2] R. Zemke et al.: *Designing and delivering cost-effective training and measuring the results* (Minneapolis, Lakewood Publications, 1981), p.29.

[3] S. Lusterman: *Trends in corporate education and training* (New York, The Conference Board, 1985), p. 11.

[4] These principles are discussed in considerable detail in another ILO publication. See M. Kubr (ed.): *Management consulting: A guide to the profession* (Geneva, ILO, second (revised) edition, 1986).

COMPENDIUM OF TECHNIQUES

GENERIC APPROACHES TO NEEDS ASSESSMENT

3

Part II of this book provides a wide choice of needs assessment techniques suitable for various purposes and situations. In choosing among these techniques, however, it will be useful to keep in mind that there are a few generic or basic approaches that are used in one way or another by every technique. The understanding of these approaches, to which chapter 3 is devoted, will help the reader to look at each technique with an open mind, to choose among alternative techniques and to combine techniques flexibly. It should help, too, in developing and trying out new techniques for diagnosing training and development needs, thus enlarging their portfolio.

3.1   Problem identification and analysis

First of all, any training and development need can be regarded as a management or organisational problem, and needs assessment as problem identification. A training need *is* a problem in its own right, which has its own characteristics, causes and solutions. In addition, it is often part of a wider and more complex personnel or organisational problem, and may be interwoven with other problems, more or less complex and significant. As explained in section 2.1, in business practice the assessment of training needs is in many cases preceded by the finding that the organisation concerned is facing problems. The identification of these organisational problems is the first step, or entry point, of training needs assessment. Training is then considered as the means, or one of the means, for solving the performance or other problems of the organisation.

How is a problem defined?

A problem is normally defined as a difference or discrepancy between what is (or will be) actually happening and what should (or might) be happening. A problem can also be an uncertain or disturbed situation. Any problem can be identified by the following five principal dimensions or characteristics:[1]

---

(1) substance or identity: low performance, growing costs, shortage of competent staff, lack of new ideas, etc.;

(2) location: divisions, departments, plants, buildings, offices, etc.;

(3) problem "ownership" (people affected by the existence of the problem and primarily interested in resolving it): managers, staff specialists, supervisors, workers, secretaries, the whole organisation;

(4) magnitude (in absolute and relative terms): importance of the problem to the unit and whole organisation, e.g. in terms of waste, idle capacity, money lost, potential savings, etc.;

(5) time perspective: Since when has the problem existed? When was it first observed? Has it been recurrent? Has it been growing, diminishing or stabilised, etc.?

Steps in problem-solving

The process of problem-solving can be broken down into several steps:

o   creating awareness;

o   defining and describing the problem;

o   finding and analysing facts;

o   establishing and verifying real causes;

o   developing alternative solutions;

o   choosing the optimum solution;

o   implementing the solution chosen.

A short description of these steps is given in the following paragraphs.

Creating awareness

The process starts with the realisation that something is going wrong, not as planned and expected, or not as well as in other organisations. This may be only a feeling, or a finding based on hard data measuring profitability, productivity, quality, market position, deviations from long-term objectives, etc. For example, a high (or increasing) personnel turnover (the ratio of staff leaving in relation to the total number of personnel in the organisation) might be an indicator of poor employee morale, as well as involving increased costs of recruiting new personnel. The failure to achieve the long-term organisational objectives could be identified through a strategic audit, which includes a systematic examination and appraisal of how an organisation fits into its environment and opportunities. For this purpose, such measurement tools as ratio analysis and variance analysis can be used.

Table 3.1. Signals of undesirable trends

Indicator	Situation
Output	Low/falling
Standards of service	Low/falling
Scrap/waste	High/rising
Standards of human performance	Low/falling
Time taken to perform tasks	Long/rising
Level of accuracy	Low/falling
Use of equipment	Low/falling
Accident rate	High/rising
Labour turnover	High/rising
Absenteeism and tardiness	High/rising
Recruitment problems	Continuing/increasing
Labour disputes	Excessive/increasing
Market share	Low/shrinking
Delays in delivery	Excessive/increasing
Customer complaints	Excessive/increasing
Growth rate	Low/diminishing

There could be various warning signs or symptoms of unwanted developments and trends in different parts of the organisation or its hierarchical and functional levels. For example, changes in the indicators shown in table 3.1 can signal existing or latent problems.

As regards potential future problems, it is important to watch signals that have not yet been reflected in current performance indicators of the organisation, but could be reflected soon if corrective action is delayed. The warning signs concerning future changes and potential future problems include the general economic and industry outlook, changes in markets and competition, new government policies and regulations, new import-export barriers, major changes in technology, and so on.

It would not suffice merely to identify and measure these symptoms and signs. There must be some awareness of the need to look under the surface, and a will to reveal the full dimensions of the problems and their real causes, even if this is going to be a difficult, costly and painful exercise.

Defining and describing the problems

In this step the symptoms and signals indicative of potential problems are reworded into specific and precise statements of deviations that name the object, the kind of malfunction whose cause is to be discovered and explained or the conditions and people who have created and are sustaining the problem. The objective is to go beneath the symptoms and identify the "real" problems.

The procedure starts with the identification of the reasonable expectations, allowable tolerances and the comparison of actual situations against the expectations.

An example of the problem-finding procedure is the operation of a standard cost-accounting system. The first step is to establish standards for unit direct materials and unit direct labour costs and allowable variances from these standards. Periodically, the actual unit direct materials and direct labour costs are compared with these standards. Variances that exceed the allowable ranges are flagged for the attention of production management. They indicate that there is a problem requiring analysis and action.

Finding and analysing facts

The main purpose of this phase is to gather and analyse necessary facts in order to solve the problem. This phase often overlaps with the previous one since new facts and data help to sort out the symptoms from the causes of the problem, and identify the resources and conditions required to develop the solution and implement it. The scope of the data to be collected reflects the scope and purpose of the particular problem-solving exercise (for example, different data would be gathered for research purposes). This includes the definition of data content, degree of detail, time reference, extent of coverage, and criteria for classification and tabulation.[2]

There are three main sources of facts:

o   records (files, reports, publications, computer files, etc.);

o   events and conditions (actions and processes to be observed);

o   memories (information stored in the minds of people).

Facts and data can also be classified by their internal or external sources. Internal sources, which are those within the organisation, can be of a general inter-functional nature (policies, strategies, global plans and results), or comprise sectoral and functional data (indicating resources, activities and results in various areas of activity). External sources are sources outside the organisation, such as social, economic and demographic statistics, or data on markets and competitors.

The following techniques are widely used for collecting data needed for problem-solving:

o retrieval of recorded data or special recording;

o observation;

o interviews;

o questionnaires;

o data-gathering meetings and workshops;

o attitude surveys;

o document gathering;

o charting;

o estimates;

o corporate audit, etc.

Analysis of facts and data aims to describe correctly a problem, its nature, events and causes and to establish how to develop solutions and solve the problem. This step helps to avoid hasty conclusions and ideas that are formulated before examining the facts. It helps also to identify relationships, proportions and trends. For this purpose a variety of statistical techniques can be used, including averages, dispersion, frequency distribution, correlation and regression, etc.[3]

This analysis helps to establish whether specific qualitative and quantitative relationships exist between various factors and events described by facts and data and to examine their nature, and the most substantive relationships. Among the best ways to express and measure relationships are *ratios*. They help to evaluate output generated by a certain input, to analyse the balance of different resources and commitments, or to express the structure of a specific resource or factor.

Establishing and verifying real causes

An important feature of fact and data analysis is causal analysis, which aims to discover causal relationships between conditions and events. When causes of certain situations or problems are known, action can focus on these causes to influence them. To analyse causes, it is essential to proceed systematically by examining whether a hypothetical cause could really have created the problem effect observed.

The principal task is to identify the forces and factors which are causing the problem. The exercise starts with some preliminary knowledge or assumptions on what the causes might be. It is useful to formulate several hypotheses about possible causes, and to keep an open mind when investigating the alternatives. If data to support a hypothesis are difficult to find, this does not necessarily mean that this hypothesis is wrong and should be dropped.

The established causes may require verification. If contradictions or inconsistencies appear, it is necessary to re-check the facts used for reference and the statement of the causes in order to find the true cause. This may be difficult if we deal with potential future problems, which may be affected by various mutually interrelated factors.

For example, it may be necessary to speed up the introduction of results of research in the normal production process, and the solution is sought in increasing the numbers of researchers and technicians, using new project planning and control techniques, introducing an incentives scheme to speed up innovation, putting one vice-president in charge of research and production, and providing training for all the research and production staff involved. In such a case, the testing of the real causes of the problem cannot be done before actually implementing the solutions envisaged, and making corrections during this process.

Testing for cause is a process of matching the details of cause with the details of an observed effect. It identifies the most likely possible cause that explains the deviation better than any of the other possible causes. Verification aims to prove that a likely cause did produce the observed effect.

After the necessary facts, causes and problem statements are verified, it is time to start to work on developing solutions.

Developing alternative solutions

This phase aims at developing and selecting the effective solution to the problem, as well as a plan for implementing the solution. The effective solution is the one which has sufficient technical quality to resolve the problem, and has the best chance of being accepted and supported by those who are to implement it. Acceptance here means readiness to invest time and energy with sufficient confidence of success. The solution should meet the criteria of efficiency, adaptability, cost, time and reliability.

Solutions could be classified into *creative* and *selective*.[4] The first variant means actually creating or inventing a range of new alternatives, while the second one involves making a choice between a number of given alternatives.

It is essential to generate as many alternative solutions as feasible from the very beginning. Generating alternative solutions is a creative process like generating new ideas. A variety of well-defined approaches and techniques that blend experience and the creative process are available.

Choosing the optimum solution

After alternative solutions are developed and refined they should be evaluated to determine the preferred solution. It is important to start this process with preliminary evaluation to reduce the number of alternatives on which more work will be done and a more comprehensive evaluation undertaken. If the preliminary screening has retained more than one alternative, a phased approach may help. For example, work may be started on two or three alternatives but carried only to a pre-project or sketch-plan level. This will make it possible to collect more factual data, including tentative figures on potential costs and benefits. An evaluation of alternative pre-projects can result in the conclusion that from that moment only one will be pursued, or, on the contrary, that the client wishes the design of two or more alternatives to be completed.

Each alternative should be evaluated, using the same criteria, against all other alternative solutions. In this way it is easy to eliminate those alternatives that do not promise the desired improvement.

The criteria for analysing alternatives include economic, operational, technical, scheduling, and legal. Other factors to consider include organisational culture, attitudes, traditions, values, and so on, of workers, managers and customers, who will be affected by the implementation of the solution.

When trying to develop or choose the alternative solutions to interpersonal problems, which is often the case in management practice, the parties involved ought to establish a mutual interest and believe that each has gained from the solution. A situation in which one party is a winner, while the other feels a loser, is loaded with new problems.

Implementing the solution chosen

The purpose of problem-solving is to develop solutions that can be implemented, and to make sure that these solutions are put into effect. Without implementation, even the most rigorous process is ineffective. During implementation, unexpected new problems may be uncovered and the optimum solution originally envisaged may need adjustment to new conditions. A creative and open-minded approach to implementation is therefore necessary. However, the development of a plan for implementation and gaining commitment from those participating in implementation are of crucial importance.

Analysis of future problems

Analysis of future problems is the mode of thinking that enables managers to identify and improve the future of their organisations and employees. It is a

---

practical and preventive process which enables us to make necessary changes well in advance. The basic questions in future problem analysis are: "What could go wrong?", "What can we do about it now?", and "What future opportunities can be foreseen now and how can we prepare ourselves to take them?"

Five sorts of practical activities could provide the framework for analysis of future problems. They include:

(1) identifying vulnerable areas in the organisation's resources, activities and environment;

(2) identifying specific potential problems within these vulnerable areas;

(3) identifying likely causes of these potential problems and actions to prevent them from occurring;

(4) identifying contingent actions that can be taken if preventive action fails or where no preventive action is possible;

(5) identifying measures creating new capabilities for taking future opportunities (e.g. spare capacity or new systems design skills).

The determination of the type of actions to take – preventive, contingent, and so on – will depend on the subject of the future problem analysis, the economic and technical feasibility of implementation, the element of risk, and common sense.

Issues in problem identification

Errors in defining problems can limit the possibility of solving them. Therefore it is useful to be aware of the most frequent errors, and of the ways they can occur in the identification of training needs.

Preconceived ideas about the causes of problems. The lack of training is often regarded as a cause of inferior performance without any analysis of whether there are not concurrent causes, or causes other than the lack of training.

Looking at problems from one technical viewpoint only. This happens if the analyst (manager, trainer, etc.) has a strong bias in one technical area and is not able to take a balanced interdisciplinary view, for example, seeing the causes of all problems in distorted interpersonal relations, and the solutions in communication and training in managing people.

Ignoring how the problem is perceived in various parts of the organisation. For example, an explanation provided by a factory manager is accepted without verifying whether his views are shared by marketing management. This can be particularly misleading in examining processes and procedures (and related skills) that cut across various units and functions in an organisation.

Unfinished problem diagnosis. The analyst may be so happy "to have found the cause" that he or she does not bother checking the findings, and looking for further information, which may reveal additional or different aspects of the problem.

Mistaking symptoms for problems. When one is dealing with training needs, this can happen very easily. The fact that certain skills are not developed and used may not be the problem, but only a symptom of problems such as nepotism in personnel selection or remuneration practices that do not encourage risk taking and innovation.

Failure to discern cause and effect. Frequently conditions are observed that influence each other and an effect risks being mistaken for its cause. What is the cause and what would be the effect of poor financial results and low staff morale in an organisation? If a static view is taken, these conditions influence each other and there may be a vicious circle. If a training need is involved, the questions that must be asked are: Is the lack of training the main cause? Or is it an effect of another more profound cause?

The potential to solve the problem

This potential has several dimensions. If a training need is identified, it is equally important to establish whether there will be material and financial resources, as well as technical expertise and human authority, needed to solve the problem. The time perspective is also important. It may be that there were attempts to solve the problem in the past – e.g. through a training programme arranged in the company. If some deeper causes inhibit training and development, will the organisation be able to – and be prepared to – tackle these causes? It may be difficult to remove the causes relating to factors such as employment policy, legal terms of employment, political forces, tensions between ethnic groups, and so on.

Closed-ended and open-ended problems

In assessing training needs, it is also helpful to distinguish between closed-ended and open-ended problems.

A closed-ended problem has a unique solution, which can be found if a problem-solving technique is properly applied, step by step. Once the solution is found, it is usually the end of the problem. Often the causes of the problem will be technical, such as insufficient knowledge of maintenance principles concerning a particular type of equipment, or lack of skill in analysing the company's financial statements. Such training needs can be defined, and remedial action suggested, with considerable accuracy.

An open-ended problem is more difficult to handle since it is influenced by many factors and has more possible solutions and no clear-cut answers. Its main causes will not be easy to establish and there may be confusion in respect of various causes and their effects. Technical and human aspects will be interwoven. The attitudes and the behaviour of the people involved will be an essential part, and may even be the principal factor, of the problem. The solution may appear to be straightforward and easy in strictly technical terms, yet there will be open or hidden forces and barriers that make it difficult. Examples of open-ended problems are high absenteeism, low work morale, reluctance to take risks, absence of creativity, lack of capability to improve product quality, lack of interest in customers' demands and needs, slow product innovation, and so on. Defining training needs in these cases is a delicate issue. First, the causes of the problem will often be "non-training" factors. Second, even if there is a need for training, it may be impossible to determine it fully at the beginning of the problem-solving process. What consultants prefer to do in these cases is to start the problem-identification and problem-solving process, involving those people who have the greatest influence on the existence of the problem and on the possibility of finding and implementing a solution. Training needs – if any – are identified and met gradually, as the problem-solving process requires and the progress made permits.

3.2   Comparison

Comparison is inherent in the very concept of training and development needs. When dealing with needs, we are constantly comparing at least two – but often more – different conditions. Therefore, comparison is extensively used in needs assessment techniques, as indeed in any other problem identification and diagnosis. As shown in chapter 1, when training and development needs are diagnosed, factors and conditions affecting competence and its applications are being compared in addition to, and in parallel with, competence and performance.

Comparing what is comparable

Finding appropriate bases for comparison is the most difficult and responsible part of the exercise. Against the bases, the current condition will be compared and assessed. Important conclusions may be drawn on the inadequacy of current competence, the urgency of training needs and the magnitude of the immediate and future training task.

If an error is made in choosing the comparison base – the standard – not only will wrong conclusions be drawn on the content and magnitude of training needs, but such an error may become a pretext for designating comparison as

---

meaningless and rejecting it completely. The analyst who chooses to use a standard as a comparison base must be able to explain and defend his or her choices; otherwise the whole exercise will become futile and inconclusive.

The simplest case

The simplest case of comparison is one where there is an accepted standard against which current competence and/or performance can be assessed. It may be a job description, a competency profile, a technical performance standard, or an output and performance plan of a unit or a whole organisation. It is useful to look for these standards in preparing for training needs assessment and make wide use of them in order to enhance the objectivity of the exercise. The standard may not be sacrosanct and it may require corrections, but it is tangible, is likely to be expressed in quantitative terms, and makes the discussion of training needs concrete and serious.

Standard to be achieved in the future

The use of future-oriented models of managerial competence is quite popular in management education and training circles. There have been many attempts to identify and describe characteristics of the "managers of the future". Some of these attempts will be mentioned in part III. By comparing the profiles of current managers with ideal future profiles, it is possible to get some ideas on the sort of training and development that will be required. Such an exercise would be used mainly for revising training policies, reorienting training programmes and institutions, and providing ideas to managers on what they may expect in the future. However, experience has shown how risky all future forecasting and modelling is in business and international economy: these lessons must be kept in mind in drawing up and using ideal models of future managers.

Determining future training and development needs as part of a specific enterprise or sectoral development programme is a different matter. In such cases the time horizon is likely to be shorter (say 3-5 years) and the main planning and investment decisions will provide enough information for determining specific future standards to be achieved in training managerial and other staff.

Using foreign models

In assessing both current and future needs, the achievements and practices of enterprises in other countries are often used as references. For example, a leading and innovative international firm may be used as a standard, or a particular feature of Japanese management (e.g. quality management) or the management of Japanese firms as a whole. An enterprise in a least developed

---

country may be interested in achievements of comparable enterprises operating in relatively more advanced developing countries. The use of such standards can be inspiring and useful if foreign experience and its applicability are critically analysed and the environmental differences well understood.

Rating

An important issue in making comparisons and evaluating the intensity or span of any management development or training problem is the measurement of skills, knowledge, attitudes, behaviour, and so on. This can be done with the help of varying rating techniques. Rating is a process of evaluating and classifying by judgement, which may be adjectival or numerical, and may or may not use a scale to describe, rate and compare behaviour or another characteristic chosen at several levels. Thus, rating is a universal tool for quantitative measurement and comparison under any kind of needs assessment method.

A wide range of rating techniques is available to the analyst. They include several *comparative rating techniques*, used to compare performance or other characteristics of two or more managers with one another, and a number of *absolute rating techniques*, which assign absolute values to selected characteristics or performance levels on a fixed scale without any reference or comparison to other persons. A detailed description of different rating techniques is given in appendix 1.

3.3 Expert opinion

In diagnosing management training and development needs we are constantly faced with the question of whether and how to use "hard" data (precisely defined, identified by scientific techniques and quantified), or "soft" data (opinions, impressions, feelings, predictions of what "should have been achieved" or "might happen" or "might be required" in the future). Many researchers make genuine efforts to increase the use of hard data in order to increase the objectivity of needs assessment – for example, by measuring differences in individual or unit performance and trying to establish a causal relationship between an existing training need and a performance difference that can be explained by the existence of this need. However, while these efforts are certainly in the right direction, they cannot be pushed beyond reasonable limits. The assessment of needs, as indeed the evaluation of training, will always combine "hard" and "soft" data, and facts and opinions.

The possibility of basing all needs assessment on hard data is limited by the nature of the needs concept. On the one hand, we have the real (current) condition. This is being compared to an ideal or desired condition (a standard).

The new condition does not exist at the moment of needs assessment, and can only be visualised and described by analysing a number of factors, by extrapolating, or by seeking inspiration and guidance in a suitable model. The choices involved in such an exercise are not possible without expert opinion (judgement). By definition, this expert opinion will be a subjective one, and will be based on both rational and intuitive mental processes.

The more complex and uncertain the management setting within which the training and development needs are being diagnosed, the greater will be the role of expert opinion. Typically, studies of future training and development needs will use expert opinion as their principal tool for examining future trends and identifying the most likely but not certain implications for management education, training and development.

Who is the expert?

The choice of the experts who will be consulted is infinitely more important than the choice of the techniques to be used for tapping expertise. The question is: *Who is the expert* able to give meaningful advice or even an authoritative opinion on what the problems are, and what is likely to happen, or should happen, in management training and development? This is not an academic question. Many needs assessment studies suffer from a wrong choice of experts whose opinions are sought. There have been quite a few self-appointed "experts" in the management development and consulting profession.

An expert is not defined by the position he or she occupies in an administrative, managerial, consulting or business-school hierarchy. Rather, an expert is an individual who:

o   possesses the technical knowledge and/or practical experience concerning the issue in question;

o   is able to take a detached view, minimising personal biases and preferences;

o   is able to synthesise and conceptualise, taking a holistic view and perceiving emerging trends behind vast amounts of events, data, and other people's opinions;

o   is able to carry out a dialogue with other experts, including individuals representing different disciplines and defending different opinions;

o   is prepared to admit ignorance, uncertainty and error.

Such a person has to be hand-picked and the reasons for choosing him or her must be clear. It is not possible to choose experts by random sampling.

The experienced manager

The experienced manager or business owner is the obvious first "candidate" for the expert function.

First, there will be the managers who constitute the target population, that is, those whose needs are being diagnosed. Their role in needs assessment was already mentioned in section 2.3. Technically they will be the persons with the most appropriate practical experience and knowledge of facts for judging the context in which they operate. More importantly, they will be emotionally involved in the situation under scrutiny and will expect that their expert opinion would be sought, in addition to facts indicative of the presence or absence of certain competencies. Thus, managers in this group will play a double role of objects and subjects of needs assessment, or, put in other terms, of those who are being assessed and those who are making the assessment. This is best expressed in self-assessment techniques, and in consulting groups of experts representative of the experience and the views of the target population.

Second, there are managers who are outside the target population, but are close to it and can be of help. For example, higher management would be interviewed for expert opinion on the training of lower-level managers and supervisors. Managers in client enterprises may provide useful information on training needs of their suppliers. A bank manager or credit officer is likely to have useful views on the management training needs of the bank's clients.

Third, the managers' expert opinion will have to be tapped in broader (sectoral, national, etc) forward-looking studies and surveys of needs. The prevailing practice in these studies is to review opinions of representative samples of managers and to include directly a small number of excellent managers in the study team responsible for co-ordinating the study and drawing conclusions. We can only endorse this practice. However, it is advisable not to involve those dignitaries from management circles or the civil service who want to see their names on the list of committee members without actually intending to do any expert work.

Professional experts

Management trainers, teachers and consultants, accountants, economists, sociologists, lawyers, political scientists, development planners and other professionals are another major source of expertise in assessing needs. Managers have been their clients as course participants or users of consulting services, or else these professionals have done research and gathered experience on various aspects of the environment in which managers operate, and on management functions, methods and processes. The choice of experts from this group must be made cautiously. Experience with training or research is in itself insufficient for assessing senior managers' needs and giving opinions on probable future trends. Thus it will be necessary to differentiate between various roles played in needs assessment by the professionals – planning, co-ordination, data collection and analysis, and the expert role.

Techniques based on expert opinion

The reader will see in the following chapters that expert opinion can be tapped and used through various needs assessment techniques. They range from simple interviewing of one or more experts and collective consultations and task groups to research studies using the Delphi technique, whereby a number of experts are questioned through an iterative process of gradual reviews and approximations. In using these techniques, analysts should always ask themselves whether they are identifying facts or opinions, whose opinions they are, and what their basis is (scientific knowledge, practical management experience, a biased or unbiased view of the business reality, conservative assessment of trends or wishful thinking, etc.). If managers who belong to the target population are also consulted as selected experts on the subject, this would normally be done separately from the interviews or questionnaires administered to the population surveyed.

Analysts should not take it for granted that it is enough to gather experts and pose a general question in order to receive exactly the sort and amount of information that they hoped for. Working with experts to obtain maximum unbiased information and useful advice is an art that requires careful preparation. For example, some experts will tend to broaden the subject under review or will be unable to appreciate the importance of the arguments put forward by experts from other sectors or disciplines. Some experts will be more and others less active in defending their position, and so on. When assessing training needs, analysts will find that poorly prepared and poorly managed meetings with experts often produce trivial information.

Consulting a small number of selected experts may be a useful preparatory step in planning and structuring a needs analysis. For example, needs assessment guide-lines provided under the ARIES project of the United States Agency for International Development (AID)[5] suggest that advance interviews with experts help analysts:

o   to be more precise in delimiting the target population;

o   to find out about past efforts to solve the problems (when, where and how solutions have been successful);

o   to appreciate special circumstances that may strongly influence the problems;

o   to be better prepared for interviews conducted at the site;

o   to save time and money.

Talking to groups of experts is most useful if an analyst is to prepare a survey of needs in an environment which is new to him or her. This is often the case in preparing new technical assistance programmes in developing countries.

An example of applying expert judgement in manpower planning and vocational training needs assessment is *the key informants approach*, pioneered by the ILO.[6] The key informants are carefully chosen individuals who are knowledgeable about current and emerging trends in the given sector, concerning questions such as supply and shortages of particular skill categories, changes in demand for particular skills, changes in the nature of skills and resulting changes in training requirements. Key informants are interviewed systematically for both qualitative and quantitative information concerning trends, not specific numbers.

3.4 Case: Surfside Seasonings consult Frank Roby

The application of the three generic approaches to needs assessment is well demonstrated by the following case.[7]

The manufacturing vice-president of Surfside Seasonings, Willis Angel, is dissatisfied with the performance of his plants. He assigns three groups of people to conduct independent studies to tell him which performance improvement programmes he should invest in. When Angel reads the three reports, he can hardly believe that the studies were independent because their recommendations are so similar. They finger the first-line supervisors of the workforce in the processing area as the culprits most responsible for the poor showing in the plants. The once stable, but ageing, hourly workers have been largely replaced by young women from disadvantaged social groups. The reports agree that the old first-line supervisors are unable to manage this type of worker. A training programme in new styles of supervision and in human relations will be required and one management consulting firm offers to develop such a programme for US$78,000. For a US$400-million business, this does not seem too large an investment in good supervision.

Although Willis Angel is impressed by the agreement of the three studies he has commissioned, the US$78,000 of training costs for an operation that has been losing money gives him trouble. He cannot quite make up his mind and decides to get another opinion. He has heard of Frank Roby, a consultant with a mixed reputation. Some say that Roby is a charlatan, while others insist that, although his methods are truly unorthodox, Roby gets results. The word "results" sounds sweet to Angel, so he hires Roby at US$750 a day and decides to watch him work.

Roby shows up one morning and makes the mandatory tour of a manufacturing plant, seemingly without noticing a thing. He then spends the rest of the day talking with the corporate accountant, the plant production manager and the chief quality control inspector. To Angel's surprise, Roby appears in his office at the end of the day saying that he is ready to present his report and suggesting that they conclude the study in the nearest bar.

Angel begins the interview with suspicion, but within an hour Roby has completely convinced him that the best way for Surfside Seasonings to waste time and money would be to train first-line supervisors, and that, indeed, the company has an extraordinarily competent corps of foremen in the processing areas (even though Roby never so much as interviewed a supervisor). Besides, Roby tells Angel where he thinks the problem is, why it is there and what can be done about it. He is so convincing that the next morning Angel seeks authorisation to spend the US$150,000 that Roby said would be required for the programme.

Eighteen months later, Angel has sufficient data to prove that the adoption of Roby's programme is bringing in the company a return of several million dollars a year in greatly increased labour productivity, reduced waste, lower employee turnover and fewer grievances. And Angel finds himself taking all the credit. This was not his ambition, but how could he ever explain to anyone that an outsider could walk into a seasonings plant for the first time and after one day suggest how to turn the plant around − and against all the advice of seasoned professionals?

Let us look at a sample of the data that Roby studied to reach his conclusions. Table 3.2 shows production data for three representative supervisory groups at Surfside Seasonings (in the real case, there were 32 groups; three are chosen here to simplify the argument).

Of course, Roby did not depend on these data alone, but they contributed far more than anything else to his remarkable conclusions. In examining the data, Roby could see at once that the potential for improving the performance of the hourly employees was considerable, but that the differences among supervisors were small. Even though supervisor B had the best supervisory performance in the company, getting other supervisors to perform as he does would not improve matters greatly. If the situation were reversed and there were large differences between the supervisors, Roby's conclusions would have been quite different.

The average production per employee is 96.93 and the best employee produces 194 units; so the employee performance improvement potential (P), assuming that costs and quality are the constants, is:

$$\text{Employee } P = \frac{194}{96.9} = 2.00$$

Table 3.2. Comparative manufacturing productivity

Supervisor A		Supervisor B		Supervisor C	
Employee No.	Hourly productivity	Employee No.	Hourly productivity	Employee No.	Hourly productivity
1	163	11	194	21	172
2	149	12	138	22	137
3	118	13	137	23	136
4	108	14	131	24	135
5	106	15	110	25	127
6	93	16	89	26	100
7	60	17	61	27	56
8	57	18	49	28	52
9	42	19	48	29	41
10	30	20	41	30	28
Average 92.6		Average 99.8		Average 98.4	

This figure shows that the average hourly employee could double productivity. But the supervisory P is negligible – unusually low, in fact. Roby looked at these variances and noticed that the job employees had to do was to operate low-tolerance equipment. A lot of learning is required to master this job. He also heard people say that it simply took a lot of experience to reach maximum production. And he learned that the hourly employees got no formal training – mostly because production managers did not think that formal training was as good as on-the-job experience. He considered this to be a nonsense, and advised Angel that US$150,000 invested in proper training in the theory and trouble-shooting of the equipment could get any new employee producing at about 150 units an hour, thus reducing the employee P to less than 1.3. Roby proved to be right – and the most important information he had was the P measures. Management had these data in the books, but not in the form of table 3.2.

The case of Frank Roby shows how important it is to trace problems to real causes and to use comparison and expert judgement in proper ways. Thanks to his approach, Roby could suggest training for completely different people (workers) than suggested by others on the basis of superficial analysis (supervisors), and in completely different topics (equipment utilisation and maintenance instead of management styles and human relations).

---

[1] See Ch. 8 in M. Kubr (ed.): *Management consulting: A guide to the profession* (Geneva, ILO, second (revised) edition, 1986).

[2] ibid.

[3] See, for example, V.T. Clover and H.T. Belsey: *Business research methods* (Columbus, Ohio, Grid Publishing Co., 1979).

[4] J. Prokopenko, J. White, L. Bittel, R. Eckles: *Modular programme for supervisory development* (Geneva, ILO, 1981), Vol.2, Module II-9, p. 9.

[5] ARIES: *Training needs assessment manual* (Minneapolis, Control Data, 1986).

[6] See L. Richter: *Training needs: Assessment and monitoring* (Geneva, ILO, 1986), pp. 44-49.

[7] Adapted, with acknowledgement of the origin, from T.F. Gilbert: "Measuring potential for performance improvement", in R. Zemke, L. Standke and P. Jones (eds.): *Designing and delivering cost-effective training and measuring the results* (Minneapolis, Lakewood Publications, 1981)

TECHNIQUES FOR ASSESSING INDIVIDUAL NEEDS

4

The individual manager is both the main object and the main actor of any exercise in management development needs assessment. Even sectoral and national surveys must deal with the individual manager (e.g. by interviewing a representative sample of managers). Therefore, our review starts at this level – by describing the principal techniques used for assessing individual needs. Later on we shall see how these techniques are used as components of group, organisational and even macro-economic needs assessment. At the same time, we shall see that macro-economic and global techniques generate information, and questions, for assessing individual needs.

Without going into much detail, we shall review job analysis and job descriptions first of all (section 4.1). It could be objected that these are not, strictly speaking, needs assessment techniques, but techniques for defining the scope, content and qualification requirements of any job, including management jobs. However, we shall see that job analysis and job descriptions serve as a sort of "basic building block" in needs assessment and can be used in conjunction with several other techniques.

Following the discussion of job analysis and job descriptions, 12 groups of individual techniques will be reviewed in the following sequence:

o   tests and examinations (4.2);

o   questionnaires (4.3);

o   interviewing (4.4);

o   observing (4.5);

o   critical incidents (4.6);

o   diary method (4.7);

o   management by objectives (4.8);

o   action learning (4.9);

o   performance appraisal (4.10);

o   self-assessment (4.11);

o   career planning (4.12);

o   assessment centres (4.13).

We have chosen techniques that are common and on which a fair amount of practical experience has been collected. Experimental, research and special laboratory techniques, as well as proprietary techniques used only by certain consulting firms, are not included. Our review also provides, whenever appropriate, comments on the advantages and the limitations of individual techniques covered.

4.1 Job analysis and job descriptions

Job analysis

Job analysis is the process of assembling, recording and interpreting information relating to essential characteristics of individual jobs. Usually job analysis is organised within the context of a functional breakdown of activities of an individual. It involves a systematic examination of jobs in order to uncover the nature of the tasks performed, the working conditions, responsibilities and skills required. Job analysis provides information on particular job components, the way in which the job is performed, the relationships to other jobs, acceptable performance standards, the complexity of specific tasks, the equipment and materials to be used, and so on.

From this information, trainers and personnel officers can derive objectives and standards for skills, knowledge and personal attributes required to do the job, information for designing job descriptions or personal specifications, performance tests and training programmes.

In practice, the primary purpose of job analysis is to collect data for job evaluation. However, job analysis can also be used for a wide range of personnel and management decisions, such as recruitment, selection, promotion, performance review and appraisal, manpower planning and, certainly, as an important technique for identifying management training needs.

Job analysis uses a job breakdown, which can be as follows:[1]

Element: the smallest unit into which work can be divided.

Task: a distinct identifiable work activity which comprises a logical and necessary step in the performance of a job.

Duty: a significant segment of the work performed in a job, usually comprising several tasks.

Post (or position): one or more duties which require the services or activities of one worker for their performance; there are as many posts as there are workers and vacancies in an organisation.

Job:	a group of posts that are identical or involve substantially similar tasks.
Occupation:	a group of jobs similar in terms of the knowledge, skills, abilities, training, and work experience required.

For example, for a plant manager's position the job could be broken down into several duties such as planning, organising, controlling, staffing and directing. The duties in turn could also be subdivided into several major tasks which relate to methods, procedures and techniques used to carry out each duty. For example, planning for a plant manager might cover setting objectives, outlining procedures and assigning responsibilities.

The element, the most detailed level of the job, usually deals with the particular details of how methods, procedures and techniques are used to carry out various tasks. For example, elements of setting objectives of the task could be studying reports, collecting and analysing business and production data, counselling, and so on.

The process of job analysis usually begins by establishing a list of all positions in order to group those which are identical or essentially the same into "jobs". This step is generally known as "job identification".

The first operation in actual job analysis involves the gathering of information about jobs: what the employees actually do (the duties and tasks they perform); how they do it (the manner in which they perform each task); why they do it (the purpose of each task, or of the output produced); what materials, tools, procedures, equipment, principles, guide-lines, etc., are used in the execution of each task; and under what conditions each task is performed.

The second operation is to ascertain the knowledge (in terms of education, training and experience), skill, abilities and attitudes required to perform each task at an acceptable level of proficiency. When this is being done, one has to keep constantly in mind that job analysis seeks to determine objective job requirements and not to assess the personal skill of the job holder.

Though it is clear that a manager tends to influence his or her own job content, a job is seldom so deeply affected by the holder that it is changed dramatically. The job of a production manager, for example, has certain basic requirements, which are definable irrespective of the qualities, views and personal biases of the incumbent. It is these basic requirements that are the focus of job analysis.

The main questions to be answered about job characteristics during the information-collection stage could be as follows:[2]

A.   The job:

(1)   Who does the work? What is the job title?

---

(2)   What are the essential tasks?

(3)   How are these tasks performed and with what equipment?

(4)   Why are these tasks done and what is the relationship between the tasks of the job and the tasks of other jobs?

(5)   What are the jobholder's responsibilities towards colleagues and towards the machines?

(6)   In what conditions (hours of work, noise, temperature, light, etc.) is the work carried out?

B.   Qualification requirements for satisfactory performance of the job:

(1)   Knowledge.

(2)   Skills, including experience.

(3)   Level of education.

(4)   Physical ability.

(5)   Mental ability.

(6)   Aptitude (initiative, tact, etc.).

An example of a practical and simplified form for using job analysis in identifying training needs is given in figure 4.1.

The main information-collection methods used at the first stage of job analysis include interviews (both group and individual), observation, questionnaires, technical meetings, the diary method, critical incidents and analysis of technical documentation (see the following sections).

Figure 4.1.   Example of a job analysis form for a shop-floor supervisor

Area of work	Main elements	Supervisor's responsibility	Knowledge	Skills	Training needs
Personnel selection	Requisition for new labour	Total	Requisition procedure: limits of authority		
	Information on wages and condi- tions of employment	Shared with Personnel Department	Wage rates; working conditions		
	Second interview	Total — makes final selection	Systematic selection procedure	Fully competent to inter- view	Better know- ledge of systematic selection procedure

Job description

The job description is the end-product of job analysis and summarises its essential information. Therefore it assembles all important elements of the job, such as the main tasks and responsibilities, the qualifications required and the functional relationships of the job to other jobs. It should be put in simple descriptive language and a uniform phraseology to facilitate comparison of different jobs and to be easily understood by the person who holds the job or applies for it.

There is no universally accepted standard format for job descriptions for the good reason that there are many different jobs. However, effective job descriptions usually contain the following information:[3]

Identification. Job title of person employed on the job, location in the organisation chart, location defined by plant, department, machine, etc.

Work performed. A concise description of what the worker does, and how and why he or she does it, defines the scope and purpose of the job. Detailed descriptions, including work assigned, specific tasks, areas of responsibility, inherent authority, working relationships, specific methods, equipment and techniques, working conditions, and specific examples, are written in a chronological or logical order.

Job specification. Mental skills such as basic education and job knowledge and responsibility, and physical skills and working conditions, are the basic components of job specifications. Judgements regarding these attributes and their degree of importance may be highly subjective since requirements are often inferred from duties actually performed.

The drafting of a job description can be broken down into four major steps: planning, gathering information, writing the job description and validating it.

Step 1: Planning. The objective is to define sufficient information from which to write a good job description, whose main ingredients are duties, responsibilities and control:

o   What is the job trying to achieve (duties)?

o   How does a person try to do it (responsibilities)?

o   How is the job performance measured (control)?

First it is necessary to define the scope and importance of the job. It could be done by asking what the inputs and outputs are, what raw materials are required, and what should be achieved. The analyst's task at this stage is to prepare a draft analysis of the job, and to produce a plan covering the major areas involved and a list of the questions to ask.

Step 2: Gathering information. It is important to collect sufficient information to set the job in the context of other related jobs, and to place it

---

within the organisation's structure and reporting relationships. A job's position in the organisation structure is best shown diagramatically.

The main areas of activity that make up the job are responsibility, communication, output and economic conditions. Responsibility has two facets: assigned and discretionary. As regards discretionary responsibility, one needs to know whether the job holder acts according to his or her own judgement, acts with prior approval or delegates the authority to act to others. For example, it is important to find out how much financial authority the manager has. May he or she appoint staff members or other managers and direct their work, determine methods of work and decide task priorities, or can he or she authorise capital and current expenditure?

Communication requirements refer to the type of information being received and issued by the holder. Is it oral or written, how important and how complex is it? Who are the job holder's normal contacts? At what level are they? Are they inside or outside the company?

Finally, it is necessary to find out what the job holder produces:

o   Is it in the form of instructions, recommendations, advice, or a service?

o   If a tangible output is produced, what is it used for? Is it someone else's input?

o   What salary and other benefits go with the job?

Step 3: Drafting the job description. This means turning the information gathered into a job description to help the job holder, his or her manager, the personnel department and other interested parties to form the same mental picture and scope of the job.

Job descriptions can be written by the job holder or the manager alone, by a personnel officer, a consultant, or even by a committee. Sometimes a personnel officer writes a draft after talking to the job holder and the manager. Then the former checks the text and the latter approves it before producing the final version. When a committee is formed for this purpose, a trade union representative may be a member if appropriate.

When editing the information and translating it into a job description, the following headings are useful:

Job purpose: Why does the job exist? It is usual to describe the purpose of the job before drafting the rest of the job description. One can then go back and modify the statement of purpose after completing the job description.

Main duties/responsibilities: If a job comprises several main areas of activity, this should be reflected in the layout of the job description. In particular, the job description should be written to help in grasping the underlying structure and scope of the job. A good job description delineates the job boundaries and sketches the job content in some detail, but stops well short of a detailed account of routine day-to-day procedure.

Reporting relationships: Whom the job holder reports to.

Results to be achieved: How performance is actually measured.

Economic conditions: What salary and benefits go with the job.

Step 4: Validating the job description. The job holder and the manager concerned have to review the job description and agree to it (in writing). In addition, it is necessary to check whether the job evaluation unit (or committee) is able to understand the description and assess the scope and complexity of the job. The actual job holder and the supervisor or manager must be able to agree on how to determine if the job holder meets the requirements of the job.

Experience suggests that before proceeding to lower levels of management, job descriptions should first be written for the top and other most senior executives to ensure that the organisation's objectives are defined and have been adequately reflected in the job descriptions at the highest level. Each senior executive should then proceed with his or her subordinate managers to agree on their respective job descriptions, ensuring that the sum total of jobs covered satisfies, without gaps or overlaps, both organisational and individual job objectives.

Job specification

As mentioned, the job specification (also called personnel specification, job requirements, qualification requirements, and so on) is prepared in conjunction with the job description and constitutes its important section. The focus is on qualifications regarded as necessary for satisfactory performance. This helps us to relate individuals to jobs. The objective is to provide information about the knowledge, skills, aptitudes, attitudes and experience required by the job. This can be done by considering four groups of factors:

o   qualifications and experience;

o   physical characteristics;

o   circumstances;

o   attitudes and attributes.

Qualifications and experience are considered both in a positive and a negative sense. For example, to become a trainee chartered accountant it is essential to hold a suitable university degree, but no experience is necessary. In contrast, a company looking for a new sales representative to boost flagging sales may be uninterested in formal qualifications but will view practical experience as essential.

Physical characteristics vary by type of job. For example, a field service or project manager will need to be physically very active. A design engineer or research manager who works in a laboratory may be someone who, for instance, is physically handicapped and cannot move about easily.

The *circumstances* in which people live influence the way they do their jobs. Some jobs require much individual time commitment. A travelling manager or consultant needs to be free to spend a lot of time away from home.

Attitudes and attributes are the areas of greatest ambiguity and risk in selection and training and are often the most difficult to describe and evaluate. When converting a job description into a job specification, we try to describe the sort of person we are looking for. For example, jobs which require extroverts can hardly be done well by introverts, and vice versa.

Example of job description: Assistant Personnel Manager

Title of post:	Assistant Personnel Manager (Recruitment and Selection)
Responsible to:	Personnel Manager
Staff:	Two interviewers, one secretary, two record clerks, and one secretary/receptionist

Duties and responsibilities: To maintain a flow of suitable employees to fill vacancies as and when they occur. The Assistant Personnel Manager will undertake the following specific tasks:

(1) Keeping informed of future requirements in manpower, using the following sources of information, as relevant:

- longer-term estimates arising out of probable developments in the company's activities (new products, new markets, new lines of research, extensions to new areas, etc.);

- shorter-term estimates of current rates of labour turnover, retirement, promotions, etc.;

- immediate vacancies arising from resignations, dismissals, and other forms of separation.

(2) Knowing and developing sources of recruitment from which suitable applicants may be drawn (advertising media, employment agencies, universities, personal contacts, recommendations from existing employees).

(3) Keeping himself informed of the requirements of jobs, in terms of qualifications, experience and other personal qualities essential to their efficient discharge, including causes of failure.

(4) Ensuring that all applicants are dealt with in a manner which enhances the image of the company.

(5) Responsibility for the initial interview of all applicants for higher-grade posts, and through the interviewers for other posts. Responsibility for the quality of personnel recruited.

(6) Actually offering a post to a new employee, and ensuring that the terms and conditions of employment are known and accepted. Direct responsibility for fulfilment of the relevant labour legislation making sure that all other formalities of the actual engagement are properly completed, and that arrangements for starting work are effectively made.

(7) Maintaining employee records, and ensuring that an accurate picture of the company's personnel is available at any time, presenting periodic analyses of wastage and turnover figures, and bringing these to the notice of the Personnel Manager, with a diagnosis of the cause and suggestions for dealing with the situation.

(8) Responsibility for movement within the company and for all transfers, promotions, etc. Implementing company policy concerning the priority filling of posts by promoting existing personnel.

(9) Dealing with the routine administration of suspensions and dismissals and suggesting and sometimes initiating action on these, involving trade unions when necessary.

(10) Under the Personnel Manager, responsibility for the company's wage and salary structure, continuously reviewing the relative earnings of various categories and grades of personnel and calling attention to any anomalies that may occur or be foreseen.

(11) Assisting the Personnel Manager generally as circumstances may dictate.

Working conditions: Normal office hours, with canteen and other facilities on the middle management level. The holder of the post will have an individual office, forming a part of a suite which comprises the secretary's office, a waiting-room and two interviewing rooms. In view of their effect on applicants, the decor and furnishing of these rooms will be maintained at a higher standard than similar accommodation in other departments.

Economic conditions: The post carries a salary which will attract a suitably qualified and effective person in the early thirties. In present-day terms this would imply an annual salary in the US$30,000-40,000 range, but with changing values in the company's annual bonus, which is linked with the company's overall trading results. Three weeks holiday with pay, full salary during illness up to three months, and then subject to review, and participation in the company's contributory pension scheme which is open to all staff on completion of three months of service.

Opportunities for promotion within the Personnel Department are limited as the only post above this one is that of the Personnel Manager himself. There is, however, the possibility that the job itself may be upgraded if it proves to be making a significant contribution to the company's efficient operation. Promotion to other departments of the company will be open to anyone with a suitable record and personal qualities.

Training and skill required: This post calls for formal training in personnel work of the level represented by graduate membership of the Institute of Personnel Management. It also requires at least three years' experience in a related personnel department during which some acquaintance with all aspects of the personnel function has been acquired. Skill and experience in systematic interviewing are essential and knowledge of the underlying theory of selection methods is necessary. A qualification in the application and interpretation of psychological tests would be an added advantage.

Using job descriptions in assessing needs

At the beginning of this chapter job descriptions were labeled as "basic building blocks" of needs assessment. In management practice there is an urgent need to know and understand the competencies – the knowledge and skills – which underlie effective job performance. Without clear competency criteria, recruiters select, managers manage, trainers train and career planners plan according to different (and sometimes even conflicting) images of the capabilities required to do a job.[4]

Firstly, through job descriptions work areas are distributed among the positions (posts) established, thus helping to avoid gaps and duplications. The definition of training needs can thus be related to the real content of established jobs rather than to mere wishes and passing fads. For example, a group of managers may be keen to learn a new computerised budget control system, but are they going to use it? How does it relate to their roles? Does the whole group have this training need, or only one or two of its members?

Secondly, job descriptions are essential in individual performance appraisal (see section 4.10) and constitute a useful starting-point for interviewing managers about their training needs and demands (section 4.4). Such discussions can not only provide excellent information on training needs, but also help to discover gaps and shortcomings in job descriptions.

Thirdly, job descriptions can be reviewed and updated from time to time to take account of any changes which may occur and to establish new training requirements. If this is not done, the practice of job descriptions could create barriers for management and organisation development and play a negative role – there may be individuals who would resent participating in new training and development programmes, if they saw no relationship to their actual, formally valid, job descriptions.

However, the functions of job descriptions in management development needs assessment should not be overestimated. Even if they are systematically updated, they cannot reflect all short-term changes within the organisation and its environment that may require short-term training solutions. Even the best job descriptions cannot be specific and detailed enough to reflect all facets of jobs and their mutual relationships. Also, as a rule job descriptions can be only general and are often quite vague as regards the "soft" – predominantly attitudinal and behavioural – aspects of managerial positions. However, in many situations training and development has to deal with exactly these aspects rather than with technical knowledge and skills.

Competency models

A competency model is a variant of a job description that describes the key capabilities required to perform a job. In certain cases it can be more reliable and useful than a conventional description, which sometimes pays more attention to describing the job and less to the necessary skills and knowledge. Competency models are particularly suitable for describing jobs that require high levels of imagination and creativity, considerable judgement, learning, flexibility and tolerance of ambiguity, and which are difficult to describe in conventional ways.

Competency models of managerial positions typically focus on elements of managerial behaviour and the underlying behavioural skills. A detailed example of such a model, used by the American Management Association, can be found in section 8.1 in part III. The model concentrates on those behaviours that are "characteristic of superior performance" and distinguish superior (excellent) American managers from their peers whose performance is only average. The model is used for assessing training needs of individual managers by comparing their individual skills with those shown in the model.

A competency model can be produced for a particular organisation or its units, or even individual positions. For example, a major division of Phillips Petroleum has developed a competency model including a list of 37 managerial competencies expected of the company's managerial employees;[5] these are communicated to managers as expected standards. These competencies concern personal, management, leadership and employee development factors. Some of them (e.g. energy level, ingenuity) are personality traits that are more appropriate as criteria in selecting managers. Other competencies can be influenced by various types of on-the-job and off-the-job management development activities.

Figure 4.2. Description of competencies

Analytical thinking
Discriminates between important and unimportant details, recognises inconsistencies between facts and draws inferences from information.

Forecasting
Accurately anticipates changes in workloads, resources and personnel needs, etc., as a result of changes in the work situation, technology or external developments.

Goal orientation
Ensures that the results to be achieved by the division, units, teams or individuals are clearly defined and understood at all times.

Knowledge of subordinate jobs
Thorough understanding of the purpose, general tasks, knowledge and skill requirements of the jobs under one's supervision.

Knowledge of user support areas
A basic understanding of the various user areas being supported, their needs and technical requirements.

Multiple focus
Effectively manages a large number, i.e. 10-15, of different and often conflicting objectives, projects, groups or activities at one time.

Organisational knowledge
Thorough understanding of organisational policies, procedures and key personnel that enables a manager/supervisor to effectively carry out job responsibilities.

Priority setting
Identifies and separates those tasks that are most important from those that are less important; maintains a clear sense of priorities and a vision of the larger picture.

Risk taking
Takes risks when the consequences are difficult to predict but payoffs are likely to be great, even when proposals may be rejected by supervisors or when one's image may suffer if wrong.

Source: R. Mirabile, D. Caldwell and C. O'Reilly: "Soft skills, hard numbers", in *Training*, Aug. 1987, p. 54.

Most management competency models currently in use focus mainly on behavioural and interpersonal skills, general managerial abilities and elements of corporate culture. An example of descriptions of such competencies is given in figure 4.2. Companies use these descriptions in various ways, including ranking (by raters working separately) of the importance of the competencies for particular jobs (priority ratings), the rating of the proficiency level required in each competency area and the rating of the actual proficiency of an individual in that area. The results can be used for designing training programmes that react to both the priority requirements of the job and the specific competency gaps of each individual.

Competency models can also be used to determine technical and business knowledge and skills specific to sectors and to enterprises. A competency model of managerial positions at a certain level in a company (e.g. division managers, vice-presidents) can define the technical and business knowledge and skills that every manager promoted to that level should possess. Individualised training and development programmes can then be formulated for all persons who are being considered or prepared for taking up these positions, although their backgrounds and career paths may be different.

4.2   Tests and examinations

A test (examination) is a means of observing and describing how an individual performs in a specific controlled situation. The test sets the verbal or numerical tasks that are used to report different kinds of information about the person who takes the test. Thus, tests are one of the simplest and most direct methods of assessing training needs by asking specific questions and checking and evaluating answers. It is important to use questions that enable one to test actual knowledge or skills, not impressions or intentions to do something. For example, "How many warnings must an unsatisfactory performer be given before dismissal?" is a clear and precise question.

In management development, tests are used to:

o   classify and group the trainees properly for the courses;

o   measure the effectiveness of training and development programmes;

o   inform senior managers about the progress that managers are making in their performance improvement;

o   define immediate (and sometimes future) training and development needs.

The various types of tests are described below.

Question and answer tests

Question and answer (paper and pencil) tests consist of carefully constructed test items in the form of "true or false", matching, completion, multiple choice or arrangement items. The examinee marks answers directly on the test sheet, on a separate answer page, or on a card or sheet which can be scored by a computer or another data-processing machine. More and more tests are fully computerised and the manager introduces answers through the keyboard.

Advantages

o   Scoring is quick and easy;

o   objectivity in scoring is ensured;

o   tests can be administered to large groups simultaneously;

o   tests can be designed to be essentially self-administering.

Limitations

o   It is difficult and time-consuming to design effective tests;

o   it is impossible to measure validly all types of behaviour;

o   these tests are restrictive in terms of managers' response;

o   some tests in which people choose answers from several alternatives make it easy to fake answers or to give answers which aim to please the examiner.

Objective oral tests

These tests are almost the same as the above in content, except that the manager responds orally.

Advantages

o   These tests are easy to administer;

o   they allow examinees to qualify and classify their answers;

o   they offer the examiner an opportunity to clarify the questions or answers.

Limitations

o   They are difficult to design;

o   they can be administered to one examinee only at a time;

o   they are difficult to score unless they are of the short-answer type;

o   they may turn out to be less objective than desired because examiners may give more assistance to the examinee than was intended by the designer of the test.

Essay tests

This is an instrument that calls for written responses to questions or problem situations in that the manager is asked to discuss, compare, recall, classify, analyse, explain, criticise, organise, apply, describe, evaluate, solve, etc. In writing an essay, the manager discusses the issue freely or under a few headings.

Advantages

o   They are relatively easy to design;

o   they offer the examinee an opportunity to select, organise and integrate facts;

o   they are suitable for identifying conceptual and synthetic skills, as well as ideas for improvements;

o   they provide an opportunity to evaluate effectiveness in written communication.

Limitations

o   The reliability and validity may be low because of the small number of test items and the subjectivity involved in scoring;

o   they are time-consuming to administer, examine and score;

o   they are demanding on the evaluator's own competence.

Performance tests

The present state of management is best evaluated by obtaining and evaluating first-hand information on the process of management and on ways in which managers behave in specific work situations.

Such information is best acquired through observing the manager working on the solution of a practical problem (e.g. preparing induction training for new employees or analysing the causes of excessive scrap in a particular section of the works). This will be discussed later in this chapter in connection with several other techniques, but performance tests are one of the techniques that apply this principle.

Performance tests require managers to demonstrate some practical application of their knowledge and skills. During the test, performance is observed and evaluated in accordance with a predetermined standard. Scores may be based on completion time, accuracy, quantity of work completed, or quality of the product, etc.

Performance tests may be any one of four types:

Identification. This measures ability to identify essential characteristics of procedures, processes, equipment, objects, etc.

Simulation. This involves the use of simulated conditions because of the impracticability of using the actual equipment, or any other process. Among the tools of this test are in-tray (in-basket) exercises, business games, role playing, leadership simulations, etc.

Work sample. This requires the completion of sample tasks, representative of the job, where the procedures, work products, or results are evaluated (writing a short computer programme, carrying out repairs, etc.).

Observation of a real situation. This requires the skills of observation of real events or processes, making conclusions about weak and strong points of the job performers, and deriving from this information on his or her training and development needs.

Advantages

o   They appear to be valid in that they cover a job, duty or task, in a realistic way;

o   they are relevant to the job;

o   they are usually highly reliable.

Limitations

o   They usually cover only a part or sample of the job;

o   they require more time to administer;

o   they often require tools, equipment and materials which add to the problems and expense;

o   they are difficult to design.

In-tray (in-basket) exercises

An in-tray exercise simulates the manager's workload of a typical day. It consists of three parts:

(1)   a set of instructions to the manager, which give background information (managerial position, organisation structures, type of business, company rules, etc.);

(2)   the contents of the in-tray. These could be letters, memos, telexes, messages and any kind of business, communication documents, internal or external;

(3)   notes of guidance for the trainer.

Participants are required to assume the role of a hypothetical executive in a given situation. They are supposed to familiarise themselves with the content of the in-tray against the background information provided. Then they are asked to take any decisions and actions they consider appropriate within a limited time period. They must actually do things, take decisions, write notes and memos, make telephone calls, and so on. At the end of the in-tray exercise a written record of every action of each participant is obtained.

During the exercise, the trainer (or observer) has an opportunity to observe how the participants react under particular conditions, what factors they take into consideration for the decision-making process, and how they justify their conclusions and actions taken. Administering the same exercise to two or more persons can provide most interesting information for comparing their behaviour and skills. The technique can be used easily for needs identification, or for testing candidates in a selection process.

Psychological tests

Psychological tests measure a number of things: attitudes, personality, interests, motivation, basic intelligence, mechanical aptitude, numerical aptitude, ability to think logically, computer aptitude, etc. Provided that a qualified professional conducts the test, in-depth interviewing supplemented by psychological testing is probably one of the best ways of identifying potential problems in managers being considered for recruitment or promotion.

The tests are used as indicators of traits that are required for certain jobs, and can serve as initial screening devices to spot those who do not meet the minimum qualifications for executive jobs as regards attitude or aptitude. The choice of test depends upon the requirements of the personnel specification that is to be investigated.

In general, this tool should be considered as an aid to long-term development planning rather than short-term diagnosis of immediate training needs. Psychological tests are less likely to assist with urgent training problems.

Psychological tests tend to be fairly complex. They should be designed and in most cases also administered by professional psychologists who are trained in their use. Therefore, we shall not describe them in detail but shall mention only a few of the most important ones.

Among the standardised psychological tests in use are personality tests, interests tests and intelligence (or mental ability) tests. Three questionnaires by Fineman (Self-Description Questionnaire, Work-Preference Questionnaire and Job-Climate Questionnaire) are a major contribution to testing in industry; they are short, well-researched and give coherent and useful information.[6] These questionnaires provide the basis for fruitful discussion of training needs, focusing on development in the medium to long term.

Standardised psychological tests most commonly used

o   The Wonderie Personnel Test

o   The Shipley-Hartford Test

o   The SRA Verbal Test

o   The DAT Abstract Reasoning Exam

o   The Watson-Glaser Critical Thinking Test

o   The Davis Reading Test

o   The Kuder Preference Record

o   The Guildford-Zimmerman Temperament Survey

o   The Primary Mental Abilities Test for the SRA Verbal

o   The Strong or Kuder Interest Measures

- The Early Identification of Management Potential (EIMP) Battery of Tests
- The Fineman 16-PF (Form C or D) with Self-Description Questionnaire, Work-Preference Questionnaire and Job-Climate Questionnaire
- The Occupational Personality Questionnaire (OPQ) by Saville and Holdsworth Ltd.
- The Achievement Motivation (N Ach) Tests developed by McClelland and others.

Designing and conducting tests: some general rules

During the psychological tests and interviews the psychologist should be alert to many different sorts of *warning signals of hidden problems*, such as:

- inconsistent answers by the candidate;
- inconsistencies between what the candidate says and does, or has done;
- abrasiveness or any other personality quirk that makes the interviewer uncomfortable;
- evasiveness;
- a pattern of unhappiness in former job;
- psychopathic personality;
- split personality;
- a tendency to blame others for all one's troubles;
- an attempt to dominate the interviewer.

The following rules[7] provide some *guidance for designing tests*:

(1) Select realistic and practical problems. Test items should require demonstration of specific knowledge or skill.

(2) Select important aspects or critically important elements of the job for testing.

(3) Select items or elements that are distinctive and objectively gradeable. (What are the criteria for performance, acceptable work products, or the correct or best solutions?)

(4) Make each item or situation independent of other items. The solution of one item should not give the answer to another.

(5) Fit the difficulty of the item or situation to the required level of job knowledge or performance.

(6) Make certain that the test situation is standardised. Difficulty, equipment, tools and working aids, materials, arrangement and environment must be identical for all participants.

The steps to be followed in constructing the test are as follows:

o   Construct a test plan.

o   Select items or situations to be used in the test.

o   Draft the items (draft more items than necessary).

o   Select the final items and word them carefully.

o   Place the items in an appropriate sequence and format (assemble the test).

o   Review and polish the items and finalise the test.

The next task is to prepare instructions for administration and scoring. All instructions must be specific, complete, concise, clear and standardised.

No test can be used unless its adequacy as a measuring instrument has been proved. The value of a test must be determined by actually trying it out under realistic conditions on a sample of the population for which the training needs are to be determined.

4.3   Questionnaires

A questionnaire asks the respondent to supply written information related to his or her job and training needs. Usually, a manager is asked to complete the questionnaire alone; however, the immediate superior could sometimes be asked to assist or to verify the responses.

Questionnaires can be self-administered and group-administered. A self-administered questionnaire is usually presented to respondents by an interviewer or consultant, and respondents complete the questionnaire by themselves and may return it later. This method ensures a high response rate, accurate sampling, a minimum of interviewer bias and the benefit of some personal contact. A group-administered questionnaire is given and explained to groups of respondents assembled together.

Closed-form questionnaires

The closed (closed-ended) form of questionnaire provides a list of items to be checked, alternative answers to be selected, or blanks to be filled in. It can be fully structured with scales or "yes/no" responses. Figure 4.3 shows an extract from a closed-form questionnaire aimed at collecting data on the frequency of certain supervisory management tasks.[8] Such a questionnaire provides information on the relative order of importance of specific work and skill areas, but does not indicate where the training needs are more, and where they are less, important and urgent.

Figure 4.3. Questionnaire used to examine supervisory tasks

Instructions: Place a check mark beside each task in the column that best describes how frequently you perform the task.

Tasks	Frequency					
	Several times per day	Once daily	Once weekly	Once monthly	Less than monthly	Do not perform
Develop work schedules						
Assign employees						
Order material						
Keep work records						
Confer with superior						
Check on work						
Orient new employees						

Source: M.R. Tracey: *Designing training and development systems* (New York, American Management Association, 1971), p. 121.

The closed questionnaire has certain advantages. It takes the respondent a minimum amount of time to complete the questionnaire, and tabulation is simple and less time-consuming. However, it is also dependent upon the completeness of the list of questions that are asked. The respondent tends to depend on this list and is unlikely to provide any additional information. In many cases the closed form may be difficult to design, as all possible responses cannot be foreseen in advance.

Open-form questionnaires

The open (free-response, open-ended) form of questionnaire offers an opportunity to give a more complete and comprehensive picture of a situation. It encourages respondents to go beyond the factual material and data and convey their attitudes, feelings, opinions and ideas.

Open-ended questionnaires use questions of the following type: "What do you think about the management style in your organisation?" There can be many different answers to this question. Some of them will supply a lot of useful information both on the management style and on the respondents.

Clearly, an open-form questionnaire is less rigid and restrictive; it is also less demanding on the designer. However, completing it takes much more time; it may be necessary to motivate respondents and convince them of the usefulness of their efforts. Besides, people may understand the same questions differently (the failure to understand a clearly worded question may already suggest that there is a training need). Tabulation and analysis are more difficult as well.

Some tips for designing questionnaires

(1) Define the objectives of the questionnaire, and consider the group to whom the questionnaire is to be addressed and how the results will be used.

(2) Select the topics or factors to be covered in the questionnaire, keeping in mind that these factors should be relevant, specific and understandable to all respondents.

(3) Group similar or related items and establish a logical sequence.

(4) Draft the questions using standard terms and definitions, keeping them clear, direct and short; use checklists if necessary.

(5) Avoid questions that can be answered with "yes", "no", "it depends", and so on, and those embarrassing to the respondent.

(6) Select the format for the questionnaire: clear, attractive and easy to follow.

(7) Draft the instructions and a covering letter to the respondents, including the purpose, the definition of the group interviewed, the amount of time required to answer it, when and to whom the form should be returned, and what use is to be made of the data collected.

(8) Prepare a final draft of the questionnaire, with the instructions and the covering letter, and reproduce them in several copies.

(9) Ask a few qualified persons to review and comment on the questionnaire.

(10) Revise the questionnaire and supporting materials.

(11) Administer the revised questionnaire to a small sample of the target population (6 to 12 persons).

(12) Analyse the returns from the preliminary test and make final revisions.

It is important not to use a language (ambiguous, bureaucratic, excessively technical or colloquial) which could confuse or put off respondents. It is better to avoid negatively worded questions unless absolutely necessary. They could be misinterpreted or clue respondents into "desired" responses. It is essential not to bias respondents by hinting at "desired" answers.

Advantages

o   Questionnaires provide insights into the perceptions of real people rather than ideal types;

o   they are a sensitive barometer of organisational culture;

o   they are a suitable method for collecting data about known issues or problems;

o   the method is anonymous and may produce information otherwise concealed;

o   the method can elicit information from a wide number of respondents in a relatively short period of time;

o   the questionnaire must be structured in advance, which facilitates the processing of the results; in some cases, once the responses to the questionnaire have been verified, they can conveniently be used with little further processing to identify training needs;

o   results are easily quantifiable.

Limitations

o   Excellent questionnaires are difficult to design;

o   to ensure validity, a reasonably large proportion of the managers surveyed must respond; thus the use of this method in small organisations or at the top management level is questionable;

o   questionnaires are influenced by the level of ambiguity in both questions and answers;

o   they cannot be adjusted to suit individual reactions, interests or knowledge, and therefore have low flexibility;

o   they are difficult to use correctly with large and heterogeneous groups; in this instance questionnaires require a rather large investment in preparation and design time, as well as in tabulation;

o   the results are frequently disappointing because either respondents fail to return the questionnaire or answers are banal, incomplete, indefinite, or very difficult to interpret and use;

o   tabulation and technical interpretation of responses are difficult even under the best conditions; with open forms these problems are multiplied;

○ because considerable subjectivity in interpreting the answers is inevitable, this method could be inefficient and subjective when used as the only means of collecting data.

4.4 Interviewing

Interviewing, a universal and powerful fact-finding technique, is used for many different purposes and in many different ways. In diagnosing management development needs, interviewing is undoubtedly the principal technique. If a diagnostic exercise is confined to one technique, it will be interviewing in 90 per cent of the cases. However, interviewing is also one of the most often misused techniques since it is seemingly very simple: anyone can go, without any preparation, to a manager and ask about his problems and training needs. Unfortunately, this is what happens in many organisations and institutions.

The purpose of interviews is to gather relevant information in face-to-face contacts. This information may concern events, work results, knowledge, behaviour, attitudes, opinions, values, habits, perceptions, and so on. Properly prepared and conducted interviews produce a considerable amount of information on numerous other problems in addition to training and development needs. Unlike the normal conversation, the interview focuses upon a specific subject that is relevant to a specific situation.

Sometimes the interview could be the only feasible method of getting the necessary data. However, in most cases the interview is used in combination with other needs identification techniques. For example, interviews often supplement survey questionnaires.

Two basic types of interviews are used in needs identification: structured (directive) and unstructured (non-directive).

Structured interviews

A structured (directive) interview is planned in advance around topics on which it is necessary to get information. The interviewer uses a list of questions that will throw light on the interviewees' training needs. The same sort of information is thus collected from all managers who are interviewed.

The questions could be, for example: "Do you have a written statement of objectives for your job? When were these last reviewed? Should they be reviewed more frequently, and why?"

A structured interview can be *scheduled* or *non-scheduled*. If the interview is structured and scheduled, every manager is required to give precisely the same information; the interviewer therefore asks identical questions following a schedule prepared in advance.

An example of part of a typical scheduled structured interview is given below.

(1) How long have you been a supervisor in this department?

    a.   Less than 6 months

    b.   6-12 months

    c.   1-2 years

    d.   Over 2 years

(2) How would you rate your performance?

    a.   Unsatisfactory

    b.   Below average

    c.   Average

    d.   Above average

    e.   Superior

(3) What is the most difficult task for you in supervising people?

    a.   Planning

    b.   Organising people

    c.   Communication

    d.   Work control

    e.   Technical tasks

    f.   Motivating people

    g.   Others (please specify)

If this form is used, responses can be relatively easily tabulated, analysed and used to reach conclusions on training needs. Therefore, scheduled interviews are quite popular among management training professionals.

In non-scheduled interviews, standardisation has to be achieved without using a prepared schedule. Instead, the interviewer is thoroughly briefed on what information is required and is then allowed to alter the wording and the sequence of the list of questions when talking to individual respondents.

An example of a non-scheduled structured interview form is given below:

(1) What sorts of things in your job give you the most satisfaction?

(2) What changes would be necessary to make your job more effective? Who could make these changes?

(3) What sorts of activities take up a lot of your time? Does this please you?

(4) How far are you responsible for planning the way you spend your time?

(5)   What proportion of your activities depends on choices made by other people?

(6)   What aspects of your work interest you the most? The least?

(7)   What training have you had? Do you remember any particular training activities as useful or useless? Why?

(8)   What training do you think you need, because either you know about its availability or think that it should be introduced?

Structured interviews usually generate more useful information than other interviews, but they take more time.

Unstructured interviews

This category of interviews is used to explore broad problems that may be difficult to determine, or to find an explanation for unexpected situations.

An example of questions may be as follows: "Do you think this unit is as effective as it should be? Is there anything you would like to say about how your unit is managed? What changes in management are necessary to improve the performance of your unit?"

It is clear that this type of interview demands more time and more competent interviewers; it tends to be less reliable.

An important purpose of non-directive, unstructured interviews, besides fact-finding, includes achieving understanding and building confidence, inviting self-expression, and encouraging interviewees to talk easily about feelings, attitudes and values important to them. This type of interview is sometimes called the employee-centred approach.[9]

Individual and group interviews

Although they are time-consuming, individual interviews are more popular than group (board) interviews since they encourage frank discussion, provide for more flexibility in getting the data required and offer a better opportunity for evaluating the credibility of responses.

In a group (board) interview a number of managers are called together to provide information about their jobs and training needs. In some cases the managers are asked to complete standardised interview forms (questionnaires). Group interviews are less popular than individual ones as they often provide incomplete and less accurate data.

Planning for the interview

The success of an interview depends on careful planning. The plan should cover such elements as setting objectives, choosing the persons to be interviewed, evaluating available information about the interviewees, designing questions and arranging the physical setting. So the first step is to decide about the objectives of the interview, i.e. what must be accomplished. In this case the objectives should comprise the identification of development and training needs or/and problems, or the verification of available information.

It is certainly very important to decide on who should be interviewed and why. The prospective interviewees should be given advance notice, for example, through a memorandum explaining the purpose of the interviews and the planned use of the facts obtained, taking confidentiality into consideration.

Gathering information about interviewees and their performance is a most important preparatory step. It is essential to determine their job requirements, observe some of their jobs if possible, familiarise the interviewer with the duties and responsibilities of the interviewees, and try to understand the latter's personal problems and relations with others. Such preparation saves time and mental effort during the coming discussion and enables the interviewer to sketch at least a general picture of the situation in advance.

Then the interviewer prepares the questions likely to reveal the required facts. These should merely serve as a guide and a check that the interview covers all necessary areas, and should in no case impede the exploration of potentially important topics.

An important step in interview planning is allocating sufficient time for each interview. Time is needed before the interview to review the available information, during the interview to ask all questions and to allow for discussion, and after the interview to write up notes and reflect on what occurred during the interview. Generally speaking, if the actual face-to-face interview runs beyond 90 minutes it tends to become tiresome for both parties. Normally, approximately 30 to 45 minutes should be allotted for the face-to-face meeting.[10] However, these figures are only indicative.

Interview success can be enhanced by a suitable physical setting, which should include privacy, comfort and freedom from interruptions and distractions. Privacy is very important if managers are expected to talk freely with assurance that the conversation will not be overheard. This is particularly important when they are discussing sensitive and confidential matters.

The comfort of interviewees is also important. It is good to offer interviewees, for example, a choice of seats that provide an opportunity to relax. If they must perch uncomfortably on the corner of a table, for example, it is unreasonable to expect them to lower their guard and reveal what is on their mind.

An important element of the physical setting is freedom from interruptions and distractions. A telephone call during the interview may spoil everything. During the interview the interviewee comes first. Interruptions and distractions only emphasise the fact that lower-level managers and employees are considered to be unimportant.

These considerations are summarised in the following checklist.

Checklist for interview planning

(1) Determine the objectives of the interview.

(2) Select the managers to be interviewed.

(3) Identify what kind of information about a manager (his or her job performance, knowledge, skills, attitudes, etc.) is to be sought.

(4) Retrieve and review available personnel information on managers to be interviewed (job descriptions, specifications, performance appraisals, etc.).

(5) Select the relevant topics or factors to be covered in the interview.

(6) Draft the questions using standard terms, keeping them clear, direct and short.

(7) Draft the opening statement on the purpose of the interview, the target group and the use to be made of the data collected.

(8) Prepare a timetable for interviews so that the later interviews could build on information from those preceding them.

(9) If possible review your interview design and plan with another (experienced) interviewer.

(10) Find a room that will be free from interruptions, situated near the activity to be examined.

(11) Inform the interviewees of the purpose of the interview in advance (when making appointments) and make appointments at dates convenient to them.

Carrying out the interview

Any performance or needs analysis interview could be broken down into three distinct parts: opening, conducting and closing the interview. Some useful general principles may benefit both the interviewer and interviewee.

Opening. Common sense suggests that an interview should be started with a friendly smile and a few interested (but not banal) remarks that could enhance communication and a favourable relationship, put the interviewee at ease and establish the beginnings of a rapport.

It is then important to give detailed explanations to the interviewee about the purpose and structure of the interview, and to assure him about confidentiality. Although the introduction should be prepared in advance, it should be delivered in a conversational manner.

At the outset, the interviewer should also refer to specific positive results achieved by the interviewee. A friendly and sincere introduction will put the interviewee at ease and convince him that what he has to say is important.

Conducting the interview. The main purpose of the interview is to encourage managers to talk about their feelings, attitudes and opinions concerning their jobs and the organisation, and to explore their own solutions to their personal and organisational problems. To achieve this, it is important during the interview to use methods of behavioural simulation (such as listening, smiling, nodding the head, etc.) and verbal simulation (acceptance, repetition, probing and interpretive statements).[11]

During the interview performance shortcomings should be interposed between discussion of two positive results. The interviewer should be specific and orient discussion towards comments on performance, not personal criticisms. It is useful to stress that the purpose of bringing up the specific issues is to alleviate the problem in the future, not to criticise the past.

A few other suggestions could be useful to follow during the interview:

o   Do not dominate the conversation, encourage the manager to talk as much as possible, avoid interrupting, do not argue, avoid stating your own opinions and being critical about statements made by the interviewee.

o   Aim your questions at the required information; however, allow the interviewee to follow his own line of thought.

o   Show that the views expressed are understood and taken seriously.

o   Use the interview to supplement facts already obtained. Identify and investigate any inconsistencies and distinguish hard facts from opinion. Ask specific questions to allow quantitative responses.

o   When questions are answered vaguely, pursue them in a pleasant way until they are fully clarified.

o   Refrain from asking strong, direct questions too early in the interview. Open-ended questions are more useful in enlarging upon and enriching the fund of information already available. Early closed-ended questions could provoke a one-word or "yes or no" response.

Too many questions fired in quick succession may turn the conversation into a grilling and reduce the flow of spontaneous replies, thus increasing tension and distorting the outcome.

The interviewer may encounter unexpected resistance. This can be expressed in various ways, e.g. the interviewee does not answer questions or his replies are evasive and too general. The interviewer should consider whether he is not himself provoking resistance. Asking the manager directly how he feels about the course and value of the interview may unblock the situation.

Closing the interview. As the interview draws to a close, the interviewer should thank the manager and ask whether there is anything else he or she would like to add. The main points covered should be summarised, and the interview should conclude with positive comments and overall evaluation of the results. If possible, the manager should once more be told how his or her contribution will be used in planning for performance improvement and management development.

After the interview

After the interview the interviewer should read over the notes taken, lists and points to be checked, and should complete an interview record form if this has not been done during the interview. Use information from one interview to prepare additional questions (e.g. cross-checking or tentative) for other interviews when necessary.

Advantages

o   Obtaining, in face-to-face contacts, information that can be immediately checked, clarified and completed;

o   an opportunity to draw out information and to take advantage of small clues, including non-verbal ones;

o   a possibility to form an impression of the manager's personality;

o   a good return of data in relation to the time spent;

o   an opportunity to explore previously unexpressed ideas;

o   flexibility: if one line of questioning fails to produce the required data, another can be tried.

Limitations

o   Interviews are costly and need considerable time for preparation, execution and evaluation;

o   the main problem is that information is subject both to choice by respondents and to understanding and interpretation by interviewers (do they hear what is said, what they want to hear or what they enjoy hearing?);

o   the interview is strongly influenced by the competence, background, views and experience of the interviewer; the reactions of the interviewer tend to be subjective and patterned in his or her own image; if less competent or ill-prepared trainers or consultants interview highly competent and busy senior managers, the whole exercise can be an utter failure;

o   with some interviewees there is a time-lag before useful information starts to emerge;

o   there is a danger of distortion: the interviewee may have a faulty memory or may distort information unconsciously, or sometimes deliberately mislead the interviewer;

o   the data obtained from interviews often contain much irrelevant and useless information; this must be carefully eliminated.

4.5   Observing

Many training and development problems become apparent simply by systematic and careful observation of work and management processes, i.e. of what is actually happening in the organisation. For example, observing a regular management meeting, watching a manager dealing with individual people or problems or observing a manager full-time during his working day – all these are sources of invaluable information on organisational and management problems, and, possibly, on related training needs.

This can be effectively combined with analysing results achieved by individual managers. In this way the deficiencies in the skills of the manager are brought to light by current problems and difficulties which could be the result of poor management.

Observation techniques are particularly useful for analysing managerial behaviour and working (rather than organisational and administrative) relationships between individuals and teams in the same unit, as well as among various units within the organisation. It is possible to obtain qualitative information (what is actually happening and what positions and attitudes prevail in various situations), as well as quantitative information (e.g. frequency of particular contacts or relative importance of collaborative relationships), that lends itself readily to various analyses.

It is difficult to ascertain whether managers behave differently when they are being observed. However, observation is more likely to produce abnormal behaviour in its early rather than its later stages. An analyst who chooses this method should also appreciate that the data will be voluminous and probably quite confusing, as well as rich and potentially powerful. It is important not to be misled by placing too much weight on something that may be a unique event, unrepresentative of the situation as a whole.

Selective rather than permanent observing (e.g. by applying the work-sampling technique to managerial jobs) may make it possible to collect information on groups of managers over longer periods of time, while maintaining the cost of the exercise under control. Work sampling is a fact-finding technique which measures directly the overall activities of people or machines. It can provide the answers to basic questions such as what percentage of their time maintenance craftworkers spend in actual craft work or how a production manager shares his or her time among various daily tasks. Work sampling consists of a series of snaps, or instantaneous observations of each of the people in the group under study. The observer classifies whatever activity he or she sees in a predefined series of categories. The results of work study are given as a set of percentages or proportions for each category, which reflect the structure of the overall activity.[12]

Advantages

o   Useful for getting an overall picture;

o   may highlight information (especially on behaviour and relationships) that would not be revealed by interviews or questionnaires, either because the respondents are unaware of it or unwilling to disclose it, or because the interviewers do not know about its existence and fail to ask for it.

Limitations

o   Only shows what is observable on the surface; therefore further investigation is needed to explore events in depth and to discover underlying issues, causes and motivations;

o   if done properly and systematically, observation is time-consuming and requires qualified and specially trained staff.

4.6   Critical incidents

Critical incidents are those particular and distinct events in the life of the organisation that are different from the ordinary daily routine. In facing and handling these events, it is assumed, managers will apply and demonstrate certain skills, or will be unable to take appropriate action since they are ill-prepared for such a situation.

Examples of critical incidents are:

o   the unexpected resignation of a plant manager;

o   the cancellation of a major order by an important customer;

o   an explosive consulting report on promotion practices;

o   lack of work in one production department while another department works overtime;

- o   loss of an important file due to computer breakdown;
- o   a convincing demonstration by a subordinate of competence higher than that of his or her manager;
- o   refusal by a senior person to do work which is clearly his responsibility;
- o   considerable plant damage caused by a natural disaster;
- o   high absenteeism due to an epidemic;
- o   an unexpected strike;
- o   a sharp increase in prices of raw materials.

When this technique is used, managers are asked to recollect and describe particularly difficult situations and problems they had to face, say, within the last 4-6 weeks. Alternatively, an arrangement can be made for recording such situations, events and problems over an agreed period of time. The managers concerned can do the recording themselves, or the job is undertaken by a trained observer.

Critical events are then classified and the categories thus established are subjected to a more profound examination, in particular as regards the requirements of management skills, or the absence of knowledge and skill that made the handling of a critical incident difficult or impossible.

Questions are asked such as:

- o   What was done that led to effective job performance?
- o   What was done that led to ineffective job performance?
- o   What, if done differently, would have been more effective?
- o   What attitudes, values, abilities, knowledge and skills (or lack of them) contributed to success or failure?
- o   What conclusions for development and training can be drawn?

An example of a survey of management development needs based on the critical incident technique is described in section 8.1.

Advantages

- o   The critical incidents technique calls attention to critical job behaviour and indicates organisational areas where people had not thought of looking for training needs;
- o   it takes little effort to carry out, requires less preparation than other techniques (interviews, questionnaires, etc.);
- o   it is useful for performance appraisal interviews, since the evaluator can be specific in making comments on what happened at work;
- o   it helps to avoid a bias that is the result of recent information about behaviour, achievements or failures;

o   a categorised large number of incidents can help to select and classify managers for training and set training priorities.

Limitations

o   The technique becomes time-consuming and burdensome when critical incidents are recorded for all managers over a long period of time;

o   it will not give detailed and exhaustive coverage of every potentially important job behaviour and management training need;

o   the level of objectivity of the reported and categorised incidents depends to a great degree upon the skills and objectivity of the observer.

4.7   Diary method

The diary method is a variant of the previous two, i.e. of observing and critical incidents. In this case it is the manager who records activities under various headings. The coverage can be exhaustive (a complete range of activities over a given period of time), selective (certain preselected sorts of activities are recorded, e.g. activities lasting more than 30 minutes) or be confined to events regarded as critical incidents.

For example, a manager or supervisor can be asked to put a tick in the appropriate place each time he or she deals with one of the following:[13]

Activity: Talking
                               –   on the telephone

                               –   with another person face to face

                               –   with more than one person face to face

                               –   was the contact scheduled?

                     Touring (inspecting the workplace)

                     Mail

                     Other paperwork

                     Other activity (lecturing, travelling, operational work, etc.)

Contact: Alone

                     With boss

                     With secretary

                     With subordinates

	With colleagues (reporting to the same boss)
	With peers (similar level, but reporting to another boss)
	Another senior
	Another junior
	External: please specify
	New contacts
Interruptions:	Place
	− own office
	− other: please specify
Nature of activity:	Crisis (drop everything to sort out)
	Choice (need not have done that day or any particular time)
	Deadline (done for a definite time-limit)
	New work (different from anything done before)
	Recurrent tasks
	Urgent work
	Unexpected work

The manager ticks each item, and uses a code to indicate different actions required (for example, whether he or she had taken action or told someone else to do it). Analysis of this information, obtained over a period of several weeks or even months, could provide a lot of useful material on training needs.

Developing a diary

The design of a diary may go through the following steps:

(1) a pilot investigation to see what the probable training needs are, and whether they are general or specific to one or two areas of skills;

(2) decisions on specific demands to record in the diary: whether the duration of an activity is important; whether information about people is important; whether the trainer needs information about results of managerial activities, etc.;

(3) each of the desired categories is broken down into appropriate codes − one for type of activity, one for contacts, and so on. It is important to make the manager's task as easy as possible by allowing ticks rather than written answers;

(4)   a questionnaire containing the diary is assembled, with a statement of its purpose and instructions on how to fill it in;

(5)   the returned diaries are analysed and a report is prepared and reviewed with the managers. A full discussion of their comments and demands is then followed by decisions on training needs.

It is necessary to supplement the diary form with written instructions, which should stress, among other things, the need for accuracy and frankness, the danger of allowing the diary to influence one's own behaviour and the importance of filling out the diary at the requested intervals and not at the end of the period.

Advantages

o   The diary is good for recording and measuring activities within the day, when an hourly record is needed, to sum up certain activities over a period of a week or longer and to record some unobservable behaviour;[14]

o   this technique, if properly used, can produce richer information than some other methods, particularly those that are not likely to be remembered accurately over a period of time;

o   the method is self-administering and reasonably adaptable to machine processing;

o   besides its diagnostic value, the method is self-teaching.

Limitations

o   The recording is influenced by the conscientiousness of the respondents and by their understanding of the task listing and coding;

o   the diary method requires a higher degree of management commitment and participation than any other technique;

o   the method must often be closely monitored by the immediate supervisor of the respondent;

o   the method is time-consuming and requires skills and a greater degree of familiarity with the organisation than some other techniques;

o   the technique is relatively expensive, difficult to design, introduce and analyse;

o   there is the danger that the respondent's interest in filling up the diary will cause him or her to modify the very behaviour that we wish to be recorded objectively.

Table 4.1. MBO report of a sales supervisor

Objectives	Target	Results	Variance (in %)
1. Number of sales calls	100	104	104
2. Number of new customers contacted	20	18	90
3. Sales of product Z	10000	9750	97.5
4. Customer complaints/service calls	35	11	31.4
5. Number of sales correspondence courses successfully completed	4	2	50

Source: Adapted from W.F. Glueck: *Personnel: A diagnostic approach* (Dallas, Texas, Business Publications), p. 307.

4.8 Management by objectives

In addition to its use as a management technique, management by objectives (MBO) can also be used for identifying management development and training needs. In this system, a set of objectives is assigned to a unit or individual for a given period (say, 6 or 12 months). This assignment is based on joint assessment and consultation on what could and should actually be achieved; thus the method is participative. The objectives focus on, say, 6-10 key results to be achieved. These are "milestones", or "specific achievables or deliverables", rather than levels of standard effectiveness that will be acceptable on a continuing basis. Therefore the objectives can be below standard effectiveness level if clearly the manager could not achieve it within the planned period, or can exceed this level if the manager is a high performer. Thus MBO is future oriented, but focuses on objectives to be achieved in the short and medium term.

An example of an MBO report for a sales supervisor could be as shown in table 4.1.

Training and development needs are normally reviewed at two points. When objectives are discussed and fixed at the beginning of the planned period, consideration is given to training as well as non-training measures that will help the managers to achieve the objectives. This, too, is a subject for discussion between the managers and the supervisors. At the end of the period, training is reviewed when assessing the fulfilment of objectives: an attempt is made to identify whether the existence or absence of appropriate training had any impact on the actual level of accomplishment of the objective, with a view to preparing corrective measures for the future period.

Advantages

o   Shift of focus from activities (what I am doing) to results (what I want to achieve), and to what should be changed to achieve these results;

o   involvement of jobholders in the objective-setting process, with concurrent involvement of their superiors, which creates commitments on both sides;

o   ensuring clear formulation of objectives and their measurement;

o   helps to relate training efforts at all levels to company-level objectives;

o   systematic performance appraisal is enhanced, and is oriented to the future rather than to the past; attention is focused on future potential problems and measures for avoiding them;

o   training is integrated in planned organisational efforts for achieving higher objectives and improving performance overall.

Limitations

o   In some situations the definition of meaningful and measurable objectives is difficult;

o   the method emphasises a small number of specific milestones and ignores a manager's effectiveness in other areas;

o   extra efforts are required to monitor the MBO process.

4.9   Action learning

Action learning is both a practical problem-solving method and a management development method.[15] A manager who engages in an action learning exercise works at the diagnosis and solution of a real organisational problem. As a rule, this would be an "open-ended" problem, i.e. one which does not have a single straightforward solution but can be approached and solved in various ways and whose solution requires considerable judgement and "people skills", in addition to the application of management techniques. Examples might be how to reduce absenteeism in a factory, or how to make sure that functional departments start exchanging and jointly analysing information generated by their decentralised information systems. The problem chosen must be meaningful and important enough to the organisation. At the same time, to serve a training purpose, the problem must also represent a challenge to the manager working at the solutions. It must be reasonably new and difficult for him or her. In one variant of action learning, managers work not only at new problems in areas or sectors other than their own, but also in other organisations than those employing them. Interaction with the "client" organisation where the project is undertaken is very strong – the project idea has to be "sold" to it, collaboration at finding facts and searching for solutions must be enlisted, the solution must also be "sold", and the implementation undertaken as a joint task.

The contribution to needs assessment can be considerable and straightforward. The process of action learning identifies training needs at all its stages. First, these can be the needs of the individual undertaking the project – new information, knowledge or skills, that are required in order to pursue the project successfully. In action learning, these needs are not recorded for later action, but are immediately met in the course of the project. This provides the opportunity for an immediate application and feedback, and for correcting and supplementing the training provided if necessary. Second, action learning also generates information on those training needs of the client which become apparent in working on the project, or are defined as conditions of implementing the proposed solutions.

Advantages

o   Focus on needs requiring immediate action and application of results, hence quick feedback on relevance of training provided;

o   strong management motivation for meeting priority needs that will be rapidly translated into results.

Limitations

o   Definition of needs confined to areas treated under a given action-learning project;

o   The method can therefore be used for wider needs assessment only if a sufficient number of meaningful action-learning projects is taking place in the organisation;

o   limited time-horizon, focuses on immediate, short-term needs.

4.10   Performance appraisal

Performance appraisal is the process of evaluating the manager's effectiveness against predetermined, job-related performance standards or objectives usually set by job descriptions or other specific requirements (e.g. business plans). It aims to determine the relationship between individual effort and results, as well as between individual results and the attainment of organisational (enterprise, plant, unit) objectives. As we know from chapter 1, organisational performance is affected by other factors in addition to the manager's competence, effort and personal performance. For example, excellent business results can be achieved at least in the short run with mediocre management performance if the business climate is particularly favourable, and so on. Therefore performance appraisal aims to evaluate all factors together in order to distinguish what a particular manager has contributed as an individual. However, the focus on organisational performance as the principal criterion or basis for assessing individual managers' performance has always to be very strong in order to stress the ultimate purpose of the manager's total endeavour, including efforts in training and self-development.

In theory, a system of individual performance appraisals could be an invaluable, if not the principal, source of information and ideas concerning the training and development of managers. Consistent periodic performance appraisal of all managers in an organisation would reveal problems and deficiencies, some of which could be traced to the absence of required knowledge, skills, behaviour, and so on. These findings could be formulated as training needs, thus providing information on which effective training programmes can be built.

In practice, managerial performance appraisal faces many problems and is seldom applied as an ideal model, although there are companies that have used performance appraisal very aptly.

Approaches to performance appraisal

George Odiorne has identified four basic approaches to performance appraisal.[16]

Personality-based systems. In such systems the appraisal form consists of a list of personality traits that presumably are significant in the jobs of the individuals being appraised. Such traits as initiative, drive, intelligence, ingenuity, creativity, loyalty and trustworthiness appear on most such lists.

Generalised descriptive systems. Similar to personality-based systems, they differ in the type of descriptive term used. Often they include qualities or actions of presumably good managers: "organises, plans, controls, motivates others, delegates, communicates, makes things happen," and so on. Such a system, like the personality-based system, might be useful if meticulous care were taken to define the meaning of each term in respect to actual results.

Behavioural descriptive systems. Such systems feature detailed job analysis and job descriptions, including specific statements of the actual behaviours required from successful employees. A typical example is the system known as BARS (see appendix 1). These systems work well with lower-level jobs, where

---

the job requirements are known, specific and often repetitive. The approach is less suitable for evaluating professional, technical and managerial positions, where independent behaviour by the employee is required.

Results-centred systems. These appraisal systems (sometimes also called work-centred or job-centred systems) are directly job related. They require that manager and subordinate sit down at the start of each work evaluation period and determine the work to be done in all areas of responsibility and functions, and the specific standards of performance to be used in each area. These decisions then become the basis for judging the results produced by the subordinate on the job. In fact this is a form of management by objectives.

Experience suggests that results-centred (results-oriented) appraisal systems are the most useful ones for planning corrective action, including management development and training focused on real needs. Management courses based on personality-centred appraisal can often delve into personal matters in a way that produces unwanted side-effects, including psychiatric damage.

In contrast, a results-centred approach provides an objective basis for discussion with the person whose performance is being appraised, arouses less resentment and is less damaging to the individual's ego than a discussion on personality traits. However, in many cases a combination of results-based and BARS approaches could be more effective, particularly with the growing seniority of managers.

The degree of complexity and predictability of managerial jobs has a large impact on the performance appraisal system for managers. The more complex and less structured the task, the more complex the evaluation process required. Predictability is particularly relevant to appraisals based on outcomes. In the case of predictable tasks, the relationships between the quality of performance and the amount and/or quality of outcome are relatively constant. Unpredictable tasks do not allow accurate assessment of performance on the basis of results. As uncertainty tends to rise with seniority in the management hierarchy, it is precisely at the top levels of organisations that appraisal should permit more subjective grounds.

Thus, single-measurement appraisal systems should be confined only to rather routine managerial tasks. As uncertainty or complexity grow and multiple appraisal purposes also grow, a number of additional criteria and features, as well as sources of data, have to be added to appraisal systems.

However, it is not desirable to mix too many different performance appraisal purposes (e.g. salary review and management training and development) in one system design. In using performance appraisal for salary adjustments we have to:

o   look backwards;

o look at total performance, not details;

o compare individuals to each other;

o take into consideration the climate of the appraisal, which is bound to be subjective and emotional.

In contrast, in an appraisal with the purpose of improving performance through management training and development one has to:

o look forward;

o be concerned with detailed performance;

o compare individual performance with standards (objectives), and less with other people's performance;[17]

o appreciate that the appraisal climate is more objective and less emotional.

Principles of performance appraisal design

Generally, a successful performance appraisal system should use criteria that can be defined as:

o impersonal, unbiased, related to the characteristics of the job and not to the person;

o realistic but challenging (standards should be achievable but not too easy);

o relevant and significant (standards and measures of characteristics should be related to the job and to the objectives of the enterprise as much as possible);

o precise (measurable if possible);

o acceptable and justifiable (standards should not be based on guesswork);

o appropriate (differences between standards and job results should be put in concrete terms – time, costs, complaints, etc.).

To design a sucessful performance appraisal system on the basis of the approaches and criteria discussed above, the following important principles are worth considering: [18]

(1) Analyse jobs individually: job descriptions and performance standards should be written separately for every job, not for a group of jobs. Each responsibility should be described in clear, specific language, and job goals should be defined in objective and measurable terms.

(2) Emphasise behaviour at work and work results rather than personality traits; performance should be described in terms of behaviour and results. This helps managers to respond positively to their appraisal. Even when a personal trait is used, the evaluators should be able to describe and

---

discuss how that trait is related to performing a particular job or function better. Be sure that the system balances results and behaviour and that both are assessed and appraised. Assess critically the work done, not the potential for work yet to be done.

(3) Communicate expectations clearly and provide frequent feedback: the skills that the evaluator believes are necessary to do the job should be formulated specifically and clearly at the right time. It makes more sense to schedule an appraisal at the completion of a business cycle or planning period. However, an appraisal process should be conducted at least every one or two years, and even more often if specific circumstances so require (e.g. in a difficult new job).

(4) Train the managers and raters in performance appraisal (often the appraisal skill is more significant than the appraisal method).

(5) Maintain the system: job descriptions should be reviewed periodically to ensure that they continue to describe the job performed. Informal feedback should be provided frequently. Do not rely on formal performance appraisal alone to communicate about performance: day-to-day contacts must do the main job.

(6) Make personnel decisions that are consistent with appraisal results: salary increases, promotions or management training efforts for a particular manager should be in correlation with the performance assessment. The organisation should establish policy on action to be taken when an employee's job performance is unacceptable. An appraisal system should meet at least basic standards of reliability and validity and at least be able to discriminate between mediocre and good performance in order to treat these groups differently.

(7) Treat appraisal documents as confidential and limit access to them by establishing guide-lines on how they are to be handled and who can see them.

(8) Establish an appeals mechanism.

(9) Make sure that the appraisal system meets the appropriate legal requirements, agreements with trade unions, etc.

(10) Keep the appraisal system short and simple. Stick to objectives to be achieved and assessments of those achievements. Require the personnel or human resource department to audit, oversee and spot-check the appraisals.

Performance appraisal procedure

There is no ideal or standardised performance appraisal procedure since its scope depends mainly upon the organisational objectives and the purpose of the appraisal, as well as on the skills of the raters and on the appraisal methods involved.

However, certain basic steps can be recommended, with variations depending upon specific conditions. These steps are as follows:

(1) Establish performance appraisal policies (when and how often to appraise performance, who should do it, the criteria for appraisal and the methods, techniques and forms to be used).

(2) Analyse the jobs, review (or write) job descriptions, clarify functions and responsibilities, establish work standards and performance objectives, and agree on them with the jobholders.

(3) Gather data on managerial performance.

(4) Evaluate managerial performance.

(5) Discuss feedback on accomplishments, rating and areas that need improvement with the jobholder.

(6) Separate training solutions from non-training solutions.

(7) Make suggestions on training and development policies or programmes.

The following techniques tend to be used most frequently in performance appraisals:

Individual appraisal methods

o   Essays

o   Checklists and weighted checklists

o   Goal setting (MBO)

o   Graphic rating scale

o   BARS

o   Forced choice

o   Critical incident

o   Key results areas

Multiple-person appraisal methods

o   Ranking

o   Forced distribution

o   Paired comparisons

Other methods

o   Performance tests

o   Trait rating

o   Tied review technique

o   Appraisal interview

o   Assessment centre

o   Committee review

Other techniques are used less frequently. However, the major problems are not with the techniques themselves but with the way in which they are used, by whom and with what purpose. In most cases a combination of techniques gives the best results.

The advantages and limitations of performance appraisal mentioned below are confined to its use in assessing management training and development needs.

Some general problems of performance appraisal

Various factors and problems have to be taken into consideration to make performance appraisal less difficult and more valuable. The most common problems faced are as follows:

Poorly designed performance appraisal systems. Criteria for evaluation are poor, and are focused more on activities than results, while the techniques used are cumbersome. Some systems are not in operation, and enjoy low top-management support. A rating system itself does not produce objective measures of performance. The most common rating errors include:

o   central tendency, when managers tend to give everyone about the same rating or, at least, avoid extreme ratings;

o   leniency, when managers avoid low ratings because of potential conflict or belief that such ratings demotivate people;

o   recency, when raters focus on the most recent examples of behaviour rather than considering performance across time;

o   consistency, when evaluators rate managers in rank order rather than on an individual basis, and adjust scores to match the ranking;

o   inaccurate standards of evaluation, when there is too much reliance on general terms such as "poor", "average", "good", "adequate", "satisfactory", etc., which could mean different things to different raters.

But there are some other problems: for example, rating with fewer than four or more than ten categories produces inconsistent ratings; the length of service of the person being rated can affect rating quite significantly; previous review ratings tend to influence current reviews; and there also may be personal biases, when raters favour certain persons over others (because of race, sex, religion, nationality, present position and other types of discrimination).

The halo effect. This is the tendency to place an excessively positive aura or halo over the rating of a subordinate for many reasons such as past record, compatability, recent high performance, irrelevant attributes (for example, impressive appearance), too much reliance on paper records, and so on.

The horns effect. This is the reverse of the halo effect – a tendency to rate people lower than their performance actually justifies. There are various causes for this such as excessively high expectations on the part of the supervisor, lip-service to subordinates' criticism, dislike of nonconformity, "membership of a weak team", recent failure, undesirable personality traits, and so on. When the horns effect predominates, there are no outstanding performers and nobody can earn the highest performance ratings.

Advantages

o   Organisational rigour and uniformity: a standard system is established and applied throughout the organisation;

o   the appraisal form suggests that training needs must be given consideration, and the established procedures require higher management and the personnel department to react to the conclusions.

Limitations

o   The training and development problems involved may be interpreted differently by the individuals involved, so that the outcome of various appraisal exercises tends to be uneven;

o   training is often regarded as a less important aspect of appraisal;

o   if appraisal emphasises other implications of individual performance (grading, salary, transfer, etc.), the manager concerned may have an aversion to discussing training needs at the same time.

4.11 Self-assessment

Self-assessment[19] is a conceptual approach to needs assessment rather than a technique. A professional manager who enjoys his (or her) job and has a developed sense of responsibility is continuously assessing himself without being invited to do so. He may also take corrective action, learn new methods and change his behaviour, without passing through any explicit exercise of needs assessment or attending a course.

In managerial practice it is essential that the people have a maximum of self-insight and self-understanding, including insight into reactions to problem situations and to their own strengths and weaknesses. Self-insight is normally achieved through systematic self-study in a variety of situations, and by being alert to signals that may indicate problems in individual managers' behaviour and performance. By closely analysing their reactions to different events, managers also become aware of their own defence mechanisms – the tendencies to deny what happened, to blame others, or to feel guilty and blame oneself without actually changing anything. The crucial point is that each of the various ways of defending oneself are ways of avoiding the recognition of what the real problem is and what could be done about it.

The following sorts of questions could be helpful in self-assessment.[20]

(1) What feelings is this task or problem arousing within me – anger, frustration, despair, relief, anxiety, and so on?

(2) Given my reactions and feelings, what is really the problem? What areas of choice do I have?

(3) If my feelings are getting in the way of problem-solving, do I have a choice about those feelings? Can I get the feeling sufficiently under control to perceive and act on the problem? If not, and the problem is within me, what can I do about it?

(4) What am I contributing to the problem by the way I am reacting to the external situation? Is there anything I can do about my reaction?

(5) What are my options in terms of available coping responses which I know I have available within me? How will I feel about the use of these various options?

These questions focus primarily on attitudes, values and behaviour. Equally important is self-assessment which concerns the manager's technical knowledge and skills. In rapidly changing situations, often only individuals can assess whether their competence is adequate to the new nature of the job, whether they should consult other colleagues, invite an external consultant, attend a course to learn a new method or simply say that the job will soon be beyond their competence. However, self-assessment that concerns the technical aspects of the job is relatively easy. It is in the behavioural area that managers experience difficulties when assessing themselves. Paradoxically, success and achievement may function as barriers to objective self-assessment ("How can I be wrong if all objectives are achieved and the performance of my organisation is excellent?").

Various techniques, such as the critical incident technique and the diary method (sections 4.6 and 4.7), can help the manager in self-assessment. Another technique is a self-assessment questionnaire, which exists in many different alternatives. One of these alternatives is reproduced below.

Self-assessment questionnaire

The purpose of this questionnaire, developed by George Boulden, is to help you identify ways in which you can improve your own job and team performance and contribute to improving departmental and company effectiveness and think through those areas where improvements can be made. You are asked to use the attached framework to analyse your need to improve current performance in your own job, your team's effectiveness and your personal approach.

	Relevance to your work (high: 9, low: 1)	Level of skill now (high: 9, low: 1)
1. Contribution and influence		
Ability to present ideas clearly and concisely.	_____	_____
Skill in gaining attention, getting a hearing.	_____	_____
Ability to be firm, confronting and challenging.	_____	_____
Skill in explaining technical material to people of different disciplines.	_____	_____
Ability to be persistent and assertive without being stubborn.	_____	_____
Ability to question and debate decisions passed down from above.	_____	_____
Ability to get commitment from managers in other functions.	_____	_____
2. Working with other people		
Skill in listening and clarifying the subject-matter of what another person is saying.	_____	_____
Skill in asking questions to obtain good information.	_____	_____
Willingness to see things from the other person's point of view.	_____	_____
Judging the balance of the amount you talk and the amount you listen.	_____	_____
Judging the impact you have on others.	_____	_____
Ability to be supportive and build on the ideas of others.	_____	_____
Ability to give and receive feedback.	_____	_____
3. Decision-making and problem-solving		
Skill in being explicit about problems and issues.	_____	_____

	Relevance to your work (high: 9, low: 1)	Level of skill now (high: 9, low: 1)

Skill in collecting data and analysing causes of problems.

Ability to generate creative solutions.

Ability to evaluate alternative action plans critically.

Ability to implement decisions.

Ability to work systematically without being inflexible.

4. Personal work organisation

Skill in selecting the right activities to work on.

Effectiveness in managing time from day to day.

Skill in finding out about and understanding new ideas and technologies.

5. Dealing with subordinates

Skill in explaining and clarifying objectives and tasks.

Ability to assess personal and technical skills of subordinates.

Ability to use a flexible management style.

Ability to judge which style is appropriate for different situations.

Skill in delegating and controlling the work of others.

Ability to understand employee relations issues.

Skill in diagnosing underlying problems and issues involved in employee relations.

Ability to assess the training and development needs of subordinates.

Skill in giving feedback to subordinates to help them develop in their role.

	Relevance to your work	Level of skill now
Skill in resolving conflict and disagreement between subordinates.	_____	_____
Skill in recognising and understanding the feelings and motives of others.	_____	_____
Ability to motivate and get commitment from others.	_____	_____

6. Managing project and organisational issues

Skill in setting and controlling project deadlines.	_____	_____
Ability to represent your project or department with other functions.	_____	_____
Ability to understand your manager's viewpoint and problems.	_____	_____
Ability to get your manager to share in goal setting/feedback, etc.	_____	_____
Ability to be open and honest with your manager.	_____	_____
Ability to complete jobs on time and to budget.	_____	_____

Self-assessment for performance appraisal

Self-assessment can also be used as a first, preparatory step in performance appraisal (see section 4.10). The person who has the greatest knowledge of what he or she has actually done and what problems have been faced is the appraisee. By basing the formal appraisal on an individual's self-assessment, the appraisal form can directly invite the identification of relative strengths and weaknesses or the extent to which various goals have been achieved. However, it should be taken into consideration that a manager's self-appraisal could sometimes be subject to self-serving bias: it may give a better picture of the manager's achievements than is actually the case. This effect is much less when an appraisee carries out self-appraisal only for training and development, and not for promotion or salary review.

Advantages

o Helps to identify skill deficiencies and behavioural problems difficult to identify with other techniques;

o relates work problems to problems of family and social life;

o makes the manager responsible for his or her own development ("ownership" of the definition of the problem and of envisaged corrective measures);

o hence strongly motivates the manager for self-improvement;

o has a considerable learning effect; in particular, it helps the manager to learn from events that occur and from feedback received from others;

o can provide a great deal of information at a low cost.

Limitations

o Requires considerable skills and experience for reviewing the managers' self-assessment with them;

o can distort the needs assessment process if wrongly used;

o can be misused for self-serving purposes;

o can be misleading to the managers assessing themselves if not supplemented by another assessment.

4.12 Career planning

Career planning aims at matching individual potential for promotion and individual aspirations with organisational needs and opportunities. Its principal product, an individual career plan, suggests a career path that is both feasible and desirable from the individual's and the organisation's point of view, as well as conditions to be met in pursuing this path.

Further training and development have a prominent place among these conditions. In particular, career planning indicates what training and development would be necessary for advancing in the career (promotion to higher-level position), altering the career path (transfer to another type of work), or staying in the current position (no transfer, but broadening the scope of the function).

The focus on future needs and opportunities is the main advantage of career planning. Thus, it is possible to make suggestions not only on how to do the current job better, but how to prepare oneself, with the organisation's consent and support, for future jobs. This is why effective career planning is closely linked to strategic planning, business forecasting, managerial manpower planning and other activities that are forward looking and try to prepare the organisation to take future opportunities and cope with future problems.

The harmonisation of future individual and organisational needs, possibilities and aspirations is another advantage of career planning, which has a beneficial influence on planning training and development. The career planning process makes it possible to define needs that are real and not just an expression of wishes or unrealistic expectations. They reflect commitment of both the individual concerned and the organisation.

Properly organised performance appraisal produces a great deal of information and suggestions for career planning. Thus, there is a direct linkage between the two techniques. Also, self-assessment is an important feature of career planning since all managers whose careers are reviewed are expected to express their future expectations, aspirations and commitments, based on their own perceptions of their efficiency and further potential for growth. Thus, career planning helps to increase managers' responsibility for their own career paths, and to develop correct perceptions of their own strengths and weaknesses. In addition to serving to establish future training and development needs, the career planning process is itself an exercise that develops certain individual skills, perceptions and judgements.

A simplified model of the career planning process is shown in figure 4.4.

Career-counselling sessions

Career-counselling sessions serve as a practical tool in implementing the career management cycle and career planning. Their key steps and objectives are as follows:[21]

o   *Preparation and planning:*
    The manager and the employee independently develop ideas, facts and data about company career opportunities, and the employee's performance history and competence (skills, knowledge and behaviour).

o   *Opening the session:*
    Establishment of an interpersonal climate of trust, enthusiasm and openness. Conducted in private. The manager explains the purpose, structure and process of the career-counselling session.

o   *General analysis and discussion:*
    Mutual examination of employee's skill and knowledge inventory, performance, aspirations and options.

o   *Agreement on career options:*
    Discussion of existing competencies, and career goal options. If possible, establish skills and knowledge required to achieve ultimate career goals and all the intermediate job steps. Decide realistically on next job within the department or organisation.

Figure 4.4. A simplified model of the career planning process

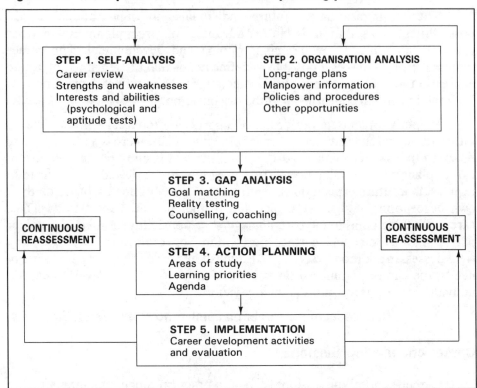

o   *Alternative action:*
Specific action steps established to acquire the knowledge and skills for next job and optional action steps over long term, necessary to attain ultimate career goal.

o   *Implementation plan:*
Agreement on mutual responsibilities to ensure actions: scheduled time, sources of skill/knowledge, costs, measurement of results. Employee takes ownership of personal development plan and career action.

o   *Closing the session:*
Manager checks for unanswered questions/concerns and creates a positive climate of achievability, common vision and expressed enthusiasm for the career action plan.

o   *Follow-up:*
Manager monitors and guides implementation plan by further discussion and counselling as needed. Until employee leaves department, manager assumes continual interest and responsibility for helping employee's career development.

Advantages

o   Career planning is distinctly future oriented, but links long-term goals with short-term goals;

o   individual and organisational objectives and commitments are matched;

o   the process of career planning is itself a training event. It improves skills, perceptions and communication;

o   the linkage between job performance and job satisfaction is enhanced.

Limitations

o   Effective career planning is a complex and costly exercise, requiring a great deal of changes in attitudes on the part of both the organisation and the individual;

o   hard data permitting realistic career planning may be too difficult if not impossible to obtain;

o   difficult to use in small organisations and units with very limited career prospects;

o   there is a risk of focusing excessively on individual managers' personal expectations and goals, which could make the whole exercise unrealistic and impractical.

4.13   Assessment centres

The basic approach of the assessment centre is to expose a manager to a range of exercises, tests, simulated situations, and so on, in a structured environment within the centre for a few days. These exercises are designed to bring out behaviour relevant to skills critical for success in a target job. The individual's reactions are observed by competent observers with practical management experience, and evaluated in terms of the individual's managerial potential and/or training and development needs. As a rule, assessment centres are used for:[22]

o   early identification of high-potential ("fast track") talents;

o   assessing an individual's experience, diagnosing strengths and weaknesses and suggesting a tailor-made training and development programme;

o   organisational planning and development;

o   encouraging self-development and stimulating interest in training by providing direct feedback to the person being assessed.

Assessment centres use a combination of techniques such as in-depth interviews, in-basket exercises, role-playing, management games, individual and peer evaluation, group evaluation, group discussions, work group exercises, fact-finding and problem-solving, questionnaires, knowledge tests, intelligence tests, psychological tests, and analysis of educational records.

In a typical centre the group of managers under assessment consists of 6-10 people, who spend about 2-3 days at the centre. The level of candidate to be assessed usually dictates the duration of the procedure. A summary report is developed on each participant, outlining his or her managerial potential and training needs and defining actions required from both the organisation and the individual to improve managerial performance. Assessment centres can be used at all levels of management, from first-level supervision to top management. The centre can be an external organisation or can be established within a larger enterprise as an ad hoc temporary project, possibly involving external consultants.

Among the most popular dimensions of managerial skills evaluated by assessment centres are impact, creativity, stress tolerance, leadership, sales ability, sensitivity, initiative, independence, problem analysis, planning and organisation, judgement, decisiveness, delegation, flexibility, tenacity, management control and risk-taking.

Advantages

o The approach involved in this technique is oriented towards both personality traits and results;

o there is minimum bias and better objectivity since all participants are assessed on the same basis by the same persons, who do not know them;

o the participants learn from the exercises and become more aware of their particular strengths and weaknesses;

o the assessment centre format is flexible and may be easily changed depending upon situations.

Limitations

o The method requires considerable skill and expertise, and should be used only by well-trained professionals;

o it is an expensive technique;

o the method may overemphasise interpersonal skills.

---

[1] ILO: *Job evaluation* (Geneva, 1986), p. 12.

[2] ibid, pp. 16-17.

[3] Cf. L.R. Bittel (ed.): *Encyclopedia of professional management* (New York, McGraw-Hill, 1978), pp. 580-581.

---

[4] P.A. McLagan: "Competency models", in *Training and Development Journal*, (Washington, DC), Dec. 1980, p. 22.

[5] H.W. Smith: "The Phillips advanced management programme – Changing to meet the times", in *Journal of European Industrial Training* (Bradford, West Yorkshire), Vol. 12, No.1, 1988.

[6] P. Saville and A. Munro: "The relationship between the factor model of the occupational personality questionnaires and the 1GPE", in *Personnel Review* (Bradford, West Yorkshire), Vol. 15, No.5, 1986.

[7] Adapted from W.R. Tracey: *Designing training and development systems* (New York, American Management Association, 1979), pp. 149-150.

[8] ibid., p. 121.

[9] R.B. Dunham and F.J. Smith: *Organizational surveys: An internal assessment of organizational health* (New York, Scott, Foresman and Co., 1979), p. 128.

[10] A. Diane: "Preparing for the interview", in *Personnel* (New York), Feb. 1986, p.40. See also M. Kubr (ed.): *Management consulting: A guide to the profession* (Geneva, ILO, second (revised) edition, 1986), pp. 148-151.

[11] For details on how to use these methods, see Dunham and Smith, op.cit., pp. 136-151; and P. Pigors and C.A. Myers: *Personnel administration: A point of view and method* (New York, McGraw-Hill, 1973), pp. 193-197.

[12] A. Stewart and V. Stewart: *Managing the manager's growth* (Farnborough, Hampshire, Gower Press, 1978), p. 70.

[13] ibid., p. 75.

[14] A.N. Oppenheim: *Questionnaire design and attitude measurements* (London, Heinemann, 1966), p. 217.

[15] There are many publications on action learning. A comprehensive description of various alternatives of this method may be found in G. Boulden and A. Lawlor: *The application of action learning: A practical guide*, published by the ILO Management Development Branch as a technical paper (Geneva, doc. Man Dev/46, 1987; mimeographed).

[16] G.S. Odiorne: *Strategic management of human resources* (London, Jossey-Bass, 1987), pp. 258-259.

[17] D.L. Kirkpatrick: "Performance appraisal: When two jobs are too many", in *Training* (Minneapolis), Mar. 1986, pp. 65-66.

[18] R.V. Romberg: "Performance appraisal 1: Risks and rewards", in *Personnel*, Aug. 1986, pp. 20-26; Glueck, op. cit., p. 295; D.G. Martin: "Performance appraisal 2: Improving the rater's effectiveness", in *Personnel*, Aug. 1986, pp. 28-33; and R. Zemke, L. Standke and P. Jones (eds.): *Designing and delivering cost-effective training and measuring the results* (Minneapolis, Lakewood Publications, 1981), pp. 30-32.

[19] For more ideas on self-assessment, including samples and checklists, see another ILO publication by T. Boydell: *Management self-development: A guide for managers, organisations and institutions* (Geneva, 1985).

[20] Cf. E.H. Schein: *Career dynamics: Matching individual and organisation needs* (Reading, Maryland, Addison-Wesley, 1978), pp. 71-72.

[21] See E.G. Velander: "Incorporating career counselling into management development", in *Journal of Management Development* (Bradford, West Yorkshire), No.3, 1986, pp. 42-43.

[22] V.R. Boehm: "Using assessment centres for management development – Five applications", in *Journal of Management Development*, No. 4, 1985, p.41.

TECHNIQUES FOR ASSESSING GROUP NEEDS 5

Group techniques are used for (i) identifying those training and development needs of individuals that reveal themselves best, or only, when people work, communicate and interact in a team; (ii) finding out about needs that are common to the members of the group; and (iii) getting a collective opinion of the group and consensus on what the needs are and in what order of priority they should be met. Again it should not be overlooked that these techniques overlap to some extent and are complementary with techniques defined as individual or organisational in our classification. This is because group techniques deal with needs that concern both the group as a whole and its individual members. On the other hand, group needs may also reflect some organisational needs, common to all or several groups in the organisation that is being observed.

The following techniques will be discussed:

o   meetings of management teams (5.1);

o   group meetings and discussions (5.2);

o   syndicates (5.3);

o   the Nominal Group Technique (5.4);

o   group projects (5.5);

o   group creativity techniques (5.6);

o   simulation training methods (5.7);

o   sociograms (5.8);

o   behaviour modelling and analysis (5.9).

5.1   Meetings of management teams

Management teams in an organisation are the most natural and logical groups for assessing training and development needs. These are more or less permanent groups of people who have developed certain characteristic patterns in working together on a variety of topics over a fairly long period. Typically, they include the top management team (e.g. the president, general manager or director-general, with deputies and main functional or division directors), functional management teams (a functional vice-president with specialist managers, etc.), and middle- and lower-level management teams. Their meetings could be regular (monthly, weekly), or ad hoc meetings on significant events (new market policy, an acquisition, a financial crisis, etc.).

Of interest is both the content and the conduct of these meetings. An evaluation of the agenda, the quality of preparation, the technical arguments put forward and the conclusions reached can reveal a great deal about management's capability to choose the right topics at the right time, to allocate discussion time according to the importance of the topic, to make conclusions on the basis of proper analysis, to strike a balance between short-term and long-term issues, and so on.

An observation of the processes during the meeting reveals information on questions such as who plays what role, who is listened to, who does not listen, who normally disagrees with whom, whose views are ignored by the group, and who has the main impact on the final outcome and why. It also becomes evident whether the meeting serves for collective diagnosis and synthesis, or is used merely for formally endorsing conclusions already made by someone before the meeting.

Advantages

o   First-hand objective information on management procedures, including processes at top level (in particular if combined with observing individual managers outside the meetings);

o   provides inside and sensitive information that cannot be obtained by any other technique.

Limitations

o   A number of meetings have to be observed to make up a fairly iomplete picture;

o   very demanding on the observer's skill and experience;

o   the sensitivity of information requires cautious treatment;

o   senior managers must be prepared to agree to this technique and refrain from adjusting the agenda to influence the observer.

5.2   Group meetings and discussions

Meetings and discussions involving groups of various sizes and compositions are a most common communication and management tool in any type of organisation. The assessment of training needs can be a by-product of group work organised for another purpose (e.g. for consulting the group on changes in production scheduling and stock control). Alternatively, a group can gather specifically for discussing training and development needs.

As in the previous case, the assessment of the training and development needs can focus on technical aspects, on group dynamics involving mainly behavioural issues, or on both. Various methods of structuring, organising and running meetings and discussions were developed for these purposes. Numerous validity studies have shown that group discussion ratings correlated quite well with performance indices. If the group operates in a constructive spirit of co-operation, the combined experience and imagination of the members is a factor of synergy. The purpose of training would be to enhance this dimension, in addition to serving the individual needs of each group member.

Normally the group would include 6-10 people drawn from one or several units in the organisation. The objective is to get this group to discuss a range of issues related to organisational effectiveness and management development needs. In most group approaches it is deemed essential to draw up a list of topics that need to be covered and the relevant issues that one would like to touch upon in connection with each of these topics. The objective is to get an open conversation going, in the course of which all of the topics on the list will be spontaneously introduced by the group members themselves.

The order in which the topics are dealt with would be dictated by the flow of thought of the respondents rather than by a predetermined scheme that should only be confirmed or completed by the group. It is absolutely essential that the purpose of the group discussion is clearly communicated to the participants. It will make them feel more at ease and enable them to focus their contributions on issues relevant to the objectives.

The question of confidentiality should be clarified if managers are to speak openly. This technique particularly requires a willingness and ability of individuals not only to be open in expressing their views in front of their peers, but also to be accurate in doing so in an interactive group.

The discussions should take between 45 and 60 minutes. The topic should be clearly structured and work oriented, yet general rather than too specific. It should allow scope for some display of emotions and attitudes, but require the group to come to a definite conclusion or decision. If the discussion is too long, momentum can be lost and interest goes down. It is preferable to meet several times than to insist on long exhaustive meetings.

It may be worth having two observers of group behaviour to increase reliability. They should be trained, and should make descriptive notes of members' behaviour, rating them on three criteria: general quantity and quality of contribution, and degree of co-operation (or their supposed correlates:

leadership, persuasiveness and social skills). However, it is important to consider whether and at what stage of the meeting the presence of observers affects group behaviour.

Any plan of the group discussion could consist of the following items:

(1) Introductory remarks.
(2) Opening questions.
(3) Discussion.
(4) Intermediate summary.
(5) Closure.

Points 1-3 can be repeated many times depending upon the number of topics to be discussed.

How to prepare a discussion

(1) Determine the overall objective.
(2) Define the topic clearly and concisely.
(3) Prepare a discussion outline.
(4) Have everything ready (date, time, place, physical facilities, handouts, etc.).

How to lead a discussion

(1) Start the meeting on time and make the group feel at ease.
(2) State the general purpose of the discussion, announce the topic clearly and concisely, explain the discussion procedures and introduce the topic.
(3) Guide the discussion by encouraging participation of all members, do not allow one or two members to monopolise and dominate discussion, draw out the shy and control the over-talkative members, avoid personal arguments, summarise frequently, re-state questions if necessary, use audio-visual aids.
(4) Summarise the discussion. Review the highlights and conclusions, re-state any minority viewpoints, get agreement on conclusions made and action proposed.

Advantages

o   Group meetings and discussions provide collective rather than individual opinions and expertise;

o   reveal relationships within the organisation;

---

o   demonstrate management and communication skills that can best be observed in group work;

o   enhance collective interest in the issues treated and provide support to conclusions generated by the group.

Limitations

o   Usually data collected on the group itself will be more accurate and useful than data on wider issues of management effectiveness and training needs;

o   technical data will be influenced by the public framework, personal relationships, loyalty, interests of strong individuals, etc.;

o   the group may be misused for individual goals;

o   considerable time may be required if all group members are to have the opportunity to participate;

o   competent preparation and interpretation of results can be very demanding on the analyst's experience and skill.

5.3   Syndicates

Syndicates are small groups (of about 10 people), whose members come from various organisations and represent various areas of expertise.[1] Their purpose is to serve as a tool for collectively exploring various possible solutions to management and business problems, and learning from other members' experience. Typically, syndicates are established within the framework of a management training programme or conference for dealing with specific problems which may have been identified by the managers themselves, or assigned to the syndicates by the course director for learning purposes.

The process is quite structured and organised. The group aims to produce a required result, which could be a report on a particular organisational problem, including solutions that the group has developed, examined and endorsed as a collective. If several syndicates are established, which is common in courses and conferences, there are also plenary sessions where each syndicate explains to all course members the approach taken and the results obtained.

Syndicates can be quite useful for examining training and development needs by groups of managers who can contribute various experiences, insights and approaches. Training problems can be presented to the syndicates as an issue on which they should work, or a syndicate can deal with training issues in connection with other, "non-training" problems. In addition, as in the previous cases, observing the syndicates at work, and assessing the quality of their "products", provides training professionals with information on the participants' training and development needs.

Advantages

o   Faster and less expensive than other approaches;

o   provides for active participation of all syndicate members;

o   brings out such problems as lack of communication, negative attitudes or cultural barriers.

Limitations

o   Provides less reliable data about individual managers' deficiencies in skills;

o   requires an experienced syndicate leader;

o   often opinions could dominate reality;

o   in programmes involving managers from various organisations, the solutions proposed by the syndicate are not always acceptable to the organisations concerned.

5.4   The Nominal Group Technique

The Nominal Group Technique (NGT) uses a group of people who "nominate" problems and issues that deserve attention. It is a data-collection method useful in situations where individual judgements must be tapped and combined to arrive at decisions which cannot be made by one person.[2] NGT can also be effectively used in organisation development, general diagnostic studies, and so on.

The process of NGT involves several non-interacting individuals who follow a structured format in developing the desired information.

The main steps in the NGT process are as follows:

(1)   Forming a non-interacting group.

(2)   Generating ideas in writing by the group members and listing them on the cards without discussion with each other.

(3)   Recording the listed ideas from each group member by the group leader on a flip chart, again without any discussion.

(4)   Clarifying, simplifying and organising the listed ideas, which should be grouped logically.

(5)   Voting on the priority of ideas (or problems) and making group decisions, rating them by each group member.

Advantages

o   Because of its structured process NGT provides reliable data and consistent information;

o   faster and less expensive than other approaches (e.g. interviews, questionnaires and observations);

o   reduces inhibitions and increases participation by all group members in needs assessment, creates a climate where communication is open;

o   emphasises job-related problems and factors.

Limitations

o   Needs an experienced group leader;

o   has to be combined with other types of interventions to be really effective.

5.5   Group projects

Similarly to group meetings discussed in the previous sections, group projects can serve a wide range of purposes. In business practice, the following two tend to prevail: (i) a temporary group is established on a part-time basis for dealing with a significant organisational problem, with the agreement and support of senior management (a senior member of the management team may be the group leader and various managers can be group members); (ii) a group is established with the combined objective of working on a practical problem and of learning specific skills in the course of this process (a group form of action learning). In both cases, the task is distinct, important and complex enough to be defined as a project. The group will have to work at it as a collective over a period of time. A number of group meetings will be required, as well as individual work on assigned subtasks in periods between group meetings.

In the course of the project, the group itself can gradually define, and redefine, its own or other managers' and staff members' training needs, and the interventions required for progressing with the project and putting its results fully into effect. If an action-learning objective is pursued simultaneously, the information on training needs uncovered would be handled in a similar way as in individual action learning (see section 4.9).

Advantages

o   Direct relationship between problems, tasks, definition of training needs and action to meet these needs;

o   feedback is therefore immediate, giving the work group good insight into training effectiveness and the dynamics of training needs;

o   it is easy to motivate the project team members for training needs assessment.

Limitations

o   Needs assessment is confined to problem areas dealt with in the project; this can give a distorted picture where certain needs are overemphasised and other needs ignored;

o   the gradual process of advancing with the project and identifying and meeting training needs is quite demanding in terms of managerial, leadership and training skills;

o   the technique can be used if meaningful projects have been identified in which the organisation is genuinely interested.

5.6   Group creativity techniques

Creative thinking is the relating of things or ideas which were previously unrelated. The basic philosophy of creative thinking is to suspend the normal logical process of looking for solutions and to concentrate in the early stages on looking at alternatives. Creative thinking does not do away with logical thinking completely; it just suspends it to enable as many ideas as possible to be generated before the logical process of identifying a solution to the problem takes place.

This approach is particularly relevant to those management problems which have a number of potential solutions but no specifically right answers. For example, if a manager is looking for ways of motivating employees to improve quality, there are many ways of tackling the problem, most of which will have been tried before. What the manager needs is a new approach which will be seen as a serious attempt to get something done. For example, instead of tightening the quality rules or redesigning the bonus scheme management may decide to involve the workers in managing their own product quality.

The following guide-lines apply in using creativity techniques:

(1)   Suspend judgement − rule out premature criticism of any idea.

(2)   Free-wheel − the wilder the ideas the better the results.

(3)   Aim at quantity − the more ideas the better.

(4)   Cross-fertilise − Combine and improve on the ideas of others.

Selected techniques that can be useful in assessing training and development needs will be briefly reviewed below.[3]

Brainstorming

Brainstorming is the best known and most widely used of the techniques. It is a means of getting a large number of ideas from a group of people in a short time. It is inexpensive in managerial time. The total exercise, including evaluation, will take less than half a day. It is highly participative, which generates commitment to an ownership of the solutions arrived at.

The first stage of brainstorming takes place with a group of several people concerned with the given situation and contributing ideas in a free-wheeling and informal manner. Every conceivable idea is encouraged, even the wildest one. Participants are strongly requested to suspend critical judgement. The main task of this first stage is to generate the maximum number of ideas in a short time. Each person stimulates the others in the group, and in turn each person is stimulated by the group. Encouraging the suspension of judgement and criticism creates a free atmosphere for the mental process.

The second stage concentrates on the selection and refinement of ideas. Each idea is judged in the light of the objectives and requirements established earlier in the problem-solving process. Most of the ideas generated in the first stage will thus be easily eliminated. Only a few really good ideas are likely to be identified. These good ideas should be refined if necessary, and preserved as likely alternative solutions. Thus the main task of this stage is narrowing the number of ideas or alternative solutions.

The Delphi technique

This technique employs an idea-generation concept similar to brainstorming. However, the Delphi technique isolates the participants from one another. There is a group of experts, but they are polled for ideas individually, and their ideas are subsequently summarised and presented to each participant. After allowing time for each participant to review this feedback, the consultant again polls the experts. Each participant can adjust and revise his or her ideas in the light of the collective responses. This feedback and polling cycle is repeated until the responses have stabilised. Then the stabilised results are summarised and presented as the refined ideas of the collective of experts.

The Delphi technique could produce excellent ideas or solutions, since they represent the refined views of selected experts. However, the method is very time-consuming. It tends to be better suited to complex problems involving forecasts than to other types of problem situations. In our case it could be very good in looking at future management development and training needs connected with complex economic and social developments.

Synectics

Synectics is another technique similar to brainstorming. A synectics group consists of a leader, a "client" and about six participants. The leader is responsible for running the session, recording ideas and ensuring that the process is conducted correctly. The leader is, however, barred from contributing his or her own ideas. The "client" has the problem and the process is directed to producing acceptable solutions for him or her. The participants need not be technically involved with the problem. The process involves analytical and creative thinking and aims for a solution in about 45 minutes. Each burst of analytical or creative thinking lasts no longer than 5 to 10 minutes and the client is continually referred to in order to ensure that the avenue being investigated is acceptable.

As distinct from brainstorming, in synectics the creative stages are relatively short and are interspersed with analytical stages. Participants may find it difficult to switch from one to the other. However, the synectics process has the advantage of leading to possible solutions in a very short time.

The SCAMPER approach

An approach that is more deliberate in nature than brainstorming is known by the acronynm SCAMPER, which stands for Substitute, Combine, Adjust, Magnify, Put to other uses, Eliminate, Reverse.[4]

In this approach each new idea represents an evolution of a presently stated idea. Thus, a new idea may emerge from asking the question: "What is a reasonable substitute for idea A?" Another new idea may develop from the combination of ideas A and B.

Because the SCAMPER approach is more deliberate and systematic than brainstorming, it allows time for incubation. This process requires several sessions. During the first iteration the more obvious alternatives can be listed. During the second iteration you might allot a preset period of time to substituting, combining, rearranging, and so on. Then, after a time lapse, you might allot another preset period of time to recycling the SCAMPER functions once again.

A possible drawback of the SCAMPER approach is that it tends to limit the range of likely idea. Revolutionary ideas are not likely to emerge from this evolutionary approach.

Advantages

o   Creativity techniques can produce very interesting ideas for training, related to innovative ideas on how to improve technology, the management system, marketing approaches, etc.;

o   these may include non-conventional approaches to training;

o   the motivation of the managers involved is increased.

Limitations

o   The techniques are not suitable for systematic assessment of needs;

o   the exercise requires competent group leaders;

o   it may be impossible to meet some of the expectations created.

5.7   Simulation training methods

Simulation training methods can be used not only for training itself but as a tool for identification of management training and development needs. Even when these methods are not used intentionally for this purpose, an attentive trainer can nevertheless derive valuable information on many aspects of management skills, knowledge, attitudes and shortcomings in a situation that is close to actual practice. Alternatively, an observer may be present during the training sessions to collect and evaluate this information.

Role playing

Among the simulation methods, role playing is perhaps the method that is most appropriate for identifying training needs. In a role play, participants assume an identity other than their own, and try to cope with real or hypothetical problems, mostly in human relations, personnel or communications. However, there can be role-playing exercises whose content is highly technical, e.g. a management meeting analysing the company's balance sheet and other financial statements (each participant contributing the viewpoint of a different senior management position), or two company teams negotiating a merger or an acquisition. Playing their roles, managers try to behave in a way they believe characteristic of these roles and specific situations. Role playing allows a player to simulate reality, make and detect mistakes, try out alternative responses, and so on.

Generally, there are two approaches: structured role playing, when a leader (or the group itself) selects the situation, the roles, specified goals and activities, and spontaneous role playing, when the problem situation arises from group discussion, without advance planning. Both approaches relate to learning through *(a)* doing; *(b)* imitating; *(c)* observing; *(d)* feedback; and *(e)* analysis.

Besides gaps in different technical skills, the trainer can identify analytical, evaluative, creative (or suggestive) and communicative capabilities of players, especially in human relations, and also some important leadership features, which probably need to be improved or developed.

Business games

Generally speaking, business (management) games are a training technique in which participants are grouped in teams, consider a sequence of steps in dealing with problems, make decisions and receive feedback which reflects the action taken by the opposite team(s). It is a form of simulated, sequential decision-making exercise structured around a hypothetical model of an organisation's operation, in which participants assume roles as managers of the operations involved.

The purpose of business games is to increase an understanding of:

(1) specific organisational problems (marketing, production, etc.);

(2) the interrelationship of different functions and sectors and their relationship to the environment;

(3) the problems of company policy and decision-making;

(4) the fact that some factors and developments are not under the organisation's control and that decisions made by competitors, supervising ministries, price control bodies, etc., may have a major, if not decisive, influence on the company's performance;

(5) the problems of working in a team and being efficient and effective under time pressure;

(6) participants' training needs or areas for performance improvement.

There are several varieties of business games which differ in their particular goals, structures, timing, etc. However, certain elements or procedures are common to most:

o   participants are grouped in teams, representing organisations, and briefed on the objectives and rules of the game;

o   each team is provided with initial information about the status of the organisation, its competitors and the environment;

o   teams are required to analyse information and make decisions within a limited period of time; these decisions are to be recorded on special forms (or fed into a computer);

o   feedback is provided, requiring further decisions in a new situation;

o   at the end an overall review session is usually held, in which the teams and the game leaders discuss the performance.

Business games allow all participants to be involved in the game, give an opportunity to make and correct mistakes, exchange ideas and learn through expressing opinions, trying to understand other people's points of view, defending decisions, etc.

During this whole process an observer may follow participants' actions and reactions, recording all problems, difficulties, mistakes and other symptoms of existing and potential training and development needs.

However, it is not advisable to use business games only for the identification of training needs since the method is expensive, complex and time-consuming, while it cannot detect training needs in those skill areas which are not put to work in the given game.

Case studies

The case study method simulates the analytical and synthetic work involved in preparing and proposing solutions to business problems. The individual preparation of the case study, discussion in a small group or by the whole class, the exposure of opinions and confrontation of alternative solutions proposed by various individuals or teams – all are meant to develop a range of skills needed by managers in real-life situations.

Since case studies are usually very close to real life (most of them describe actual business events), the trainer (or a separate instructor charged with observing) can detect gaps in knowledge and experience that prevent participants from viewing the problems from the correct angle (i.e. proceeding methodically from facts to solutions, and making full use of information and opinions contributed by others).

One of the variations of the case study is the *incident process* (see also section 4.6). This involves only a bare "incident" which is reported to the group together with limited relevant information (usually only a minimum) to facilitate analysis. The group is supposed to ask for more specific information to solve a problem. Following the fact-finding stage and clarification of the problem, each member writes his or her own solution and then all proposed solutions are discussed collectively. Finally, the trainer reports the best "real-life" solution.

Advantages

o   Simulation training exercises provide useful and fairly reliable information as a by-product of the training process, and hence at a low cost;

---

o   during simulation, participants tend to be very open about their knowledge and skill gaps, readily asking for help and advice.

Limitations

o   These techniques can be used for needs assessment only if the relatively important training activity of which they form a part is already taking place;

o   separate observation may have to be arranged since the trainer is already fully occupied in running the training exercise;

o   even the most perfect simulation is not a real-life situation – for example, it is impossible effectively to simulate risk taking.

5.8 Sociograms

The sociogram is a means of highlighting the interrelationships between different people in a group. The basic process is concerned with recording the transactions that take place between individuals. This is done using a sociogram, as shown in figure 5.1. The observer sits outside the group and writes down the names of the participants, normally from left to right around the table. He or she then records on the appropriate line each time one individual speaks to another.

In the example shown, Derek has spoken eight times and has been spoken to nine times. He has spoken four times to John, once to Stephen and three times to Hilary. John has spoken nine times and has received ten responses. He has spoken four times to Derek and five times to Hilary, but not at all to Stephen. Stephen has spoken six times (once to John, twice to Derek and three times to Hilary) and has received two responses. Hilary has spoken nine times (three times to Derek, five times to John and once to Stephen), and has received 11 responses. Stephen is not really part of the conversation. He is trying to contribute but nobody seems to want to listen to him apart from Hilary, who is probably just being sympathetic. This information can now be fed back to the group and be used to highlight the fact that Stephen is unable, for whatever reason, to make a meaningful contribution to the discussion. This could be due to communication problems, lack of confidence or just simple lack of skills and knowledge on the subject under discussion.

Advantages

o   Sociograms are useful in highlighting the problems that individuals have when working within groups, particularly the different levels of contribution;

Figure 5.1.   An example of a sociogram

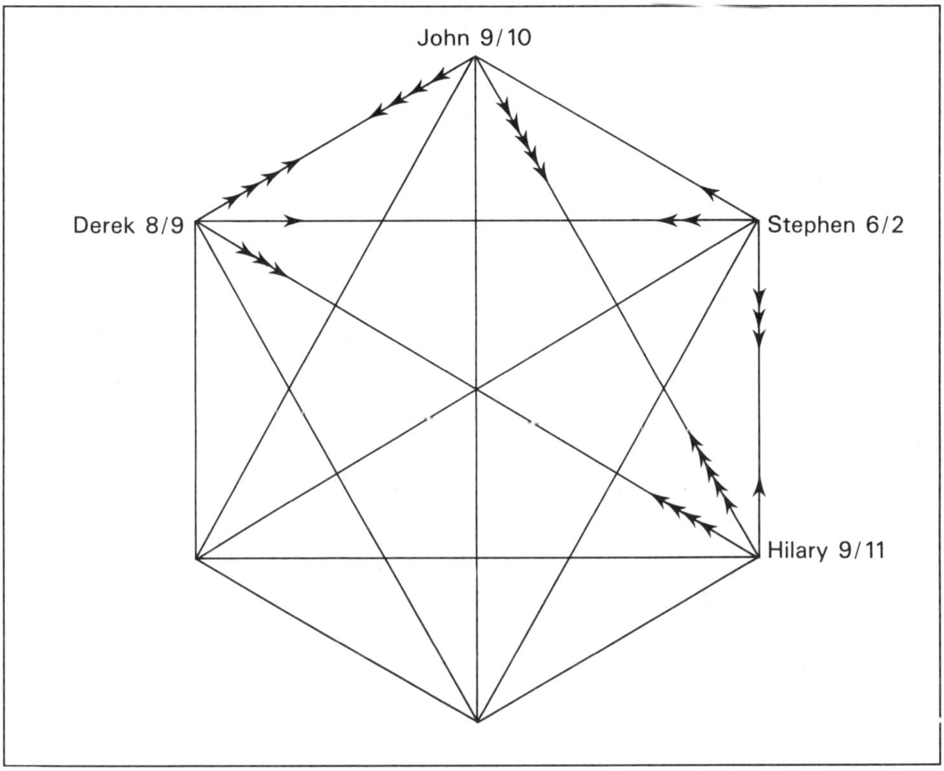

o   useful in analysing attitudes of managers to each other.

Limitations

o   More useful in identifying problems of attitudes and communication than of skills;

o   can normally only supplement other needs identification techniques;

o   require an experienced psychologist/observer.

5.9   Behaviour modelling and analysis

The aim of behaviour modelling is to modify the organisational behaviour of managers by increasing their behavioural repertoire. This can be done by providing them with information on alternative and more effective forms of behaviour relevant to their jobs. The technique can be applied both to individuals and to teams or groups of managers.

Behaviour modelling can be portrayed in terms of a five-step problem-solving model:[5]

(1) The critical forms of behaviour that make a significant impact on performance are identified.

(2) The baseline frequency of the identified behaviour is obtained and measured by determining the number of times it has occurred.

(3) A functional analysis of the behaviour is made (conditions and consequences are identified).

(4) An intervention strategy is developed in order to strengthen and stimulate the desired critical behaviour.

(5) The intervention is evaluated to ensure that performance has improved.

In individual behaviour modelling it is important to demonstrate (by role playing, video reviewing, etc.) effective behaviour in a real or simulated problem situation, make the trainees act it out and then experience it for themselves.

Behaviour analysis was described by Andrew Stewart as a special case of content analysis in which people's actions are categorised in a running analysis performed by themselves or a trainer.[6] The behaviour of each manager is monitored under a series of simple headings (supporting, giving information, criticising, making premature value judgements, etc.) and a check-mark is made every time the listed behaviour occurs. The trainer looks for the overall contribution level of each person (too high, too low) and the relative importance of the various kinds of behaviour. This relative importance can be measured by producing ratios (e.g. ratio of caught proposals to escaped proposals). These ratios can be generated again after training, thus measuring the change achieved. Feedback should be given early and often, as soon as the observations can be shown to be indicative of training needs.

Advantages

o   Helps to focus training on very specific needs in the behavioural sphere;

o   the managers concerned obtain relatively accurate information on what problem ought to be tackled;

o   not too difficult to use if properly prepared.

Limitations

o   Experience with the use of this technique is limited;

o   some managers may resent the observation and precise measurement of their behaviour patterns.

[1] The term "syndicate" is popular mainly in Anglo-Saxon countries. The technique was pioneered in the 1950s by the Administrative Staff College in Henley, United Kingdom.

[2] E.L. Harrison, P.H. Pietri and C.C. Moore: "How to use Nominal Group Technique to assess training needs", in *Training* (Minneapolis), Mar. 1983, p. 30.

[3] See also J.G. Rawlinson: *Creative thinking and brainstorming* (Farnborough, Hampshire, Gower, 1981) and section 9.1 in M. Kubr (ed.): *Management consulting: A guide to the profession* (Geneva, ILO, second (revised) edition, 1986).

[4] See S.W. Barcus (ed.): *Handbook of management consulting services* (New York, McGraw-Hill, 1986), p. 141.

[5] A. Huczynski: *Encylopedia of organisational change methods* (Aldershot, Hampshire, Gower, 1987), pp. 38-39.

[6] The description of behaviour analysis is taken and adapted, with acknowledgement of the origin, from A. Mumford (ed.): *Handbook of management development* (Aldershot, Hampshire, Gower, 1986), pp. 65-66.

TECHNIQUES FOR ASSESSING ORGANISATIONAL NEEDS

6

From a wide range of data-collection, analysis and action-planning techniques used in various organisations and countries, this chapter presents a selection of those that are most popular and appropriate for diagnosing management training and development needs. With some exceptions, the techniques reviewed below tend to take a broad view of the organisation and its problems. The focus is on facts and problems affecting business strategy and performance, relations with the environment, corporate culture, management systems and processes and management style. A common advantage of these techniques is that they relate the assessment of training needs to wider organisational concerns, although there are differences in the method and degree of establishing this relationship. Therefore they are well suited for identifying both training and non-training needs, and the relationship between these two sorts of needs.

The following techniques are examined:

o   records and reports analysis (6.1);

o   future trends and opportunities analysis (6.2);

o   inter-firm comparison (6.3);

o   management (diagnostic) surveys (6.4);

o   management development audits (6.5);

o   attitude surveys (6.6);

o   the Management Climate Survey (6.7);

o   organisation development (6.8);

o   structured performance improvement programmes (6.9).

6.1   Analysis of records and reports

Records and reports are a prolific source of information in any organisation. An obvious source related to training needs is personnel and staff development documentation, covering issues such as personal files, application forms, past performance evaluation records, requests for transfers, promotions, disciplinary measures, demotions, labour disputes, complaints and grievances, terminations, exit interviews, sick leave, overtime, training reports, and so on.

Records and reports related to activities and performance globally (financial statements, operating performance reports) and by specific technical functions (production, research and development, marketing, finance) can be equally significant.

Even looking at routine reports prepared by managers and analysing their drafting and other skills can reveal some important shortcomings (such as when facts are not distinguished from opinions, the purpose of the report is not clear, the context is missing, benefits are not stated clearly, there are grammar and syntax errors, etc.).

Thorough and consistent collection and examination of organisational records and reports is therefore an essential, and universal, technique of needs assessment. In practice this is often ignored. Looking into files may be difficult, time-consuming and boring. Thus, trainers often design questionnaires only to collect data that have already been collected and can be reviewed. Old reports on training needs are not gathered and read before starting work on a new report. This is one of the factors that reduces the credibility of training.

Advantages

o   Focuses on information that is already available, since it was produced for other purposes;

o   hence a time-saving device, which can make preliminary searches and analyses redundant;

o   can enhance the objectivity of needs assessment.

Limitations

o   Old data lend themselves to different interpretations by different people and at different points in time;

o   it is sometimes difficult to get access to really significant written information owing to confidentiality of records and reports;

o   not everything that happens in an organisation is recorded on paper.

6.2   Analysis of future trends and opportunities

The assessment of management training and development needs is an essentially future-oriented activity. Even in dealing with short-term needs requiring virtually immediate action, it is important to know enough about

---

trends – for example, to avoid spending money on an activity or product that will have to be phased out. As regards future needs, they can be considered only in the light of trends and opportunities at the level of the organisation, the sector, the whole national economy, the global markets, the new telecommunication technologies, and the like. Clearly, in some organisations the needs assessment will have to be more future oriented than in others. However, every organisation without exception should view its management training and development needs in the right time perspective.

The analysis of future trends and opportunities is environmental analysis first of all. The main questions asked are: What are our future development prospects? What should be our future strategies? What new skills will be required so that we can cope with future problems and opportunities? What current skill gaps could jeopardise our market position and chances in the future? What skills will no longer be needed? What roles will training and development have to play in the future and what will be the resource implications?

The scope of environmental changes to be considered can be very broad. They can be in any or all of the following areas:

o   products, services and markets;

o   materials and energy;

o   infrastructure;

o   technologies;

o   management techniques and methods;

o   legislation;

o   social and political environment;

o   the supply of educated and trained manpower;

o   forms of doing and financing business;

o   the growth of regional economic groupings, etc.

The most widely used approach to future trends analysis is simple extrapolation from past developments. This may be acceptable within certain limits. Unfortunately, both managers and trainers tend to extrapolate beyond these limits because they are unable or unwilling to consider at what point the current trends may change radically. In periods of rapid technological and other changes, it is normal for current trends not to continue into the future for too long. Other useful techniques include technological and economic forecasting, scenario building, the Delphi technique, brainstorming, market research, the study of demographic and social developments, strategic planning, and so on.

As a rule, only a large organisation staffed by researchers, strategic planners and internal consultants will be in a position to engage in a wide range of information gathering, research and forecasting activities needed for long-range planning and for designing future-oriented management training and development programmes. These activities are often assisted by information and research services provided by various national and sectoral associations, or by private consulting firms and information agencies. The question is then how to use this information and draw conclusions from it for a particular enterprise.

Advantages

o   Essential for making management training and development future oriented and for preparing human resources well in advance in order to meet future goals of the enterprise;

o   equally essential for building up adequate training resources and facilities in the long term;

o   makes managers alert to the fact that "the future is no longer what it used to be".

Limitations

o   Fairly expensive to organise since vast amounts of information have to be collected and interpreted;

o   with a longer time-span the degree of accuracy is low;

o   even suggested action can be quite expensive if several alternative trends are regarded as possible and the organisation wants to act on all of them.

6.3   Inter-firm comparison

Inter-firm comparison is a variant of the universal comparison technique discussed in section 3.2. It reveals how a firm's performance compares with that of other similar organisations. Further analysis can discover and explain the reasons for differences in performance, and suggest action needed for improvement. Comparison techniques can refer to examples, models and standards from other organisations, sectors and even countries. The analyst must consider whether the diversity of conditions permits such a comparison, especially if some important practical conclusions are to be drawn on which management should take action.

Inter-firm comparison usually starts by examining global indicators of performance such as profitability, return on investment, turnover, cost of sales or productivity. These ratios are then broken down and supplemented by a number of operating ratios, indicative of more specific and detailed relationships in the use of resources (see figure 6.1).

Figure 6.1. Example of a management ratio system for inter-firm comparison

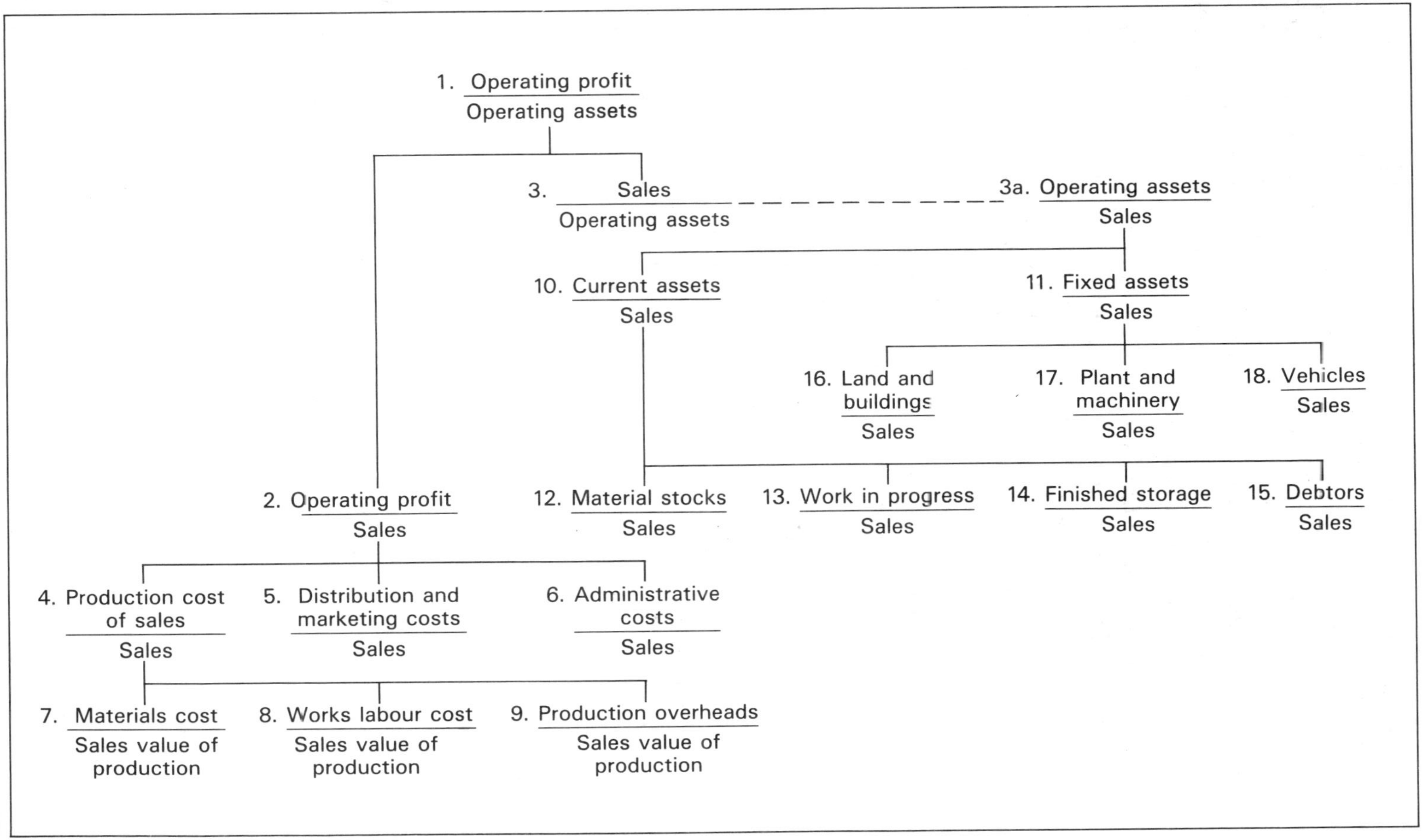

Thus, inter-firm comparison provides some basic data for analysis. Experience has shown in many cases that before seeing how data for their own organisation or plant compare with data from other organisations, managers were completely unaware of major differences in operational efficiency and of related training needs. Therefore the use of figures, and models of other companies whose performance could be considered as good or at least average, puts needs assessment on solid ground, in a way that the practitioner understands and is prepared to accept.

The next level in inter-firm comparison is comparing qualitative factors of performance. These can include the management techniques and systems used, corporate cultures, value systems, management styles, personnel and training policies, and so on. This comparison can lead to the definition of standards reflecting "good practice", which can serve as models at sectoral, national and even international levels. Publications such as *The art of Japanese management* or *In search of excellence*, and several others that followed along the same lines, suggest this approach to managers and trainers.[1] Even if the models of excellence described are not replicable as such, they are presented to the readers as standards for inter-firm comparison. The suggested question is this: If company X can operate as described and be successful, why could we not operate in the same way? If we cannot be the same as company X, what can we learn from them? What is applicable in our setting?

Even if not always so called, the inter-firm comparison approach is widely used in diagnosing training and development needs. It is used both as a rigorous technique, working with complete sets of global and analytical ratios, and as a study of models that provide useful experience, inspiration and ideas for action.

Advantages

o   Gives most useful information on relative managerial and organisational performance;

o   enables a firm to compare its general performance and potential with other companies and find the weakest points in its structure;

o   useful source of information and ideas on where to look for improvements;

o   emulates performance.

Limitations

o   Requires good co-operation and trust between managers and different companies to supply often confidential information for inter-firm comparison;

- o   information on what others actually do and how their actions relate to performance must be well analysed; superficial, impressionistic and journalistic information can be misleading;

- o   requires additional research to link identified performance problems to specific managers, their skills, styles and other factors.

6.4   Management (diagnostic) surveys

A management or diagnostic survey[2] is a fact-finding and analytical exercise whose main purpose is to provide an overall picture of the organisation's performance and effectiveness, strengths and weaknesses, development potential and possible improvements.

These surveys comprise two principal types. Most management surveys are of the first type. They are carried out by management consultants in preparing specific consulting projects. The survey is relatively short (1-4 days, or 5-10 days if a more complex assignment is being prepared) and is completed by a diagnostic report, or a proposal to the client for undertaking a consulting project. The second type of survey is a detailed in-depth study that is usually carried out in preparation for important decisions on the future of the business. Such a survey may precede major restructuring, turnaround, reorganisation, acquisition, merger, nationalisation or privatisation, or a decision to close down the business. In this second case the consultant's mandate is to help the client prepare correct decisions; the consultant may also act as an objective and neutral expert who gives a professional opinion on the health, strengths, weaknesses and prospects of the business. A diagnostic survey of this second type may be a fairly extensive, long and difficult assignment. It is often undertaken in an atmosphere where "business is not as usual", as it is already obvious that some critical decisions cannot be avoided.

Although management surveys can differ quite considerably in their scope, depth and degree of detail, they always aim at a comprehensive view of the organisation, its main results, functions and activities. Therefore they provide good orientation and an introduction to an assessment of training and development needs by identifying the main problem areas where corrective action will be required, and suggesting how to orient further diagnostic and problem-solving efforts. Detailed management surveys invariably include an in-depth assessment of senior management personnel and of human resources management, including management and staff training and development.

Advantages

o Provides quick global information on main problems faced by the organisation, including the indication of areas and units where training needs might be important;

o helps to orient further work or more detailed needs assessment.

Limitations

o The survey consultant must be a very experienced professional, alert to management training and development needs;

o some conclusions from a quick global assessment may have to be rectified in subsequent detailed analysis.

6.5 Management development audits

A management development audit is a fact-finding and evaluation exercise which provides a comprehensive picture of management development within an organisation.[3] It can be held at any time, provided it does not overlap with a similar ongoing exercise with implications for the development of managers (an in-depth diagnostic survey, major policy changes in progress) and management is willing to participate and take some action on the findings of the audit.

Normally the audit starts by identifying official management development policy (e.g. by reviewing policy documents and interviewing top management). Questionnaires are then issued to a representative sample of managers throughout the organisation to reveal *(a)* what happens in practice as opposed to theory, *(b)* what the managers' evaluation is of the effectiveness of existing programmes, and *(c)* what changes they would like to see introduced.

The central issues examined involve training and development, staff appraisal and career development. Within each subsystem the key factors analysed can be, for example (examples in brackets concern the training subsystem):[4]

(1) involvement (whether managers are involved in the decisions concerning their future);

(2) information downwards (whether information about training opportunities is made known to managers);

(3) information upwards (whether managers can communicate their training needs to their superiors);

(4)   planning (how much planned development there is in the organisation's training scheme);

(5)   assessment (how valuable managers find the training programme);

(6)   activity level (in the opinion of the trainees, how much training actually takes place?).

Such an audit can be undertaken by a company, using its own expertise, or with the assistance of external training and development consultants. In any case confidentiality must be guaranteed.

Interpretation of findings aims to provide an overall picture first of all. Reports are then issued to each manager on issues highlighted by the audit concerning his or her function, and suggestions are made in respect of issues that require further investigation and action.

Advantages

o   A relatively simple means of obtaining the perceptions and opinions of managers;

o   takes solid and comparatively objective evidence into account;

o   the managers' views and wishes are considered as very important;

o   prevents the managers from taking entirely subjective decisions to show that "some action" has been taken.

Limitations

o   Provides only a broad orientation and initial data for detailed needs assessment and planning of training programmes;

o   could be a superficial exercise limited to generalities if not properly planned, executed and followed up.

6.6   Attitude surveys

The main purpose of attitude surveys is to determine the opinions and feelings of large groups of individuals in respect of an issue or set of issues. An appreciation of these opinions or feelings can lead to a better understanding of the causes of different problems, anticipate undesired events, identify some management development and training needs and generally improve the quality of the decision-making process and management style. Attitude surveys are most often used to identify probable causes of dissatisfaction, such as inadequate supervision, wrongly focused wage policy and administration, interpersonal clashes, uninteresting work, and so on.[5]

Generally, the attitude survey is a good tool for finding out how employees and/or managers feel about their jobs, their bosses, and their organisation; it can provide valuable information on what and how to change, most of which could be considered in determining management training and development needs. An attitude survey can help to identify and eliminate barriers to better performance, improve communication throughout the organisation, demonstrate management's commitment to listening and improve morale and productivity.[6]

There are four more reasons for employee attitude surveys:

o   employees possess a vast amount of accumulated information and experience and a wealth of good ideas about their jobs;

o   solutions to operating problems are provided by those people responsible for implementation; hence, solutions have more chance of being workable and are likely to meet less resistance;

o   the involvement of employees satisfies their need to contribute more to the company rather than merely to perform routine tasks;

o   problems can be identified and solved before they become intractable.[7]

More specifically, the following main objectives of attitude surveys have been put forward:[8]

o   to receive feedback on the state of organisational health and the management climate to be used in organisational audits, planning, assessing future changes and identifying management training and development needs. This is especially important for executives in large, decentralised organisations;

o   to explain or predict critical organisational events such as turnover, absenteeism, tardiness, downwards trends in productivity, etc. Understanding of these events and their reasons could make management decisions preventive and more effective;

o   to serve as a communication device providing a direct "safe" upward communication channel from workers to management, and from lower-level supervisors and managers to middle and top management, and to stimulate downward communication;

o   to provide managers, by involving them in the survey, with enlightening experience and a direct opportunity for developing new insights and skills and for improving their understanding of organisational processes.

For example, IBM uses surveys of employee opinion as a measure of the quality of its own managing skills. The answers are grouped into a "moral index" and every manager gets an individual index score as recorded by the people he or she manages. This is a high-status measure to which managers throughout the organisation pay keen attention.[9]

Main areas of attitude surveys

The main areas covered by attitude surveys are normally the following:

o   management styles;

o   training and development;

o   payment systems;

o   physical environment and working conditions;

o   organisational value systems;

o   communications, including reporting relations between a boss and a subordinate;

o   industrial relations;

o   job satisfaction;

o   accident prevention;

o   stress at work;

o   autonomy, authority and responsibility, etc.

The attitude survey process

A typical attitude survey process (stages and tasks) is given in table 6.1.

Attitude surveys use anonymous questionnaires (designed to assess attitudes) for identification of problem areas, and face-to-face interviews for in-depth analysis. Sometimes observation is used to check and supplement information obtained through interviews and questionnaires. Furthermore, there are various tools to measure attitudes, such as the following:

(1)   *The Employee Relations Index* (developed by General Electric) attempts to measure the extent to which groups of employees (managers) accept the objectives and policies of the company, and perform in accordance with them. This index synthesises eight different behavioural manifestations (absenteeism, all types of separations, initial visits to the dispensary for occupational reasons, suggestions, disciplinary problems, grievances, work stoppages, and participation in the insurance plan.)

(2)   *The Attitude-Scaling Method* is a relatively crude measuring instrument whose main function is roughly to divide people into a number of broad groups, with regard to a particular attitude. There are also techniques for placing people on a continuum in relation to one another, in relative and not in absolute terms. Among these methods are social-distance scales, Likert scales, Factorial scales, Scalogram-analysis, etc.

(3)   *Projecting techniques* are indirect techniques for measuring attitudes. They are less obvious to the respondent than the scaling method, and therefore more objective and reliable. Projecting techniques could be effectively

Table 6.1. A typical attitude survey process

Stage of survey	Administrative tasks
Discussions with management and trade unions on survey proposal	— Agree wording of announcement of survey and who is to issue it — Agree overall timetable for survey — Set up liaison arrangements
Agreement for survey to go ahead	— Fix date for discussing draft questionnaire — Issue announcement
Exploratory research	— Review sampling frame. Select participants for group discussions and in-depth interviews and send out invitations to attend with reply slips for return — Inform supervisors of names and times — Arrange for interview rooms or for distribution of self-completion questionnaires
Questionnaire drafting	— Type and circulate draft questionnaire — Discussions of draft questionnaire — Draw pilot and main samples about now — Send out invitations and reply slips for pilot interviews and inform supervisors — Retype questionnaire and copy for piloting
Pilot survey	— Draw up timetable for main survey. Start issuing invitations and reply slips about now with copies or list of names and times to supervisors — Finalise questionnaire. Agree once more with management and trade unions, if necessary
Main survey	— Type and print final questionnaire — Brief interviews or distribute self-completion questionnaires — Check completed questionnaires. Monitor response by department/shift for early identification of any group non-response — Start coding responses to open-ended questions about now, and preparing data for computer analysis — Postal survey: send out reminders
Data analysis	— Agree dates for initial presentation of results to management and trade unions — Type and copy report
Report and presentation	— Determine follow-up action, including arrangements for further feedback of results to other employees
Follow-up action	— Take action — Monitor and evaluate action taken

Source: T.K. Reeves and D. Harper: *Surveys at work: A practitioner's guide* (Maidenhead, Surrey, McGraw-Hill, 1982), p. 209.

used for purely exploratory purposes – to identify the main areas where more precise, direct techniques such as scales should be used later on. Projecting techniques can also help to penetrate some particular barriers:

- the barrier of awareness, when people are unaware of their own motives and attitudes and cannot give an accurate answer;

- the barrier of irrationality;

- the barrier of inadmissibility, when we fail to admit that we are unable or find it difficult to meet some standards;

- the barrier of self-incrimination, when some feelings might lower the respondent's self-esteem;

- the barrier of politeness, when people prefer not to say negative, unpleasant or critical things.

Indirect (projecting) techniques include sentence completion, cartoons, interpretation of pictures, stories, pseudo-factual questions, play techniques, experiments and so on, which are all broadly used in attitude measurement and analysis.[10]

Advantages

o Attitude surveys are especially useful in large organisations (more than 200-300 employees), where information about opinions is notoriously liable to distortion and editing when being transmitted up the hierarchy;

o well-conducted attitude surveys provide information that cannot be obtained by the usual management communication channels and fact-finding techniques, and can be much more systematic;

o they are an effective instrument for communicating suggestions to management;

o they are the only reliable instrument to provide information on management attitudes and measure their intensity.

Limitations

o Attitude surveys require high management commitment and willingness to face unexpected findings;

o they are time-consuming;

o a highly experienced professional has to design, and in most cases also conduct and analyse the survey.

6.7   The Management Climate Survey

The Management Climate Survey (MCS) is a technique that aims at measuring how people view and react to the organisation's culture, values and norms, and other aspects of the organisation's health. Normally, people behave in accordance with their understanding of the organisation's norms and values. Their perceptions affect the management team's performance, as well as the individuals' motivation, and, as a result, organisational effectiveness. Thus, any discrepancies between real and perceived organisational norms and values among managers and employees could be considered as important pieces of information on existing management development and training needs.

A typical MCS aims to measure the following factors:[11]

o   clarity of the organisation's goals and overall direction and how well these are understood and shared by managers and supervisors;

o   effectiveness of the decision-making processes;

o   the level of organisational integration, co-operation, and vitality;

o   effectiveness of individual managers and leaders;

o   the degree of openness and trust;

o   the level of job satisfaction;

o   the level of performance measurement, evaluation and accountability;

o   the effectiveness of teamwork and problem-solving;

o   the level of overall confidence in management.

Answers throw light on organisational culture, which in turn depends very much on management style. The latter could and should be influenced positively by management development processes.

An MCS may include from 25 to 100 questions or even more. It can be customised to focus on certain aspects of an organisation's internal relationships. For example, a series of questions can be developed to answer the question: "How well do departments/subsidiaries respect and service each other's needs in terms of quality, service, timeliness, cost and overall responsiveness?"

In practice, MCSs have been used mainly for the following purposes:

o   to clarify perceptions concerning an organisation's mission, objectives, strategic directions;

o   to identify management development needs;

o   to reallocate resources;

o   to prepare background for cultural changes;

o   to improve personnel selection in accordance with new (or expected) cultural values.

Advantages

o   MCS is one of the effective tools for identifying organisational culture and management styles;

o   to use it is relatively simple, though extensive use of questionnaire techniques is required;

o   it can be used as part of an organisation development or another organisation-wide process for performance improvement.

Limitations

o   MCS concentrates more on perceptions of organisational norms and communication and interaction problems, and less on individual management skills and techniques;

o   it is effective only in combination with other needs analysis tools.

6.8   Organisation development

There are many definitions of organisation development (OD). The most common and constructive one defines OD as a planned activity or organisation-wide effort managed from the top and directed to increasing organisational effectiveness and health through interventions in the organisation's processes using behavioural science knowledge and techniques. OD aims to help members of an organisation to interact more effectively in pursuit of organisational goals. It is intentionally based on an awareness of human behaviour and organisational dynamics, provides for harmonising individual and organisational goals, and promotes participative management. Indeed, much of an organisation's inefficiency can usually be traced to employees' disinterest in, or even hostility to, the organisation.

D.D. Warrick compiled the following set of OD characteristics which identify it as a unique approach:[12]

o   the focus of change is a whole system and its interrelated parts;

o   the OD goal is to improve present and future organisational health and effectiveness;

o   OD is a long-range approach to change that emphasises lasting rather than temporary change and seeks to influence an organisation's culture and norms by changing values, attitudes, knowledge, behaviour, processes and structure;

o   OD is a top-to-bottom strategy for change that recognises the importance of gaining the commitment and involvement of top management and any other person or group that could significantly influence the outcome of the effort. Change is initiated at the top of organisations and is gradually applied downwards;

o   it is a collaborative strategy for change that involves those affected by the process and recognises the importance of involvement in development of commitment to OD;

o   it is a data-based approach that uses data for analysis, problem-solving and stimulating change rather than making assumptions about what the real issues are;

o   its programmes are guided by internal or external agents of change or by a combination of both; these agents play firstly a facilitating role and only secondly an expert role;

o   OD focuses firstly on organisational and group change and secondly on individual change;

o   it involves planned interventions and improvements in an organisation's processes and structure and requires skills in working with individuals, groups and the organisation as a whole.

The OD process itself thus consists of the following stages:

(1) *Entry stage:*   Preliminary needs assessment, programme design and negotiation, commitment building

(2) *Diagnostic stage:* Analysis of organisational strengths, weaknesses and needs; processing the results and feeding them back through the system

(3) *Change stage:*   Improvement changes in an organisation using OD intervention techniques such as programme design re-evaluation, problem-solving, team building, conflict resolution, confrontation meetings, feedback, training, strategic planning, etc.

(4) *Evaluation stage:* Another diagnosis and comparison of the results with the previous ones, analysis of changes in productivity, profit, turnover, etc., identification of new problems to be resolved in the future

(5) *Follow-up stage:*   Used to sustain the improvements made during the OD programme

Several important features of OD are of interest for our purpose. First, the process is oriented towards problems and results. Second, it concerns both individual and organisational changes, rather than to training. Third, OD draws heavily on various needs analysis methods and techniques, in particular at stages 1, 2 and 4. Fourth, OD can use training as a part of the overall process, and can make a number of useful suggestions for training, to be taken up outside this process.

Thus, there is a multiple relationship between OD and its various techniques, on the one hand, and training and development needs assessment and various training interventions, on the other hand. A number of OD interventions and activities serve the double purpose of organisation development, and management or staff training and development. It is not difficult to see that almost every step of this sequence involves some aspects of identifying managerial development and training needs and even uses a number of techniques which have already been discussed (questionnaires, interviews, group discussions, appraisal systems, report and record analysis, critical incidents techniques, etc.). For example, the first two steps (entry and diagnosis) of an OD programme are usually based on personal interviews about job problems with every member of the team, group interviews with managers from different departments or functions, supervisors' group discussions, activity sampling and an analysis of the data already available. The third step can reveal such symptoms as frequent complaints of poor communication, other departments being blamed, hostility between managers, indecision, and so on.

The evaluation of the change process can supply interesting and practical information on present and future organisational and management weaknesses, on problems that OD failed to resolve and on further management training and development needs.

Thus, nearly all information obtained during an OD programme could be used to identify management training needs and design management training programmes as an integral part of the whole OD process, or as its continuation.

Advantages

o   Since OD is a learning and an action process, individual managers become involved in all its main phases – diagnosis, learning, action and feedback;

o   if it is properly done, the OD programme can be more effective than many other approaches since it combines management development and organisational improvements;

o   provides a useful opportunity for applying many needs identification techniques as a part of the OD process;

o   the focus is on behavioural aspects which are difficult to ascertain and influence by other techniques.

Limitations

o   The process is complex, takes a great deal of time and requires full commitment from all parties concerned, not only managers;

o   if OD is not carried out skilfully it can create more problems than it solves;

o   fully competent OD practitioners are rare;

o   since needs analysis is only one part of the OD programme, it is not effective to start OD only for the sake of data collection, without aiming at radical organisational changes.

6.9   Structured performance improvement programmes

This section refers to structured organisational projects and programmes launched with the specific purpose of bringing the organisation, over a definite period of time, from one condition (regarded as unsatisfactory, or below a feasible standard) to another condition (standard or optimum). Various methodologies have been developed and applied for this purpose and their full descriptions would exceed the scope of this publication. We will therefore limit ourselves to pointing out their main characteristics, referring to the example of the PIP (planning, or programming, for improved enterprise performance) methodology which has been used by the ILO and other organisations.[13]

These methodologies apply a structured interdisciplinary approach. In developing and implementing a set of performance measures, the company rigorously follows a particular procedure in order to respect the technical logic, maintain momentum and ensure co-ordination and control of the whole exercise, which may involve a large number of managers and units within the organisation. In addition, the methodologies apply various elements of the OD approach to enlist participation, generate commitment to the action agreed to and taken, and deal with behavioural problems. Thus, these approaches are characterised by definite commitment and leadership from the top, but are different from special projects and proposals entrusted to small groups of selected individuals, as they involve decision-makers at various levels, as well as many staff members. They are also broader and more comprehensive than the classical OD approach.

Turning to the example of PIP, this approach usually includes the following major phases:

(1) *Preliminary diagnosis of enterprise problems*

At the beginning, the objective is to establish that potential for improvement exists and that the senior executives are willing to embark on organisation-wide performance improvement programmes that may be demanding on their time and require some painful decisions. If the enterprise is found to be receptive to the idea of a programme of change, a number of preliminary diagnostic surveys are undertaken to provide current baseline data and some indications of major existing problems. This may include a management survey, a financial appraisal, comparisons with other enterprises, a preliminary analysis of trends and opportunities in the given industrial sector, and so on.

(2) *Orientation for senior managers*

During this phase, meetings and workshops are organised to explain the nature, implications and methodology of the programme. Preliminary information and assessments produced in Phase 1 are used to demonstrate the magnitude of the problems to be tackled.

(3) *Preparation for implementation*

The timetable and organisational arrangements for the programme are established. These include decisions on the possible use of external consultants and the roles assigned to internal consultants and trainers. If necessary, training in diagnosis, problem-solving, systems analysis and other methods is provided.

(4) *Analysing and defining the mission, objectives and key performance indices*

At this stage, the exercise focuses on analysing and defining the enterprise's mission, long-term objectives, position in the national or sectoral economic system, and operational indices and targets. Stage 4 is usually completed in a special performance-improvement workshop attended by senior management.

(5) *Identification and analysis of key impeding and impelling forces*

The objectives suggested in the previous phase are confronted with the factors and forces that will hamper their achievement, as well as with positive driving forces from which the enterprise will be able to benefit. The analysis is both external (environmental factors) and internal (the enterprise's own resources, capabilities and potential). Both impeding and impelling forces are ranked in their order of priority, with assessments of their strengths. It is important to determine what constraints *(a)* can be removed by the enterprise itself, *(b)* require a dialogue or negotiation with the government on some other external institutions, and *(c)* cannot be changed and will continue to limit the development possibilities in the future.

(6) *Evolving strategies and action programmes for improving performance*

Teams of managers and specialists from various sectors and functions of the organisation are then engaged in finding realistic solutions to the problems identified. Various methods of problem-solving are applied at the discretion of the enterprise, including brainstorming and other group creativity techniques. The process is co-ordinated to maintain a focus on the objectives chosen and respect the necessary relationships and linkages between various functions and areas of activity.

(7) *Arrangements for implementation*

Various sorts of projects and actions will be the outcome of the previous stage and will now require management's approval, an allocation of the necessary resources, assignment of responsibilities and arrangements for continued co-ordination and monitoring.

(8) *Implementing action programmes*

This phase provides for the implementation of those action programmes (e.g. finding new distributors of products, reorganising the production departments, establishing a strategic planning unit, etc.) that require some time for both technical reasons and for getting the changes accepted within the organisation. Individual managers and/or task forces are responsible for these programmes. Top management, with the help of internal or external consultants, and a special PIP co-ordination unit (if appropriate) monitors progress and adjusts the individual projects and the timetable to new conditions and needs.

(9) *Evaluation and feedback*

As with any organisational change programme, at some point in time the major PIP exercise is considered completed and the results are assessed. The methodology and organisation are assessed as well. It may be decided that some action programmes will have to continue. In any event, conclusions are drawn on how to approach performance improvement in the future: As another, perhaps modified, PIP exercise? A campaign using another methodology? A series of small steps and measures chosen, planned and implemented on a continuous basis?

Once more, we stress that we are providing just one example of the wide range of approaches and programmes that have been developed for this purpose. If an organisation decides to use PIP or a similar method, the opportunity to deal with management training and development needs must not be missed. Each one of the nine stages described above has specific implications for management development and the totality of these stages provides a comprehensive approach to the management development cycle described in chapter 2.

Advantages

o   PIP integrates the management development cycle with the total organisational improvement cycle;

o   ensures a consistent focus on results to be achieved;

o   helps to select specific training events and techniques that will be of immediate practical use;

o   enhances motivation for an objective assessment of needs and for taking action to meet defined needs.

Limitations

o   There must be a favourable attitude and proper conditions for embarking on a PIP programme which is rather demanding on management's time and on resources;

o   trainers who want to make use of this opportunity must have enough practical experience and be versed in a broad range of problem-solving and consulting skills, in addition to training proper.

---

[1] T. Peters and R.H. Waterman: *In search of excellence* (New York, Warner Books, 1982); R.T. Pascale and A.G. Athos: *The art of Japanese management* (New York, Warner Books, 1981).

[2] See M. Kubr (ed.): *Management consulting: A guide to the profession* (Geneva, ILO, second (revised) edition, 1986), Ch. 7 and Appendix 4, for a detailed description of a management survey.

[3] Cf. M. Esterby-Smith, E. Braiden and D. Ashton: *Auditing management development* (Westmead, United Kingdom, Gower, 1980). The booklet describes an audit methodology used by the Durham University Business School in the United Kingdom.

[4] ibid., pp. 5 and 9.

[5] M. Lo Bosco: "Employee attitudes surveys", in *Personnel* (New York), Apr. 1986, p. 64.

[6] *Training* (Minneapolis), Aug. 1987, p.12.

[7] G. Cole: "Employee attitude surveys: A new role for trainers", in *Journal of European Industrial Training* (Bradford, West Yorkshire), Vol. 5, No. 6, 1981, p.12.

[8] R.B. Dunham and F.J. Smith: *Organisational surveys. An internal assessment of organisational health* (Glennview, Illinois, Scott, Foresman and Co., 1979), p. 36.

[9] D. Dreunan and S. Walker: "What does the team think?", in *Director* (London, Institute of Directors), Nov. 1987, p.99.

[10] A.N. Oppenheim: *Questionnaire design and attitude measurement* (London, Heinemann, 1966), p. 162.

[11] Adapted from R.L. Desatnick: "Management climate surveys: A way to uncover an organisation's culture", in *Personnel*, May 1986, pp.49-50.

[12] W.R. Tracey: *Human resources management and development handbook* (New York, AMACOM, 1985), pp. 916-917.

[13] See R. Abramson and W. Halset: *Planning for improved enterprise performance: A guide for managers and consultants*, Management Development Series, No. 15 (Geneva, ILO, 1979); and V. Powell: *Improving public enterprise performance: Concepts and techniques*, Management Development Series, No. 22 (Geneva, ILO, 1987).

FROM CONCEPTS TO APPLICATIONS

HOW ENTERPRISES DIAGNOSE NEEDS

7

This chapter opens part III of the book, which is devoted to practical applications. Following a detailed review of individual, group and organisational needs assessment techniques, we now attempt a synthesis. Our questions will be: What are we to do with all these techniques? How can we combine them and make best use of them? What guide-lines reflecting proven experience can be suggested to managers and trainers who are keen to base training on solid diagnoses of needs? What is "good practice" in diagnosing management training and development needs in various organisations and various situations? How is needs assessment handled in the current context of increasingly complex and rapid environmental change? Last but not least, how can needs assessment be improved in order to increase the impact and effectiveness of management development?

Chapter 7 describes prevailing practices and points out trends in enterprise-level diagnosis of management training and development needs. The discussion will be based mainly on experience of larger industrial and commercial enterprises, private and public. However, it should also be of interest to other sorts of organisations that have to train their managers and administrators, including government ministries, public agencies and voluntary organisations.

7.1 Mapping out the enterprise scene

Most management training and development activities, including needs assessment, take place in large and medium-sized enterprises in industry, commerce, transport, services and other sectors. In the absence of generally recognised sector standards – a salient feature of the state of the art of management development – these enterprises use a wide range of approaches to the training and development of their managers and staff members. There are major differences in written and unwritten policies, traditions and practices, methods and techniques, organisational arrangements and all other aspects of human resource development. It would be impossible to find two companies that follow identical principles and practices in every respect. This has been confirmed by a number of surveys, as well as by our own observations, over the years, of how companies develop managers.[1]

Such a diversity is not easy to grasp and describe in a meaningful way. Nevertheless, it is possible to detect certain approaches and behavioural patterns that tend to be more common than others, and certain trends that seem to arouse more and more interest. On this basis, it is possible to cluster companies in broad groupings, guided by similar principles and exhibiting similar behaviour.

Three archetypes

The Ashridge study, *Management for the future*,[2] identifies three different company approaches to the role of training and development: the "fragmented" approach, the "formalised" approach, and the "focused" approach. This classification provides a useful framework for discussing company practices in diagnosing training needs, and relating this diagnosis to broader policies and practices of human resource development and managing organisational change. The typology suggested by Ashridge is in accordance with our own findings. Therefore we have adopted it for this chapter, hoping that such a typology will help the reader to understand trends and assess his or her own company.

However, any typology of enterprises is a gross simplification. Therefore it would be unrealistic to assume that a particular company could be easily classified under any of the three archetypes. As a rule, a company will belong mainly to one archetype, but will at the same time exhibit some characteristics of the other groups.

7.2   The fragmented approach

In the Ashridge study, this first approach is defined in the following terms:

o   training is not linked to organisational goals;

o   training is perceived as a luxury or a waste of time;

o   approach to training is non-systematic;

o   training is directive;

o   training is carried out by trainers;

o   training takes place in the training department;

o   emphasis is on knowledge-based courses;

o   the focus is on training (a discontinuous process) rather than on development (a continuous process).

Companies in this group do not practise any serious assessment of training and development needs, or they do it from time to time, in a haphazard way. This finding has been confirmed by other surveys. In 1985 the magazine *Training* reported on a survey which found that even in the "Fortune 500" companies a formal training needs analysis was the exception rather than the rule.[3] The most common ways of assessing training needs were informal discussions, observations and interviews, as opposed to questionnaires, group discussions and analyses of records and reports. Another survey among the magazine's subscribers found that 62 per cent of the respondents did not carry out formal and structured needs assessment for all training projects, while only 47 per cent spent enough time trying to discriminate between training needs and non-training needs.[4] Generally speaking, managers and training professionals in many enterprises pay a great deal of lip service to "the necessity to assess needs regularly, systematically and thoroughly". However, the actual practice is often different.

How to choose a wrong programme

This fragmented approach was well illustrated by W.S. Mitchell, who compiled the following list of reasons referred to by many companies in deciding on training programmes:[5]

o   "Look at all the big companies who use this programme. It's got to be right for us."

o   "Here are some new subjects that many big firms are starting to include in their programmes. We should too."

o   "We researched dozens of management programmes. These are the subjects that are common to most of them."

o   "We're going to get professors A, B and C to do our programme. Everybody's talking about how great they are."

o   "Our programme includes all the things that textbooks say managers should do."

o   "We asked senior management to give us a list of the subjects they felt should be in the programme. About a third responded, and we've included everything they suggested."

o   "We sat down and thought of all the things our managers should do better."

o   "We sent out a 20-item subject list to a sample of senior managers and this is what they chose. They confirm the need for subjects we had recently identified as critical."

o   "All we really have to do is to upgrade the programme we have been using, give it a new title and move it to a nice conference centre."

o   "A consulting firm talked to our senior manager and they recommend a programme they've successfully presented for years now."

o   "A consulting firm did a survey and the results show we need their "excellent management" programme, but with a lot of tailoring to our environment. It's expensive, but they guarantee results."

o   "The more we thought about it, the more sure we became we don't need a programme designed especially for us. Let's use one of the institutional programmes."

7.3   The systematic approach

Stimulated by the human resource development movement of the last 20 years, many enterprises in various countries have made considerable efforts to introduce management training and development as a systematic and regular activity, harmonised with other enterprise activities and helping the enterprise to achieve its main goals. In this approach, needs assessment is given a prominent place and is also practised on a regular basis, as systematically as possible.

In the Ashridge study, this approach is called "formalised" and is described as follows:

o   training becomes linked to human resources (HR) needs;

o   training becomes systematic by linking it to an appraisal system;

o   the emphasis is still on knowledge-based courses but the focus of the training course broadens, with greater emphasis on skill-based courses;

o   the link which is made between training and HR needs encourages organisations to adopt a more developmental approach. Broadly speaking, development in a formalised organisation means career development;

o   in terms of the emphasis that organisations place on training and development (apart from certain key areas), the value of the traditional training course is viewed with some scepticism, whereas development through career planning is highly regarded;

o   training is carried out by trainers, but the range of skill demands placed on a trainer develops with the new breadth of courses offered;

o   line managers become involved with training and development through their role as appraisers;

o   pre- and post-course activities attempt to facilitate the transfer of off-the-job learning;

o   training is carried out off the job, but through career development the value of on-the-job learning gains formal recognition;

o   there is more concern to link a programme of training to individual needs.

Usually this situation is found in well-established and fairly stable companies, which do not achieve overall performance improvement through major breakthroughs or projects, but mainly through a large number of successive incremental improvements and smaller projects in running their regular operations. This determines the overall role of training, which is seen as a regular feature of running the company. A great deal of management training is provided on the job, i.e. learning by doing. There may be an established pattern of job rotation, coaching, counselling, planning of management succession, and so on. When courses and seminars are used, there is a tendency to organise them within the company, either calling on the company's own training resources or bringing in external experts. External consultants and trainers may also be brought in to assist in assessing training needs. Every year a smaller number of managers would be sent on external courses and seminars.

The total volume of training activity will not be the same in all companies in this group. Although data permitting precise conclusions are difficult to obtain, it appears that the level of technological sophistication and the pace of technological change are the main factors that determine the importance attached to all training – technical, administrative and managerial. In "high-tech" companies and companies working for rapidly changing markets, this figure will be considerably higher than in other companies.

Definition of organisational responsibilities

The fact that training needs assessment is viewed as part of the personnel and training function does not mean that it would be fully handled by personnel and training specialists. On the contrary, all managers are expected to keep an eye on training needs in running their units. Management meetings where personnel issues are discussed also deal with training needs. Action can be taken immediately within the unit concerned, or the personnel department would be asked to help by locating a course, arranging for a transfer or detachment within the company, and so on.

As a rule, technical (functional) knowledge and skills are reviewed and assessed in collaboration with the technical departments concerned. For example, the development of financial know-how is primarily the province of the financial manager, while marketing competence is looked after by the marketing manager. They would be responsible for the conception and the planning of all training in their functional area, i.e. including the marketing training of production people, and so on. The director of training, or of management training and development, focuses on overall aspects of training needs and of the organisation and methodology of training. Thus, marketing training needs in various parts of the company are normally identified by the marketing specialists, with methodological guidance and organisational collaboration of the training specialists.

Interdisciplinary and people management skills are reviewed and assessed separately from technical and functional skills. The personnel department and the training managers play a key role in this, although all unit managers are expected to participate in assessing general management skills and related training needs, and in designing and organising appropriate training interventions.

Using performance appraisal and career planning

Companies in this group try to use performance appraisal (section 4.10) for assessing training needs. If performance appraisal is poorly used for its main purpose, i.e. for encouraging efforts to improve performance, its usefulness to training needs assessment is also considerably lowered. Therefore, companies that are keen to relate training to specific problems in individual performance aim to make sure:

o   that there is a formal provision for describing training needs in the appraisal form, discussing training with the person being appraised, and examining and summarising, at unit and company level, the suggestions for training made in all individual appraisals;

o   that follow-up is given to comments and suggestions thus collected; if such follow-up is impractical because too much costly training was requested, or a training request is regarded as unnecessary by higher management, these reasons are reviewed with the individuals concerned and their managers;

o   that the instructions for the overall performance appraisal system also include clear guide-lines on how to handle the question of training needs in every single performance appraisal exercise.

In a similar vein, career planning (section 4.12) can be a valuable technique for needs assessment if a clear relationship is established between career objectives and the suggested career path, on the one hand, and the relevant training, on the other hand. Career planning would focus mainly on longer-term training and development needs, requiring participation in longer courses, transfers and detachments within the company, special individual or group projects, and so on.

Using self-assessment

Self-assessment of individual training needs (section 4.11) is increasingly used as a major source of information for planning tailor-made and action-oriented training. Self-assessment should be encouraged as a matter of principle. Information should also be provided so that proper use may be made of self-assessment, which may require some formal procedures, e.g. combining self-assessment with performance appraisal and making sure that everyone receives constructive feedback on his or her perception of needs.

Self-assessment can create misunderstanding and conflict if people come up with an assessment of their potential and needs that is not shared by management, and with training demands that cannot be justified by the company standards. However, any such findings provide opportunities for discussion and for clarifying individual and management criteria and expectations.

Using training to collect data

Ongoing training activities provide a great deal of information on training and development needs. Therefore many training managers make use of this information for planning further training. The following can be arranged within the company:

o asking participants for their views on what training needs were not properly covered by programmes they attended;

o including sessions and exercises in training programmes that can reveal further needs (see chapter 5 on group techniques);

o gathering the participants' opinions and experiences in respect of training needs of their collaborators who do not attend the programme;

o evaluating the overall quality and practical impact of the training that has been provided, with the view to identifying training needs that have not been met.

Dealing with different management levels

A great advantage of regular training needs assessment carried out within companies is the possibility to look at every need from various angles as stressed in section 2.4. The most obvious and generally applied approach is asking higher managers about training needs of lower managers and staff specialists. The reversed approach is useful, too. It may not be convenient to ask people directly about the training needs of their superiors. However, indirect ways of finding out can be used, including the analysis of information sharing, communication, decision-making, leadership styles, and so on. Finally, lateral information, obtained from managers in other collaborating units, is most useful. For example, many people in various sectors of the organisation will have their particular experience and views concerning the profile, competence and work style of the corporate planning manager, or the EDP department manager.

Planning human resource development

Finally, companies in this group tend to practise some sort of planning of human resource development. There is likely to be an annual (or two- or three-year) plan defining the nature and volume of training to be undertaken, on the basis of needs assessment carried out regularly, as described above. The very existence of such a plan introduces regularity and discipline in assessing needs and programming remedial action consistent with company objectives and resources. The plans tend to provide for both training and non-training approaches and actions in the development of human resources.

7.4 The future-oriented strategic approach

Despite its many advantages over the fragmented approach, the systematic approach described in the previous section may not meet all needs of companies that operate in rapidly changing environments, and whose ambition is to achieve and maintain a leadership position in conditions where continuous change is the only constant. More and more companies find themselves in this situation. This has been reflected in the emergence of a new model or archetype of organisational behaviour, which can be labelled as "future-oriented and strategic".

In the Ashridge study, this third approach is referred to as "focused", and the organisation using this approach is defined as "the learning organisation" and described in the following terms:

o   training and development and continuous learning by individuals is perceived as a necessity for organisational survival in a rapidly changing business environment;

o   training is regarded as a competitive weapon;

o   learning is linked to organisational strategy and to individual goals;

o   the emphasis is on on-the-job development, so that learning becomes a totally continuous activity;

o   specialist training courses are available across the knowledge/skill/value spectrum;

o   self-selection for training courses;

o   training is generally non-directive, unless knowledge based;

o   new forms of training activity are utilised, e.g. open and distance learning packages, self-development programmes, etc.;

o   more concern to measure the effectiveness of training and development;

o   main responsibility for training rests with line management;

o   trainers adopt a wider role;

o   new emphasis on learning as a process;

o   tolerance of some failure as part of the learning process – *droit d'erreur*.

Many characteristics of the systematic approach described in the previous section will also be found in enterprises endeavouring to use the future-oriented strategic approach. The principal new features include strong focus on environmental change, and future needs, emphasis on continuous organisational self-assessment and learning coupled with lifelong individual learning (hence "the learning organisation"), flexibility, and viewing human resource development as investment for the future rather than current cost.

There are high-technology industries such as computers or telecommunications, in which companies tend to adopt this third approach as the most natural one. However, in addition to the nature and pace of technological change in particular industries, there are other significant trends that call for the future-oriented strategic approach: the internationalisation and globalisation of markets; the growth of regional economic groupings and communities; the information explosion; the changes in consumer taste and demand; the developments in education, social values and lifestyles; the new patterns of international finance; privatisation and deregulation in many countries; and so on.

Focus on future needs

As regards training and development needs, in the future-oriented approach the concern for future needs clearly prevails over the concern for current needs. Of course, current needs cannot be ignored and programmes have to be provided to meet them promptly. However, the best brains and the innovative decision-makers concentrate on the question of how to prepare the workforce, and managers in particular, for the future. This calls for increased use of future-oriented needs assessment techniques, such as study of future trends and opportunities and of the behaviour of the sector leaders, creativity techniques, and other ways of tapping the best expertise and expert opinion both within and outside the company. The challenge is not merely that of adapting to environmental change. The objective is to anticipate change, know early enough what change is most likely to occur and be prepared to take the most interesting opportunities created by technological and environmental change. Some companies are important enough to think of how they might influence the development of products, technologies, services or markets in their own or new areas of activity, thus influencing the direction, magnitude and pace of environmental change.

Relating needs assessment to corporate strategy

In this approach, the development of the workforce focuses on what the company wants to achieve in the future. This is impossible without strategic thinking, which is needed even if a company rejects an elaborate formalised system of strategic planning. Training and development needs assessment is geared to strategic choices and goals of the organisation. In addition, management development is used for increasing competence to think strategically and make strategic choices.

Some allowance for error is necessary, however. For example, considerable training may be undertaken to master a new marketing approach that will have to be dropped eventually. Calculated risk, and spending some resources on options that will not be pursued in the long run, are features of the strategic approach.

Organisational and individual needs

Organisational learning implies that organisational needs are continuously assessed and reassessed, and are used as the basic criterion in defining and meeting the needs of individual managers and other employees. There is, however, as the Ashridge study rightly points out, a corresponding focus on the learning needs of individuals: "Responding to the needs of individuals is seen as a way of releasing energy, securing commitment and enabling individuals to be pro-active and take responsibility in a climate of rapid change."[6] According to the Conference Board, "managers are seen as the key to the implementation of new or revised strategies that seek variously to increase competitive strength, enhance productivity, raise the quality of products and services, and meet circumstances altered by deregulation and other events. ... Some firms have been anticipating the need for a new generation of managers."[7]

In such a climate, individuals are encouraged to diagnose their own needs taking a long-term perspective, and actively contribute to the definition of wider needs of organisational units, departments and the whole company. This changes the role of training and development professionals: their formal authority to define the training and development needs of others may be reduced, but their professional role of collaborating with functional and line management in defining organisational needs is considerably enhanced.

Viewing human resource development as an essential investment

While research and development concerning products and technologies is increasingly regarded as an investment ensuring the company's future, the cost of staff training and development continues to be viewed and calculated in most companies as current cost. Companies lack specific routines and procedures for investing in human resources, a "soft" side of the business. This attitude, however, may change with the adoption of the future-oriented strategic approach. There are several reasons for this. The importance, volume and cost of training and development tend to grow. Both companies and individuals want to be sure that an enhanced learning effort will create a capability that is really needed and directly related to the strategic choices that are already decided or intended. Companies will be most keen to retain highly competent personnel in whose training they have invested considerably.

Clearly, approaching management and human resource development as a long-term investment will require major improvements in needs assessment, staff development and career planning, costing of training and development, and the discipline and quality of programme implementation. For example, companies that are currently endeavouring to link management development to their business strategies find little information and guidance on how this investment is justified, and how it should be linked with other strategic options and resource allocations.

There is likely to be more dialogue and interaction between company management and individuals in defining future training and development needs. However, it would be unrealistic to foresee zero managerial mobility. Some individuals whose training was very costly will leave any organisation, while others whose training needs were met at another company's expense will join. Investing in management development requires some allowance for mobility and wastage which can be kept under control, but not fully eliminated, by sound human resource development policies.

7.5   How to improve needs assessment in your company

The reader who has gone as far as this section is certainly keen to see his or her organisation making better use of needs assessment for improving management training and development. From the foregoing sections, it can be seen that there is a progression from the first (fragmented) approach to the second (systematic) approach, and from the second to the third approach (future-oriented strategic). This progression can be used as a framework for planning improvements, bearing in mind what is feasible in a given context. A significant feature of this progression is a reorientation towards "needs-driven" training and development strategy, as reported by companies such as IBM,

Xerox or General Electric, which have long been regarded as leaders and exemplars in this field.[8]

Clearly, a company which has no information on needs and does very little training cannot aspire to implement the strategic approach in the short run. This would have to be planned and achieved step by step. It may be useful to start by a well-prepared survey of needs, or by one or a few projects for organisational change which pay proper attention to management development based on a thorough assessment of needs. The strategy and tactics chosen will probably aim to regularise needs assessment, thus achieving the second approach, before thinking of a "front-line attack" to apply and internalise the third approach.

Eventually, a large and complex organisation may exhibit elements of all three approaches. Human resource development, including the underlying diagnosis of needs, will become a regular and – in a sense – a routine activity (second approach). The focus on future strategy and the related changes in needs assessment (third approach) will be gaining ground. However, it may be found that in some areas and units it will be difficult, or too costly, to overcome the first approach, which may be allowed to persist at least for some time.

Knowing where you are

Perhaps the best starting-point is to take a detached view of how the company has trained and developed its managers and what sort of needs assessment it has practised. This can be a formal exercise, a sort of audit of management development (as described in section 6.5), or an informal assessment by general and/or personnel management. If a company faces a major change that will require a new business strategy, a reorganisation and many staff transfers, these developments can trigger off a reappraisal of its needs assessment practices since there is an immediate demand for a management training programme that can be geared to specific priority objectives. However, it is not necessary to wait for such an occasion since this would be impractical in a company where no dramatic changes are expected in the short run. In such a company it may be possible to point out the experience of other companies that are likely to be viewed and respected as models. Still better, a needs assessment exercise on a limited scale, say in one department or focused on a particular problem (e.g. reducing equipment breakdown and stoppages by better planning and management of maintenance), may produce tangible benefits that will convince the key decision-makers about the usefulness of the exercise.

Major needs assessment exercises, such as company-wide surveys, should never be started as exclusive projects of the training or personnel function, without top management interest and active support. The attitude and the involvement of top management will set the tone: other managers will follow.

Eventually the support of management has to be obtained at all levels, by demonstrating and explaining to managers at each level how they can best contribute to needs assessment and what main benefits are likely to be drawn from it.

Ad hoc surveys of company needs

A company that has not regularised needs assessment may decide that a special survey (study) of management training and development needs is required. The reason may be that it is a new company, a company that underwent major restructuring or reorganisation and has new management, or an organisation that has been neglecting training and lacks basic information on training needs.

For example, when the Allied Corporation in the United States acquired Bendix,[9] a survey was designed and executed to "identify the various elements that collectively constitute the cultures". A programme for senior executives was then built around these elements, which thus did not grow out of a traditional needs analysis or performance appraisal, but from a recognition that the two parts of the organisation had to be integrated and to share an understanding of the firm's identity and future orientation.

There may be instances where a company with a regular and well-established needs assessment activity may feel that an ad hoc survey might be useful. A special survey may be part of an audit of management development, in order to evaluate past efforts and verify whether the management development policies and practices have been effective. Or there may be a forward-looking survey of future needs, which is aimed at issues not normally revealed by regular and periodic assessment of needs. Such a survey may be undertaken in connection with strategic planning, if the company is looking into future training needs likely to be generated by new technologies and various changes of a strategic nature.

Finally, a special study may be used as a "visible" campaign to increase the managers' and other employees' interest in training and make them aware of important training needs.

The planning and preparation of the survey would normally be done by the training manager. If there is none, and the purpose is to prepare and justify the creation of a training function, the personnel manager can be in charge. The top management of the company should be prepared to accept the main responsibility for actually managing the survey in its various parts and stages, endorsing the conclusions and reviewing them with other managers. Active participation of managers should be sought at all levels of the hierarchy.

Quite frequently, the survey is entrusted to external consultants, either from management consulting firms or from training institutions. This may be justified if the company has no training staff of its own or if the objective is to bring in new expertise, survey methods and perspectives. However, as in any effective use of external consultants, the assignment to survey training needs must never be left totally to the consultants, even if these consultants enjoy the company's full confidence. The question of "ownership" remains important. If consultants do all the work including the drawing of conclusions, and present the final results to management, it is likely that polite acceptance of the results will not imply commitment to making good use of them.

The scope of an ad hoc survey will depend on its main purposes and on the resources available. A survey can be confined to one technical area (e.g. skills and training needs in using computers) or to one unit (plant, department) within the company. Some tactical considerations will also apply: in seeking benefits from such a survey, management will have to think of the sort of study that the company can afford to launch at a particular point of time, and of the likely reactions at various levels within the company to a major and time-consuming survey.

As regards the methodological approaches to special ad hoc surveys of company-level management training and development needs, the reader may turn to chapter 8, where survey methodology is examined in some detail.

Training needs assessment in projects of organisational change

The best opportunity for trying out a new approach to training needs assessment is provided by specific actions (projects) of organisational change. These actions can be of various types as regards objectives, scope and methods used: they can range from minor organisation development (OD) exercises (see section 6.8), involving one or several units within the company, to comprehensive company turnarounds. They also include actions such as mergers, acquisitions, reorganisations and restructuring, PIP projects (see section 6.9), profit and productivity improvement schemes, cost-saving campaigns, and so on. The common feature is that these are basically one-off projects, aimed at specific objectives, with more or less clearly identifiable starting and completion dates.

The basic question concerning management training and development is straightforward: What sort and how much of it will be necessary to implement the planned change effectively and to sustain it after the completion of the project? Thus, training will tend to be results oriented and determined by the scope and objectives of the project. There will be a tendency to give priority to project-related training and to de-emphasise or postpone other training, even if it is seen as potentially useful, but not as absolutely necessary to advance the project in hand. There will be a propensity for handling training as a feature and a part of the project, harmonised in content and methods and co-ordinated in time with each stage of the overall project plan. Training may even be used as an intervention technique to help the people involved recognise the need for change and choose the best course of action at each stage of the change process. As a rule, training needs will not be established for the duration of the whole project, but for its current or next phase. They will also be met immediately by providing the required training, so that the results of training can be immediately applied. This implies considerable flexibility not only in assessing and reassessing the needs, but also in organising the training interventions at short notice. In action-learning projects (section 4.9), free-standing learning resources may be made available, so that the individual managers can flexibly define and meet their training and development needs as the project moves ahead.

7.6 Cost and other quantitative aspects of enterprise needs

Irrespective of the fact that training and development may be regarded either as a current cost or as an investment, the decision-makers responsible for resource planning and allocation in an enterprise will be interested in the quantitative dimensions and implications of management training and development needs. Even if training is valued highly and a needs assessment exercise regarded as very professional, it is impossible to ignore resource constraints and efficiency criteria. There may be a case for comparing the cost of training with the cost of alternative solutions (e.g. retraining a manager or recruiting a new one who already possesses the required competence). The principal quantitative aspects to be considered are

o   the trainees' time and its cost;

o   the trainers' time and its cost;

o   training facilities (volume, cost);

o   training materials and equipment (learning packages, computers, books);

o   the fees to be paid for participation in external programmes or for the use of external consultants in the company training programmes;

o   the costs of training administration.

Alternative ways of meeting the needs

It is important to realise that the measurement of training needs in time units and in financial terms is impossible without considering the way in which a need is to be met. Once we start dealing with the quantitative side of needs, we think in terms such as the duration of a course or a practical assignment, the number of days to be allowed for training, or the course fee and the cost of the time that will be used for training rather than for normal work.

Hence it is also essential to be sure that the best alternative way of meeting the training need identified is being considered. The differences can be quite important, as for example:

o   alternative A: four months' full-time middle management course for generalists ("advanced management programme") – 17 weeks in total;

o   alternative B: four one-week seminars, with intermittent project work requiring 20 per cent of the participant's working time over a period of six months – 8.4 weeks in total;

o   alternative C: two one-week workshops and a special work assignment (on the job) supported by coaching by a senior manager over a period of eight months, plus individual study using training packages (in private time) – 2 weeks in total.

Company training managers as well as line managers are well aware of this issue. Therefore they keep looking for those management training alternatives which *(a)* guarantee the same results while reducing the actual absence from work; *(b)* reduce the time-lag between the start of the training and the moment when results start being actually applied at work; and *(b)* optimise the ratio of benefits (results) to costs.

Balancing the needs and the resources

The basic approach consists in balancing the training needs expressed in quantitative terms with the resources that the organisation can and wants to make available. Such an exercise does not start from scratch in an organisation that has maintained training records and determined budgets, ratios or other standards defining the normal and desirable level of management training activity to meet the company's needs. For example, some companies think that on average they should provide for 5-10 days of off-the-job training and development of each manager per year. Normally such a figure would be indicative only. However, the total volume of the training budget may be an imperative and limiting figure since it will reflect what the company can actually afford to allocate.

On the other side of the balance are the training needs of the managers, established for each individual separately in connection with his or her performance appraisal and career plan, or in some other way. Summary data on needs are obtained by aggregating detailed data. This also involves screening the training proposals made, looking for the most effective solutions, eliminating demands that are not justified and establishing priorities. If resources are limited and demands high, priorities must be defined clearly enough to make sure that the most important needs will be met.

Table 7.1 provides more information on time spent by operating managers in management development programmes away from their jobs. The average

Table 7.1. Time spent by a sample of American managers in management development

Work-days per year	Current situation (% of managers)	Desirable situation (% of managers)
0	10	2
1-2	34	6
3-5	39	48
6-10	13	39
11 and more	4	5
	100	100

Source: L.W. Porter and L.E. McKibbin: *Management education and development: Drift or thrust into the 21st century* (New York, McGraw-Hill, 1988), p. 230.

yearly figure, calculated from a sample of 596 managers in American companies, is about 3.0 days, but should be 5.1 days, i.e. 60 per cent more, according to the managers.[10]

The following factors will affect the process of balancing the needs and the resources.

Dynamics of managerial manpower

Certain types of training needs will reflect the dynamics of managerial manpower in the organisation and will be determined by managerial manpower planning.[11] For example, induction training may be foreseen for all individuals newly recruited or promoted to managerial jobs. Medium- and longer-term training may be provided to a smaller group of managers preselected for future promotion to higher-level positions. Localisation of management positions, i.e. replacement of foreign managers by nationals, may be carried out in accordance with a precise plan that will also determine the sort and amount of management training required.

Major future-oriented needs

Considerable training needs, requiring upward adjustment of training plans and budgets, may be identified in connection with predicted important changes in the business and social environment, and in related corporate strategies. For example, the necessity to prepare managers for operating in the European Common Market after 1992 will generate major training needs in many European companies. This may lead to temporary or long-term increases in company training plans and budgets. The growing internationalisation of business creates major needs in language and inter-cultural training for managers.

Needs generated by special ad hoc projects

Special projects normally do not lend themselves to easy quantification of training and development needs. These needs may have to be defined, and redefined, in the course of the project, when objectives and activities become clearer. As a rule, a provision for training and development will be made in the project budget. If resources do not suffice and high-priority training needs must be satisfied, it may be necessary to re-examine the previously established order of priorities and eliminate or postpone some originally programmed training events that command less priority.

7.7   Case: Needs assessment at Hewlett-Packard[12]

Hewlett-Packard (HP) is a leading world designer and producer of computing and electronic measurement equipment and systems. It employs 82,000 people, of whom two-thirds work in the United States and one-third in 77 other countries. The role of technical and management training in HP is determined by technology, corporate culture and business philosophy. HP operates in sectors where the pace of technological change is extremely fast and the impact of technology on the knowledge, skills and behaviour of managers particularly strong. Therefore management training and development needs are not only quite considerable, but tend to change very rapidly. The identification of the needs must be fast and flexible as well. There would be no scope for lengthy and time-consuming surveys whose conclusions would be available too late to be of practical use.

An important factor that determines the role of training and development at HP is the company's culture and business philosophy. HP has developed and purposefully nurtured a strong corporate culture characterised by values such as business ethics, long-range relationships with customers, high-quality service, belief in people, honesty, openness, recognition of creativity and individual achievement, and the encouragement of self-development. Indoctrinating and training all employees in understanding the corporate culture is therefore considered as a critical common need. There are standard induction sessions ("Working at HP") and introductory seminars for new managers ("Managing at HP").

Figure 7.1. Matching corporate and individual needs at Hewlett-Packard

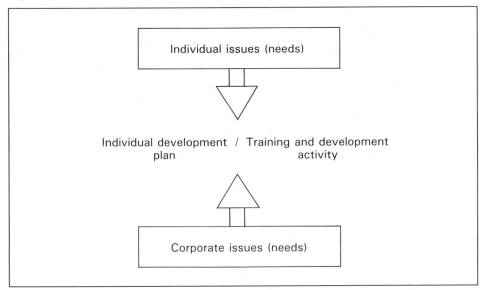

The regular process of needs assessment aims to match company and individual needs (see figure 7.1). Company needs are determined primarily by analysing the technological and business environment, choosing future strategies and assessing the impact of these strategic choices on managerial behaviour and training needs. For example, in 1984 HP began a major transformation from a company driven primarily by technology to a market-oriented firm. This strategic decision required deep changes not only in management attitudes but also in knowledge and skills concerning issues such as marketing techniques, customer relations or advice to customers on effective ways of meeting their needs for information. To facilitate this change, a programme in marketing management was developed at corporate level and distributed world-wide.

Individual needs are determined through a structured process of needs assessment related to annual performance reviews. Once a year, every employee, assisted by his or her manager, prepares an annual personal development plan. This plan considers *(a)* what training would help the individual meet his or her specific needs in the key areas agreed upon by the manager and the employee, and *(b)* what other needs, particular and unique, should be met in the forthcoming year.

Every year HP Europe issues its "management training and development guide" which lists training programmes regarded as most relevant in the current year. In-company programmes are listed alongside selected external courses. In preparing an annual development plan, a manager and his boss can choose a relevant programme from the guide. If none is found suitable, it is possible to look for another external course or seminar. In this way even an individual manager's unique needs can be met.

The company provides certain types of programmes to help meet needs regarded as common to a number of managers. For example, there is a "managing the self" programme (a two-day seminar plus a one-day refresher session six months later) to help the managers concentrate better, be more effective at work and relax better. In 1985 HP Europe introduced a "European management development programme" for senior managers, which could be referred to as an example of the focused approach in Ashridge's study terminology. Based on critical strategic issues for the years to come, the programme is focused on improving business results and enhancing self-development. It helps participants to design and implement individual projects aimed at achieving specific and measurable operational changes linked to the critical strategic issues. The concept is built on a few basic assumptions: management development has to be focused on results; management of change requires action now; improvement in results is a critical pedagogic method of improving skills in management of change; and the programme should satisfy both individual needs and the needs of the corporation.

In summary, the goal of needs assessment in HP is to help individuals achieve better results in both the short and the long run, making sure that corporate needs are met with priority. The thrust of this approach has been summarised by Ole Bovin, the HP training manager for Europe, as follows: "How to create development opportunities for managers to be successful in a turbulent and rapidly changing world".

---

[1] Among others, the following recent studies are of interest: S. Lusterman: *Trends in corporate education and training* (New York, The Conference Board, 1985); C. Handy: *The making of managers* (London, Manpower Services Commission, National Economic Development Council and British Institute of Management, 1987); J. Constable and R. McCormick: *The making of British managers* (London, British Institute of Management and Confederation of British Industry, 1987); and K. Barham, J. Fraser and L. Heath: *Management for the future: How leading international companies develop managers to achieve their vision* (Berkhamsted and Oxford, Ashridge Management College and Foundation for Management Education, 1988).

[2] Barham, Fraser and Heath, op. cit.

[3] See "Training in the Fortune", in *Training* (Minneapolis), Sep. 1986, p.61.

[4] B. Bowman: "Assessing your needs assessment", in *Training*, Jan. 1987, p.30.

[5] Adapted from W.S. Mitchell: "Wanted: Professional management training needs analysis", in *Training and Development Journal* (Washington, DC), Oct. 1984.

[6] Barham, Fraser and Heath, op. cit., p. 54.

[7] Lusterman, op. cit., p. 2.

[8] ibid. p. 11.

[9] ibid. p. 5.

---

[10] Information collected by the Futures' Project of the American Assembly of Collegiate Schools of Business (AACSB). See L.W. Porter and L.E. McKibbin: *Management education and development: Drift or thrust into the 21st century?* (New York, McGraw-Hill, 1988), p. 230.

[11] On this topic see a technical paper by A.R. Smith: *Techniques for managerial manpower planning* (Geneva, ILO, 1988; doc. Man Dev/47), or a paper by L. Dyer and N.0. Heyer (eds.): *Human resource planning at IBM* (New York, New York State School of Industrial and Labor Relations, Cornell University, 1986).

[12] Based on information provided by Ole Bovin, Hewlett-Packard Training Manager for Europe.

SPECIAL STUDIES AND SURVEYS OF NEEDS

8

In the last 15 years, "macro-level" studies of management education, training and development have become quite popular. Such a study can be sectoral (managers in the industrial or banking sector), nation-wide (the making of British managers) or international (training needs of European managers), can focus on new developments with significant impact on managerial skills (the computer and the manager of the future) or may deal with problems of one level of management (supervisory development). We are referring to "special" studies and surveys because, in most cases, the study is undertaken ad hoc as a special project, with a specific purpose in mind. Often it leads to the publication of a major report, submitted to the government, business circles and the academic community, with suggestions for policy measures.

The context in which such a survey is undertaken differs from case to case. However, the following purposes seem to prevail:

(1)   to increase managers' and policy-makers' awareness of new trends and needs (by pointing to existing or emerging gaps in competency and performance and suggesting important measures at sectoral, national or even international levels to bridge these gaps);

(2)   to plan action and mobilise resources in order to achieve significant improvements in management education, training and development;

(3)   to establish or strengthen institutions and programmes addressing these issues (training institutes, foundations, associations, information and support services, new programmes within institutions, new lines of study, etc.);

(4)   to justify and prepare technical assistance projects in developing countries;

(5)   to produce new training materials and packages.

Methodologically, the diversity of the studies can be quite considerable. Nevertheless, some common approaches tend to prevail. Also, certain mistakes are repeated again and again despite lessons from previous studies.

These issues will be addressed in this chapter. We will start by reviewing selected examples of recent studies and surveys (section 8.1). The following

---

sections will then provide guide-lines for the design and execution of special studies and surveys: on scope and purpose (8.2), methodology and organisation (8.3), quantitative aspects (8.4), producing survey reports (8.5) and use of results (8.6).

8.1 Review of selected studies and surveys

There is no shortage of examples of special studies and surveys of management training and development needs. In 1972, shortly after its establishment, the European Foundation for Management Development (EFMD) carried out the first "study of studies", identifying and critically surveying some 180 studies undertaken in eight Western European countries between 1960 and 1972.[1] National and other special studies became even more popular after 1972. Many studies were undertaken in developing countries in preparing for new technical assistance programmes.

This section provides six samples of major studies designed to serve various purposes and demonstrating practical applications of different methodological approaches.

Zambia managerial manpower and training needs survey

Context and purpose. The survey was carried out in 1975-76 by the Management Development and Advisory Service in Lusaka, assisted by a United Nations Development Programme (UNDP)/ILO technical co-operation project. It was supported and monitored by the Cabinet Office. The purpose was to provide objective information and analysis required for formulating and improving management training and development policies and plans, both at national level and in individual organisations. The results of the study were published in a major report and widely disseminated in 1977.[2]

Methodology and organisations. The principal survey method used was questionnaires to organisations with more than 25 employees. The questionnaire was returned by all public (parastatal) organisations (113 in total) and by a high proportion (488 in total) of private companies. The following information was collected:

o   characteristics of the organisations surveyed, including projections on future employment levels;

o   detailed data on numbers of managers, their salaries, present and desired educational levels, vacant posts, posts occupied by foreigners;

o   information on management training services inside and outside Zambia;

o   indications on subject and functional areas in which managers should receive more training during the coming five years;

o   comments on obstacles to developing and training managers within organisations;

o   comments on priority (favoured) approaches to developing and training managers.

The second survey method consisted of interviews with 150 selected chief executives in public and private enterprises. The interviews were structured, but non-scheduled. The following questions were provided in an interview guide used by the interviewers:

(1)   What are the most important organisational and operational problems facing your enterprise at present?

(2)   What do you consider the most important development needs of your organisation?

(3)   What do you consider the most important development and training needs of your managers? What specifically are you doing to meet their needs?

(4)   Does your industry or organisation present any special management training and development problems that you feel warrant special attention?

(5)   We are interested in exploring in detail your management problems and training needs in the following fields:

(a)   financial management;

(b)   marketing management;

(c)   industrial engineering;

(d)   personnel management.

What specific management problems and training needs do you have in these fields?

(6)   What do you see as the most important problems or obstacles impeding the development and training of managers and supervisors in your organisation, and what are their major causes?

(7)   What suggestions and/or action plans do you have for overcoming these problems and meeting your need for trained managers and supervisors over the next five years?

(8)   What will be the priority of your organisation's approaches in developing and training your managers and supervisors?

(9)   As a top manager, what is your philosophy on supervisory and management development?

(10)   As a top manager, what was the most important thing which affected your own development?

(11) What types of training and development approaches, including on-the-job training, have you found to be particularly effective in developing managers in Zambia?

(12) If your employees have participated in supervisory and management training programmes of the training institutions in Zambia, have the programmes been of practical value to your organisation? Would you suggest any additional programmes or improvements in existing programmes?

(13) Other comments (review any special problems or incomplete answers on the questionnaire).

These in-depth interviews were used to verify and complete information provided in questionnaires. Each interviewer also completed a "summary of views and recommendations" based on the interviews he had conducted.

The third survey method was an institutional survey questionnaire, completed by all ten institutions involved in management and supervisory training in the country.

The entire survey programme was planned and scheduled through the use of a network analysis and a flow chart. Detailed instructions, prepared for the handling of every stage, concerned pre-mailing and post-mailing procedures, maintaining the master lists of organisations, coding of the questionnaires, computer processing, follow-up procedures, handling of inquiries and interviewing procedures.

Principal conclusions. The survey provided synthetic data on:

o   the acute shortage of trained and qualified Zambian managers;

o   the high dependence of the country's economy on expatriate managers in key positions;

o   inadequate educational qualifications of many Zambian managers;

o   areas and levels in which management and supervisory training ought to be expanded;

o   weaknesses of training policies and programmes within organisations;

o   inadequate capacity and level of competence on the part of training institutions;

o   a wide range of "non-training" factors hampering management development and performance improvement in both public and private organisations.

Derived from these analyses, the survey made a number of policy recommendations on how to improve management development at national level and in individual organisations.

Commentary. This is an example of a major national survey in a developing country using "classical" survey methods. The coverage was fairly exhaustive and considerable attention was paid to "non-training" problems and factors affecting the managers' interest in training, and the possibility of applying the results of training in practice. Both facts and opinions were collected and analysed. Based on the results of the survey, national policies and guide-lines for management development were incorporated in the national development plan. Many organisations and several training institutions used the survey to review their own policies and embark on programmes for improving management development. However, the survey was perhaps too ambitious, time-consuming and costly, bearing in mind the country's limited resources and potential for action that could actually be taken following the survey.

Competency programme of the American Management Association

Context and purpose. The American Management Association (AMA), which provides a wide range of training and other services to managers and companies in the United States, in the early 1970s started looking for a conceptual framework for designing and structuring its management education and training programmes. The work focused on the characteristics of an effective manager and on whether these characteristics can be enhanced through training and development. A major research project was conceived in the late 1970s to identify those generic characteristics of American managers that distinguish superior performance. This research was commissioned to the Boston-based behavioural research and consultancy firm, McBer. A competency model developed from the research has been applied since the early 1980s to designing and implementing a wide range of management education and training programmes.[3]

Methodology and organisation. The research stage was based on the McBer's job competence assessment method, applied to specific jobs in particular organisations. Data were collected on 2,000 managers in 41 different jobs, employed in 12 organisations in the private and public sectors. Data were obtained through specially designed questionnaires, exercises and interviews (including the Training Style Questionnaire, the Managerial Style Questionnaire and the Picture Story Exercise).

A competency was defined as "an underlying characteristic of a manager causally related to superior performance on the job". The method was applied in five steps, as shown in figure 8.1.

The study identified a group of *managerial behaviours* that are characteristic of superior performance. Through cluster analysis, these behaviours were grouped into 18 competencies (defined by underlying characteristics) and four larger clusters of competencies. The list is as follows:

Figure 8.1.   The job competence assessment method

Steps	Activities	Results
Identification of oritorion measure	Choose an appropriate meas- ure of job performance Collect data on managers	Job performance data on managers
Job element analysis	Generate list of characteris- tics perceived to lead to effective and/or superior job performance Obtain item rating by managers Compute weighted list of characteristics Analyse clusters of charac- teristics	A weighted list of charac- teristics perceived by managers to relate to superior performance A list of the clusters into which these characteristics can be grouped
Behavioral Event Interviews	Conduct Behavioral Event Interviews Code interviews for charac- teristics or develop the code and then code the interviews Relate the coding to job per- formance data	A list of characteristics hypothesised to distinguish effective and/or superior from poor or less effective job performance A list of validated charac- teristics, or competencies
Tests and measures	Choose tests and measures to assess competencies iden- tified in prior two steps as relevant to job performance Administer tests and meas- ures and score them Relate scores to job perfor- mance data	A list of validated charac- teristics, or competencies, as assessed by these tests and measures
Competency model	Integrate results from prior three steps Statistically and theoretically determine and document causal relationships among the competencies and between the competencies and job performance	A validated competency model

Source: R.E. Boyatzis: *The competent manager: A model for effective performance* (New York, Wiley, 1982), p. 42.

Goal and action management cluster

o   Efficiency orientation − concern with doing something better (in comparison with previous personal performance, others' performance, or a standard of excellence).

o   Proactivity − disposition towards taking action to accomplish something, e.g. instigating activity for a specific purpose.

o   Concern with impact − concern with the symbols and implements of power in order to have impact on others.

o   Diagnostic use of concepts − use of a person's previously held concepts to explain and interpret situations.

Directing subordinates cluster

o   Use of unilateral power − use of forms of influence to obtain compliance.

o   Developing others − ability to provide performance feedback and other needed help to improve performance.

o   Spontaneity − ability to express oneself freely and easily.

Human resources management cluster

o   Accurate self-assessment − realistic and grounded view of oneself.

o   Self-control − ability to inhibit personal needs in service of organisational goals.

o   Stamina and adaptability − the energy to sustain long hours of work and the flexibility orientation to adapt to changes in life and the organisational environment.

o   Perceptual objectivity − ability to be relatively objective rather than limited by excessive subjectivity or personal biases.

o   Positive regard − ability to express a positive belief in others.

o   Managing group process − ability to stimulate others to work effectively in a group setting.

o   Use of socialised power − use of influence to build alliances, networks, or coalitions.

Leadership cluster

o   Self-confidence − ability consistently to display decisiveness or presence.

o   Conceptualisation − use of concepts *de novo* to identify a pattern in an assortment of information.

o   Logical thought − a thought process in which a person orders events in a causal sequence.

o   Use of oral presentations – ability to make effective oral presentations to others.

Emphasis was put on behavioural characteristics expressed at the *skill level*. In some instances competencies were described in terms of motives or trait levels, or the managers' social role or self-image. In addition, there was a fifth cluster, "specialist knowledge". However, the study did not deal with the problems of specialised technical knowledge. It could be taken for granted that superior managers possess and are able to apply the specific technical knowledge concerning their jobs and organisations.

Principal conclusions. The AMA has applied the competency model in several ways:

o   in special skill courses focused on paired competencies (e.g. "managing group process" and "use of socialised power");

o   in courses for single companies focused on topics such as team building, organisation development or human resource management;

o   in a graduate-level (MBA) programme;

o   in a professional assessment and developmental programme.

While the basic competency model defines *generic* behavioural or attitudinal characteristics, the professional assessment and development programme, through the so called "competency development laboratory", aims to discern what competencies *an individual manager* already possesses and how he or she can express them in a simulated managerial problem-solving setting. The audit exercise includes four interactive simulations, several tests dealing with the individual's learning style, power style, approaches to conflict and management style, and a behaviourally oriented interview, which is a sort of self-report on the person's specific style as applied in the real organisational context. Feedback from these exercises is provided to individual managers, and used in individualised "competency acquisition processes". In addition to reviewing the findings with fellow managers and AMA's training staff in group work, participants prepare individually tailored developmental plans to acquire the skills missing in their profiles. These plans (in six-month phases) include goal definition, ideas on how to learn more about a particular company, means to practise and gain feedback, and analysis of potential obstacles and sources of help.

Commentary. The AMA programme is probably the best example of a wide-scale application of the competency approach (see sections 1.3 and 4.1) to defining management training and development needs. Focus is not on knowledge and technical skills (whose possession, however, is regarded as necessary and is assumed), but on the actual use of behaviourally oriented skills. The empirical model of generic competencies provides a framework and a basis for assessing individual competencies and needs, and designing and implementing individualised management development programmes.

The model has been developed by analysing factors of superior management performance in the North American setting. The sample surveyed (2,000 managers from 12 organisations) was biased towards large, probably quite successful, business corporations and government organisations. Therefore, socio-cultural characteristics and skills that may be causally related to superior management performance in other settings, in particular in developing countries, are not included in the model. However, the model provides interesting ideas and approaches to identifying and developing management competencies in other environments.

Indonesia: Management development

Context and purpose. This study was initiated and co-ordinated by the World Bank at the request of the Government of Indonesia, and co-sponsored by seven agencies, among them the ILO. The study was carried out in 1982-84 and the final report was published one year later.[4]

The main objective of the study was to identify policy issues and strategic choices for management education and training for consideration by the Government. Management education and training was to be seen in the context of "broad policy and institutional environments which have strongly influenced management and institutional development and performance". The study defined the management problems faced by the country as "the deficiencies in managerial skills, practices and systems and the incompatibility of these with the requirements of modern organisations and future challenges".

It was expected, too, that various donors and technical assistance agencies would take up the results of the study and pursue the work by undertaking more detailed studies in the specific areas covered and by developing relevant action programmes and projects in collaboration with government agencies, enterprises and educational and training establishments.

Methodology and organisation. The guiding principle of the study's approach was to make use of a wide array of experience, perspectives and resources in order to obtain a large amount of information and to assess it critically. Therefore the design was kept fairly open and flexible throughout the exercise, and new aspects and special studies were added when deemed appropriate. A study team was established under the co-ordination of a team leader provided by the World Bank office in Jakarta. The team included members from various countries and international agencies. As well as the eight main members, the team included 14 members who made additional contributions. The main local contributor was the Jakarta-based Institute for Management Education and Development (LPPM).

The study started by undertaking a number of parallel in-depth studies and interviews within various sectors, subsectors and groups in Indonesian public and private enterprises, government administration, and educational and training institutions. A total of about 1,000 interviews were carried out. Tentative conclusions and first proposals were set out in 17 background papers followed up by discussions. For example, separate studies and papers were produced on public enterprise management, private sector needs, government in the provinces, agricultural enterprises, the Indonesian management environment, and some selected institutions. A draft action programme was then prepared and, together with the main conclusions from the special studies, reviewed with groups of Indonesian managers and government authorities.

These discussions were carried out as an interactive process in several steps. Finally, the results were summarised in a three-volume report.

Principal conclusions. The study identified a wide range of priority problems and needs concerning the total management environment, central and local government management, public enterprises and the private sector. On this basis, the study concluded that:

o   certain historical and cultural factors, as well as dominant management and administrative practices, tended to inhibit the development of managers, entrepreneurs and institutions;

o   the present capacity for developing and training competent managers was inadequate;

o   major changes were needed in "macro-management" agencies in order to tap the full potential of the country's human and other resources.

To address these problems, the study recommended a long-term strategy including the following elements:

o   the establishment of national forums and task forces to review, orient and harmonise efforts for improving management and developing managers;

o   a number of improvements in the institutional network providing management education, development, training and consulting services;

o   new programmes for developing training staff, management research, strengthening local consultants and training of top and senior managers.

Commentary. This Indonesian study provides an example of a broadly based comprehensive approach which deliberately

o   combines detailed fact finding with a global assessment of the situation and the needs;

o   makes use of other studies as well as of experience acquired through a number of technical assistance projects in management and public administration;

o   regards management education, training and development needs as one dimension – though a very important one – of the total management scene, or the "management problem", to use the term chosen by the authors of the study.

As a result, the study gathered, examined and presented a wealth of facts, opinions and ideas rarely found in national studies, even those in industrialised countries. It became a comprehensive state-of-the-art study of Indonesian management, including a review of some fundamental issues reflecting the country's socio-economic context, historical experience, culture, geographic conditions, links with external sources of expertise and economic and technical assistance, and other factors. However, the study did not go into detailed action-oriented assessment which would permit the design or redesign of specific programmes and projects. Where such a need was felt, it was suggested that it should be explored further under more specific and narrower studies.

Although Indonesian managers provided a great deal of first-hand information to the study team, the participation of Indonesian practitioners and professionals in running the study and writing the report was relatively small.

Study of management training needs of the SADCC member countries

Context and purpose. The study[5] was undertaken in 1984-85 in the nine member countries of the Southern African Development Co-ordination Conference (SADCC) by a team appointed by the National Association of Schools of Public Affairs and Administration (NASPAA) in the United States, in collaboration with several African experts. The purpose was to identify priority training needs and propose steps to encourage, develop and support appropriate management training programmes. The study was sponsored by the United States Agency for International Development (AID), which was interested in receiving proposals for technical assistance to the SADCC region.

Methodology and organisation. The study was based on the actual experience of managers in the nine countries reviewed. To achieve this, the team decided to give priority to two methods: the critical incident method (see section 4.6) and the diary method (see section 4.7). The team deliberately rejected the "classical" survey methods (interviews, survey questionnaires) and the opinion-seeking approach.

Critical incidents, or management events, were gathered by means of a questionnaire administered to individuals or groups of managers in public or private enterprises, and in governmental agencies. The questionnaires asked for brief reports (in 20-50 words) describing a specific experience or event (not an opinion or a class of incidents) associated with either the exercise or the absence of a managerial skill or administrative knowledge. "Most recent" or "next most recent" events were to be recorded in order to obtain their random collection. Over 3,000 events were thus collected; on average every respondent produced descriptions of about eight incidents.

The diary method was applied in collaboration with ten senior administrators or managers in each country. They were to record, over a period of 5-10 days, items that required one hour or more of their time, or seemed to be of special importance. Over 1,000 diary entries were thus collected, again providing direct access to practical management experience at various levels.

The critical events were classified and coded according to 50 different skills identified during the course of the study, as well as by sector, country, level of managerial responsibility, and a judgement as to whether the event was positive or negative with regard to the skill in question. In this way, it was possible to identify:

o   how many times a particular skill appeared in the events;

o   what skill problems were common to the SADCC countries;

o   what skill requirements were common to or different in, public enterprises, private enterprises and public administration;

o   how the skill requirements differed among various levels of management (senior, middle, junior).

The diary records were coded in accordance with 10 categories of managerial work set forth by Henry Mintzberg[6] (3 interpersonal categories: figurehead, liaison, leader; 3 informational categories: monitor, disseminator, spokesman; 4 decisional categories: entrepreneur, disturbance handler, resource allocator, negotiator).

The study also included a survey of current training efforts and existing training facilities and capabilities.

Principal conclusions. In summary, the study identified main skill areas where SADCC managers required training and assessed the existing supply of training programmes. Data on the critical events and diary entries made it possible to measure the relative importance of training needs in individual skill areas.

The following areas were identified as requiring priority treatment:

o   accounting practices;

o   management skills at senior level of government;

o   familiarity, on the part of lower- and middle-level public servants, with current rules and practices;

o   the shortage of entrepreneurially minded administrators in both private and parastatal corporations;

o   the management of expatriate personnel;

o   the negotiation of international assistance contracts;

o   management training for technicians reaching managerial positions;

o   management of training itself;

o   organisation development (OD) activities.

As regards details of management skills required, the study revealed that skills concerning the management and motivation of people were those where most improvement was required. The diary method revealed that senior managers were most concerned about their role as resource allocators.

A number of recommendations covered the strengthening of man-- agement education, and training and development facilities in the region, including the establishment of a regional resource centre in support of these efforts.

Commentary. The study was methodologically original. To diagnose needs, the team applied the critical incident method and the diary method consistently and on an unprecedented scale, thus collecting a great amount of first-hand information on what managers actually do and what problems and skill shortages they face in everyday action. Information on current problems and needs could thus be based on facts rather than on opinions or wishes.

However, it appears that these two techniques alone do not permit the completion of such a comprehensive task. Previous studies of management in the SADCC countries were not examined. No study was undertaken of economic and socio-political problems and trends of the region, and of their impact on management practices and needs. Therefore management needs could not be shown in a proper developmental and time perspective, and future needs could not be identified. For example, the issue of gradual localisation of managerial manpower, which is very important in several SADCC countries, was not examined. Limited attention was paid to non-training factors and needs, and to their impact on management training and actual management performance in the SADCC countries.

The ILO survey of supervisory training needs

Context and purpose. This is an example of a training and development needs survey of a particular management level on a global scale. The survey was undertaken in 1978-79 in preparation for the development of a new training package for supervisors.

The study, carried out by the ILO Management Development Branch, covered the nature, role and elements of supervisory development practices in a number of countries. The objective was to identify the principal supervisory development problems and suggest an effective approach to training and development in order to help a number of countries reduce the gap between the real and the desirable competence of supervisors.

Methodology and organisation. Analysis involved more than 100 different sources of published information – publications, training programmes and packages, course outlines and reports – on supervision, supervisors, and supervisory training and development. The study also drew a great deal of factual information, comments, opinions and ideas from direct contacts with trainers, consultants, institutions and ILO field experts who deal regularly with supervisory development. The main techniques used included questionnaires, discussions at meetings, analysis of reports and already existing training materials, and individual interviewing. Two meetings were held in Geneva with the participation of 40 recognised experts in management and supervisory development.

In addition to major manufacturing industries, the study covered construction, transport, banking, insurance, mining, and some aspects of office work. The data collected covered the experience of the industrialised and developing countries from different regions.

Data were sought to answer two major questions:

o   What managerial functions are most relevant to supervisory jobs in selected industries and countries?

o   How universal is each of these functions according to information received from various sectors and countries?

To answer the second question, it was established that the supervisory functions to be dealt with in the training materials have to be identified in 60-100 per cent of all information sources analysed.

The next step was to analyse the purpose, content, processes and techniques involved in each particular function. This was necessary for designing a modular programme where each module is broken down into four or five standard learning elements in order to cover both the conceptual and the practical aspects of a function, including processes and techniques to be used.

The approach in deciding on the level of sophistication of the modules was derived from an assumption that the modules should be relevant to learners with no knowledge and experience in supervision, as well as to supervisors with some experience.

Principal conclusions. The main result of the study was an overall outline, and suggestions concerning the internal structure and importance of various subjects, for the development of a major supervisory development package. Of the many different subjects or functional areas of supervisory jobs that were considered in the analysis, the following subjects appeared 95 per cent of the time: planning; communication; directing or co-ordinating; controlling (various functions); motivating; staffing; evaluating performance; human relations; wage and salary administration; work study; leadership; training and development; safety and health. Other subject areas appeared in at least 60 per cent of the information sources examined.

Besides pointing out the major supervisory training needs to cover the main functional areas, the study uncovered a number of problems common to supervisory development. Among them were the following findings:

○ The status of the supervisor still does not correspond fully to the growing role of supervisor in management. Compared with other managers, supervisors have a relatively low educational and professional background. There is confusion and misunderstanding as regards the conception and terminology concerning supervisory roles, functions, training objectives, procedures, methods, etc.

○ There is also a lack of systematic and balanced structural approaches to the design and implementation of supervisory training and development programmes. This concerns both the initial training of newly selected supervisors, and further training and development.

Supervisors are subject to influences from the informal, as well as the formal organisations. They must react to and often-yield to the contradictory expectations of different groups – line and functional managers, workers, shop stewards, and their own peers, as well as to pressures from the external environment. Thus it is not surprising to find supervisors caught between pressure groups from above and below, seeking some sort of middle ground between contradictory goals and expectations. The continuing erosion of important supervisory functions (for example wage administration, personnel policy, etc.) has resulted in the decline of the supervisor's autonomy and authority. This is another source of conflict which creates additional problems and needs for the supervisory development process.

The identification of the major supervisory job functions and problems in this case was considered to provide a fair description of supervisory development needs in a broad sense and to constitute the main information source for designing the framework and choosing the content of the ILO package for supervisory development. A modular form was chosen and the package, consisting of 34 modules covering the main areas of the supervisory function, was published in 1981.[7]

Commentary. The purpose of this study was to define global needs in order to develop international training material suitable for use in various countries and organisational contexts. This was achieved and the training package was published. However, further detailed analysis of specific needs of organisations and individual participants is necessary (i) to select training modules, and sections within these modules, for use in particular training programmes, (ii) to adapt some modules to specific sectoral, organisational and cultural conditions, and (iii) to produce supplementary training materials that could not be provided in a global package.

The Futures Project of the AACSB

Context and purpose. In 1959, two studies were completed which were to become landmarks with considerable impact on the shaping of management and business education in the United States: the Gordon-Howell study, sponsored by the Ford Foundation,[8] and the Pierson study of the Carnegie Foundation.[9] Twenty years later, the American Assembly of Collegiate Schools of Business (AACSB) engaged in a co-operative project with the European Foundation for Management Development (EFMD) to examine "management and management education in a world of changing expectations". The project, started by several colloquia attended by invited representatives of North American and European business and academic organisations, culminated in a joint conference in Paris, devoted to the topic of "Management for the XXI century" (see also section 9.5).[10]

Broad current trends, ongoing and expected changes and potential problems were thus identified. However, the AACSB concluded that, to make specific recommendations for action to its members and to the corporate world, concrete data, based on a detailed structured study, were required on (1) the current system and effectiveness of management development and (2) the views of those involved in both the university and corporate settings regarding the types of changes that would be needed in the future. This conclusion was followed by a decision to launch a national "Future of Management Education and Development" project, known as the "Futures Project". The project was carried out in 1984-87, and the report was released during to the annual AACSB conference in 1988.[11]

The overall purposes of the project were defined as follows: (1) to evaluate the current (mid-1980s) status and condition of management education and development; (2) to analyse its likely future directions if no major changes were to be made; and (3) to provide a set of recommendations concerning where management education and development should be heading in the future.[12] Thus, the project was described not as a survey of needs, but as a study of the national supply system in management education and development, including its current status, trends, problems and future changes. However, the assessment of the users' needs was implied in the definition of objectives, which emphasised the matching of supply with changing needs.

The target of the study was defined as management education and development for business enterprises in the United States (sectors such as public administration or health administration were not included and information from other countries was not collected and analysed).

Organisation and methodology. The project was commissioned to two senior researchers who had been active members of the AACSB Board of Directors. The Board provided guidance directly and through its Futures

Committee. Co-sponsoring was enlisted from 31 major industrial and professional service organisations or their foundations.

Five principal methods were applied for collecting data:

(1) Factual statistical data pertinent to management education and development were collected from various official and private sources.

(2) Literature on future trends and developments ("futures" literature) likely to affect management, and the education and development of managers, was collected and reviewed.

(3) Literature critical of management education and development and of the business schools' performance ("criticism" literature) was also collected, summarised and reviewed.

(4) Interviews were carried out with key individuals on both the suppliers' and the users' side. For the university sample, about 10 per cent of the business schools (60 out of 620) were chosen through a cluster-sampling technique by designating six different geographic areas in the country. A variety of schools were represented, but it was not a random sample. For the corporations sample, 50 larger and medium-sized companies were selected arbitrarily by the researchers among firms regarded as national leaders in corporate management development practices, or known as major employers of business school graduates. The number of interviews conducted was 525. Most interviews were conducted individually by one or both of the researchers. Within each organisation in the sample, specific categories of individuals were chosen (six in each business school and five in each corporation). The interviews were semi-structured. A list of topics to be covered was worked out, but not every topic was covered in every interview. This list directed the interviews to obtaining views and observations on management education and development, recruitment policies and practices, and future needs and requirements.

(5) Questionnaires were used to reach large samples of respondents on both the suppliers' and the users' side. All AACSB members and over 1,200 companies were contacted. About 10,400 questionnaires were returned and processed, including over 3,000 replies from deans and faculty members; over 2,500 replies from undergraduate students and some 1,800 replies from graduate students. The number of questionnaires returned by companies was nearly 1,700. The response rates were very different: between 60 and 74 per cent from the business schools, but some 10-20 per cent from the world of practice. There were 16 different questionnaires, designed for special categories of respondents within the organisations contacted. Most questions were closed-ended. The purpose was to obtain a large number of opinions, from people who can judge management education from various viewpoints, on questions of relevance and impact

of management education, the quality of institutions, industry-university relationships, and recruitment and appraisal practices.

Principal conclusions. As the study focused mainly on the supply side of management education and development, the majority of conclusions concern the business school system and its future development. Below we report only those conclusions that are directly or indirectly related to the question of needs. For other conclusions, the reader should refer to the Porter-McKibbin report referred to above.

In introducing the findings and the conclusions, the report emphasises that the management education and development system in the United States can be regarded as relevant and adequate to the needs of the business corporations. In fact, the business schools have been remarkably successful in the last 20-30 years. This, however, has led to some complacency and self-satisfaction. As a result there is "little perceived need for major changes in the way in which collegiate management education is carried out".[13] There is a shortage of innovation in some business schools, which prefer to follow the leaders and avoid the risk of being original. As regards the future, most schools are optimistic, but few of them do any strategic planning for meeting future needs and taking new opportunities. While it is likely that quantitative demand will continue to be high, qualitative demand on the content of teaching is likely to change.

The requirements for changes in the curriculum are discussed in the light of the main changes in the social and business environment likely to influence management practice, and the educational and training needs of managers. As mentioned, the views of the future are taken from the "futures" literature. The goal was not to provide the definitive view of the future, nor was it to expound the authors' own view. From the vast amount of "futures" literature, only those views were extracted that were deemed most relevant to the subject of the study. The period focused on was 10-20 years into the future, that is, the first decade of the next century. The report stresses that it would be "fallacious to seek to identify a particular scenario as a future context for any specific recommendations", and "instead of recommending changes in the system to cope with some specifically identified changes in the environment ... the system itself should be made as responsive as possible to major changes which may occur".[14]

Nevertheless, six areas in which the curriculum should be more responsive to the managers' real needs were identified:[15]

(1) Broadening the curriculum beyond technical and functional issues, with a view to transcending the analytical and the methodological and to incorporating an understanding of the importance of broad, well-rounded education in the preparation of business students;

(2) refocusing the curriculum away from the essentially internal organisational environment (how to improve operating and financial

effectiveness) to pay more attention to the external environment (governmental relations, societal trends, legal climate, international development, among other areas);

(3) increasing the attention paid to the global and international dimensions of business;

(4) adapting the whole curriculum more deeply to two major intertwined trends: the move from a primarily industrial to an increasingly service-oriented economy and the related development of a strong focus on the generation, distribution and management of information;

(5) providing an integrated approach to problems that cut across specific functional areas, which is particularly important to entrepreneurial activities and to students who will be involved in developing small, growing and dynamic businesses;

(6) putting more emphasis on the development of "soft" skills and personal characteristics required for managing people effectively in environments where the content of work is changing and which are becoming less hierarchical and more participative. This, however, should not be done to the detriment of analytical and quantitative skills, which are a major asset of business school graduates.

As regards in-company management development, and post-experience programmes provided by the business schools, the study points out that 30 per cent of the companies surveyed do not carry out any systematic needs analysis, and suggests that both companies and business schools should prepare themselves for meeting increased demands and changed needs. There will, however, by many other providers of such programmes and the free market may be the only feasible method of ensuring an adequate supply of suitable products.[16]

Finally, the study makes a number of conclusions on the development of faculty, the management of the business schools, the role of the AACSB, and industry/university co-operation in meeting the country's management education and development needs.

Commentary. The AACSB project was not an initial study of needs in an unexplored area, but a review of a major, highly structured, well-established and generally successful management education and development system serving the largest business community in the world. The overall approach was forward-looking, but cautious.

Seeking expert opinion (see section 3.3) was by far the most important generic method used. The figures given above indicate the numbers of persons interviewed as experts who have used the system and could provide some views on changing needs and the system's capacity to cope with new needs. More time was spent in obtaining the views of experts coming from the supply side than those from the users' side.

To obtain expert opinion, the researchers used conventional survey techniques, paying considerable attention to classifying and measuring the responses in order to give a picture as objective and balanced as possible. For example, from criticisms of the business school system, voiced in many articles and papers over the past ten years, only those ideas which could be regarded as valid "from the perspective of the total set of information" were pursued and developed further.[17]

The virtually exclusive recourse to expert opinion (in addition to some statistical data) was probably justified by two significant features of the study: the fact that it dealt with the needs of an extremely large and complex business community, and the focus on future needs. As the future cannot be identified and described with exact techniques, the prevailing expert opinion seems to provide the most reliable guidance for making inferences on topics such as the future of management education and development. International comparison (see section 3.2) was not used by deliberate choice of the researchers (for economy reasons).[18] The study paid only scant attention to developments outside the United States, for example in the methodology of teaching and training or in life-long management training and development.

8.2   Scope and purpose

Any special study or survey of managers and their development needs is an important project in terms of resources to be mobilised, time requirements, numbers of organisations and individuals to be contacted, and expectations that will be created, as well as dissemination and public relations efforts. Dozens of interviewers may be involved, many meetings held, hundreds of questionnaires distributed and hundreds or thousands of individual managers and professionals interviewed. Experience has shown that some basic questions ought to be addressed and fully clarified before deciding to launch such a major exercise, and working on details of its design.

Who wants the survey?

The first question concerns the agency or person who came up with the idea. This can be, for example:

o   a national policy-making and management body (president's or prime minister's office, planning ministry, manpower development committee, administrative reform commission);

o   a membership organisation representing employers or/and managers (federation of industry, chamber of commerce, management association);

o   a management development institution or foundation (management centre, national management foundation);

o   a development and/or technical assistance agency (development bank, UNDP, ILO, EEC, bilateral aid agency).

As a rule, more than one of the above-mentioned partners will become involved in any case. However, there is likely to be one "owner" of the first idea, who wants the study more than the others, because he is convinced that he will get some benefit from it. There is a significant relationship between the scope of the study and the authority and credibility of its principal promoter. The ultimate practical effect of the study depends upon active and visible backing by an authority that will be listened to and respected.

What should be achieved?

Often studies are started without clarifying the second question, namely, why is a new study needed and what will actually be achieved by doing it? It is taken for granted that if an important ministry or technical assistance agency wants a study, this decision should not be challenged, since they "must know" the reasons for it.

A deeper examination of the reasons given may reveal that there are various opinions and expectations. One partner wants a study to justify a request for resources. Another wants to stimulate thinking and get new ideas on management development policy. A third may wish to be associated with an important and visible national study without actually intending to do anything, and so on.

The definition of the ultimate purpose is essential for positioning the study within broader efforts for improving management, and the development and training of managers, in a country or sector. Is the study needed to create awareness and give a first impetus to starting such efforts? Is the main purpose to take stock of current activities because such information is lacking? Or, if we know enough on what has been done hitherto, is the main purpose to define new policies for the future?

How will the results be used?

It could be argued that only the study itself can come up with precise suggestions on how to use its results. However, the promoters and planners of the study should have the various practical uses of the final report and its recommendations in mind right from the beginning. For example, if the purpose is to justify the establishment of a new training centre of a certain size, it will be necessary to consider actual demand for external training and not only the needs. Experience shows that this demand may be as low as 5-10 per cent of the established needs. If the study is mainly a political one, to mobilise public opinion and make business and management circles aware of their growing problems and obsolescences, it will not be used for detailed course planning, but in meetings and discussions, for establishing a national foundation, for publishing a policy statement, and so on.

What is the target population?

Since management is omnipresent and some of its elements can be found in any sector and activity, special studies and surveys have to adopt some definition of the target population that limits their scope and focus for practical reasons. If this is not done, the study has to be confined to broad problems and trends common to all sectors.

This definition normally determines the following coverage:

o   the sector (public/private, economic/non-economic, modern/traditional, rural/urban, industry, agriculture/other sectors, etc.);

o   the size of units (all enterprises and organisations, enterprises with more than 20-25 employees, only small enterprises but excluding the informal sector, etc.);

o   the levels of management (higher and middle level, supervisory level);

o   the functions (general, financial, personnel, production, marketing, special functions such as export or maintenance management);

o   special groups (women managers, young managers, particular ethnic groups).

Several target populations may be covered in one study. However, their definition may be tentative at the planning stage. Target populations may be merged, or some deleted, in the course of the study, if preliminary findings show that this will simplify methodology and reduce the cost of the study without lowering the value of the results.

What studies are available?

Many designers of special studies and surveys suffer from a common disease. Once they have decided that they want a study, they will not drop the idea even if there have been other studies on the same or a similar topic, and the new study is unlikely to reveal anything new. To avoid this dilemma, they often choose to ignore the methodology, findings and costs of previous studies.

This, however, is an elementary mistake. Former studies *must* be collected and reviewed, even if the promoters of a new study do not have a high opinion of their value. A comparison of studies carried out successively in the same country or region will reveal the long-term presence of certain problems, the failure of attempts to deal with these problems, the changing structure of needs and demand, the attitudes of government and business to management development, and other important problems and trends.

8.3 Methodology and organisation

Special studies and surveys discussed in this chapter concern management training and development needs at the highest level of synthesis and generalisation. There is a long distance between findings about the needs of an individual manager XY in an enterprise AZ, and a statement that certain needs concern all or most managers in a country, and will become more significant in future years. The question is: How to find out about common and general needs in a reasonable time-frame and for an acceptable cost?

The inductive bottom-up approach consists in collecting detailed first-hand information (facts and opinions) and arriving at conclusions through gradual aggregation and generalisation. The obvious problems involved in this approach include high costs if the target population is large and diversified, difficulty in deciding what is actually common and general in the vast numbers of particular situations, and the lack of a conceptual framework and perspective for drawing meaningful and usable conclusions from the findings and for orienting future action. For example, detailed interviews of managers may produce no information on the need to increase productivity, and to train managers for managing productivity improvement. International productivity comparisons would reveal that there is a major problem in the organisations surveyed, nevertheless.

The deductive top-down approach looks at synthetic data and global processes (again using facts and opinions) and arrives at conclusions by analysing these processes and making extensive use of global comparison – with other countries and sectors, with previous periods, with organisations regarded as best performers and leaders, and with similar models.

We have seen in section 8.1 that while one study uses exclusively the first approach (e.g. the study of management training needs of the SADCC member countries), another study can be quoted as a practical application of the second approach (in particular studies based on examination of trends and emerging new needs by high-level committees of experts, and on the study of literature, such as the ILO study of supervisory training needs).

Once more, the purpose of the study will be the main factor that determines methodology. Basically, studies that are intended to raise political and policy issues, create awareness, mobilise public opinion and stimulate critical thinking would use more synthetic and global approaches. However, they must be entrusted to people with broad vision and experience, whose expert judgement can be referred to in reviewing not only single events, but sectoral, nation-wide and even international trends and concepts.

In contrast, studies that are done for the purpose of detailed resource and action planning, or establishing and reorganising institutions and programmes, normally need to be able to refer to the evaluation of more detailed analytical data, directly collected from the target population (organisations and individuals), or taken from other surveys and reports from which these data can be retrieved (e.g. statistical surveys).

Although in special cases the designers of a study have opted for using just one or two techniques, the issue of management training and development needs (including the related non-training factors and needs) is complex and complicated enough to justify a combined use of several techniques. This is actually what most studies do in various ways and proportions, trying to fit the methodology to all objectives pursued.

Questionnaires and interviews

To obtain a sufficient amount of analytical data and enlist direct participation of the target population (of its totality or a representative sample), many surveys use specially designed questionnaires and interviews, addressed to organisations (the top manager or the personnel manager replies on behalf of the organisation) and/or to individual managers (who in principle should reply without having the replies checked by their superiors). Generally speaking, questionnaires and interviews (see sections 4.3 and 4.4) are the most important techniques used in surveys.

A survey questionnaire to organisations may cover the following topics:

o industrial classification of the organisation, total number of employees, expectation for major business expansion during new few years and changes in the size of the workforce;

o inventory of managerial posts by salary level, education, experience and qualifications of incumbents, training and its sources;

o inventory of managers currently receiving training in either management or technical subjects, grouped by field of study, location of training, qualification to be obtained and expected organisational post and level upon completion of training;

o training and development needs of managers and whether the training is urgent, desirable or not required, number of managers at each level requiring training during the next years;

o   obstacles to developing and training managers (including their relative importance), priority and importance of organisational approaches used for developing and training managers.

Any survey documents should include instructions for completion of the survey questionnaire with codification of industries and managerial profile characteristics.

The verification process of the survey questionnaire should involve a number of in-depth interviews, in order to add detailed information to the survey which would not be revealed through the use of a questionnaire alone. This combination of the survey questionnaire and the in-depth interviews with the chief executives and selected managers tends to increase the level of validity of the survey information.

Interviews have to be carefully structured in such a way as to yield information – qualitative rather than quantitative – on actual competence and its application, recruitment policies, career planning, and so on. It would also be useful to find out through interviews, for example, whether organisations are setting objectives against which managerial performance can be assessed, weaknesses corrected and training needs identified, to ascertain how enterprises give managers a particular kind of training, what the managers think about training programmes and facilities, what is the general climate and what are top management's attitudes to training and development. An error to avoid is merely asking managers about the training that they want to receive.

The interview guide, and questions to assist survey personnel to build their interview plans with chief executives and other managers, should be attached to survey documents. However, such a guide should never limit the flexibility of the interview. The interview climate should provide for a completely free expression of all views and ideas of the managers on the organisational and management training and development problems and needs.

The reactions and key comments of each manager should be summarised on an interview summary sheet. Views and comments should play an important role later on when analysing questionnaire responses, identifying major problems and needs, and formulating conclusions.

Once a questionnaire and an interview plan have been designed and a satisfactory sample chosen, the next prudent step would be to have a "pilot survey", applying the questionnaire or interview to a small proportion of the sample under operational conditions, as a final check on both the questions and the sampling before launching the whole operation and incurring major costs. Such a pilot survey provides an opportunity to assess the consistency and validity of the replies and to make any necessary adjustments in the content, order and wording of questions.

With the field-work of the survey carried out, and the raw data safely gathered in, compilation of the results can begin. Provided largely verbal and descriptive, and "open ended" questions have been kept to a minimum, it should be possible to carry out the computational processing quickly – using ordinary "desk" procedures if the numbers are not too great, or a computer if large numbers and a lengthy list of questions and answers are involved. The apparent training needs of each stratum will be examined separately, and the results "scaled up" to correspond with the numbers in the population as a whole. A statistician will need to comment on the likely range of "statistical error" in the results, which can be estimated from knowledge of the sample. It is also important to evaluate the achieved response rate in order to judge the reliability of the data: for example, if a sample represents 10 per cent of the enterprise population, and the response rate is 30 per cent of the sample, it would be difficult to draw reliable conclusions from these data. If the response rate is about 80-90 per cent, the data could be considered as much closer to reliable. At all stages, the process should be monitored by a training expert, some experienced managers and a statistician or survey expert. Collectively they would decide whether the outcome is reasonably close to producing information that could have been realistically expected.

Questionnaires and interviews have become so widely applied in macro-level surveys of needs that they have been overused and often misued. This finding has led some survey designers, such as the NASPAA team responsible for the SADCC study described in section 8.1, to another extreme – to a complete rejection of these traditional techniques and to opting for a large-scale use of alternative techniques such as the critical incident technique and the diary technique. Indeed, there is considerable scope for innovation in choosing, and adapting to specific circumstances, the various analytical techniques, suitable for collecting large amounts of detailed data from individuals, groups and organisations, described in part II of this book.

The misuse of questionnaires and interviews occurs if they are applied to collecting large amounts of data which are then aggregated without sufficient further examination and analysis. Statistically valid information on what organisations and managers perceive as needs and what they would like to see happening is then presented as an objective and authoritative picture of the real needs. The authors of a study are happy with the methodology, yet the conclusions obtained may be trivial and even meaningless, conveying general knowledge or information that does not lend itself to any action. This happens, for example, if questionnaires fail to ask for the right sort of information, or if interviews are conducted by inexperienced persons who cannot establish the required human and technical rapport with managers to discuss issues as delicate as gaps and needs in the managers' training and development.

Global techniques

It is possible to prevent situations in which vast amounts of analytical data collected through questionnaires and interviews (or critical incidents and other techniques) are not properly used because of the absence of a conceptual framework and time perspective. The changing context in which the managers' needs are being identified can be examined by studies of the following topics:

o   national, sectoral (and even organisational) development trends, achievements, strengths, weaknesses and opportunities;

o   structural changes in economic sectors;

o   socio-cultural and political contexts, focusing on those factors that affect management patterns at the present time and are likely to affect them in the future;

o   ongoing and forecasted technological changes which will require changes in management;

o   a comparative study with other countries whose practical management experience, as well as expected changes in the training and development of managers, is regarded as relevant and transferrable.

Obviously this requires a wider portfolio of study techniques, making extensive use of actual economic and social development indicators, examining development plans and programmes, gathering and analysing expert opinion, making proper use of international comparisons, talking to private voluntary organisations representing various social groups, and so on.

Work programme and timetable

We have seen that there can be many different approaches to surveys of management training and development needs, and organisational schemes for formulating them. However, the following main steps should be covered in drawing up a work programme and timetable:

(1)   Seek co-operation from the highest authorities and other interested groups.

(2)   Hold very preliminary interviews and consultations with experts on the existing problems and the desirable scope and focus of a survey.

(3)   Define the objectives, scope, coverage and frame of the survey.

(4)   Establish a survey team and define main responsibilities.

(5)   Decide upon the techniques used and determine the various characteristics under investigation.

(6)   Lay out an overall timetable.

(7) Design questionnaires and draw up detailed instructions for completing various items (further staff training).

(8) Recruit and brief interviewers and other support staff.

(9) Conduct a pilot survey or test, analyse difficulties and results, and finalise the survey instruments.

(10) Prepare detailed tabulation plans and programmes.

(11) Collect the data, i.e. carry out the actual field-work.

(12) Process the data.

(13) Analyse the tabulated results.

(14) Compare the findings obtained through various techniques.

(15) Draw up and review conclusions and recommendations.

(16) Prepare the report.

(17) Distribute and discuss the report.

(18) Decide on follow-up and draw up detailed follow-up plans.

Note on sampling

A complete census of the target population means that every manager and organisation must be included in the survey. However, the time, money and human resources required to conduct a census are often prohibitive. In this case, sampling enables one to obtain an agreed accuracy of particular attributes of the managerial population with the least possible cost and effort.[19]

Three basic principles should be taken into consideration during sampling:

(1) There should be a well-defined procedure for choosing representative elements from the total target population.

(2) A sample will always represent a compromise between the tendency to increase the surveyed population in the interest of precision and completeness and the need to reduce costs, and the time taken to conduct the survey.

(3) The criterion for the sample design should be defined by the level of precision at an agreed price.

The sample design should always start with a definition of objectives and specification of the resources. Objectives should include definition of the elements of the target population as the basis for sampling units and the survey variables.

Practically the first part of the task in designing a sample will be to phrase the questions to be answered so that the answers will be unambiguous, factual and/or quantifiable. After a first list of questions has been drawn up, the next task will be to try them out on a very small scale – say by examining 20-30 jobs (and managers) or organisations – so that any snags encountered can be taken into account and revised questions prepared before the survey itself is launched.

Some attempt will also be made to estimate the total size of the population to be studied and the numbers in each "stratum" which can be identified in advance as being likely to have training needs characteristics different from those of others. For example, a production-management post will require knowledge and skills which may be quite different from those of managers in sales, exports, technical development and so on. Or organisations of different sizes may have different management structures, functions and processes, and hence different training needs. Clearly establishing different strata for the purpose of sampling must be technically justified – otherwise it could be an unnecessary complication of the task.

One important requirement of any sample is that it should be representative of the whole "population". This requirement will influence the size of the sample. Clearly, a 100 per cent sample will be wholly representative, but a 1 per cent sample of 1,000 people is scarcely likely to be. In most cases, when the size and composition of a sample is determined, the advice of a statistician or survey expert will be helpful. The size will depend at least in part on the number of different strata of which the population is believed to be composed, and their relative sizes. Each stratum should be adequately represented in the sample.

If all the strata are of broadly similar size, then it may be adequate to decide upon a sample of, say, 10 per cent across the whole population, selecting every tenth organisation (person or post, etc.) from a list in which there is no reason to suppose bias, or selecting them by a "random" process. In surveying training needs, in practice it is often decided to survey all large or very large organisations in the sector or country (100 per cent sample), a relatively high proportion of the medium-sized organisations (20-50 per cent sample) and a smaller representative sample of the remaining organisations (say 5-15 per cent). These figures correspond to the size of samples found adequate in a number of surveys.

Having decided upon the size, nature and method for selecting the sample, it is important to ensure that it is sufficiently representative. Figure 8.2 shows different types of sampling.

It is not the task of this book to give a detailed description of all sampling methods, since this can be found in the specialised literature[20] and, besides, a statistician may have to be consulted. However, a few general comments on selecting sampling methods may be of interest to our readers.

Those who prefer to use the most common probability sampling methods should avoid the following four problems in designing reliable sampling frames:

Figure 8.2. Sampling methods

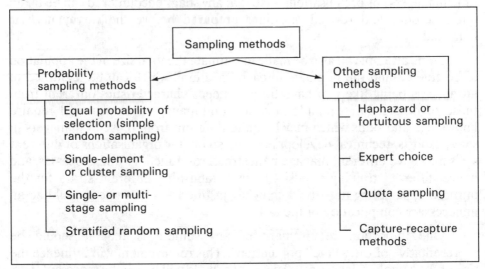

o   The frame may be inadequate because not all sampling units belonging to the managerial population are included – there may be missing elements.

o   The frame may be presented in terms of clusters of elements, rather than individual elements.

o   The frame may include foreign elements which do not belong to the survey population.

o   A single element may be duplicated in the sampling frames.[21]

8.4   Quantitative needs

If a national study deals with the quantitative side of management training and development needs in addition to the qualitative side, it is usually for the following reasons:

o   to indicate the magnitude of the challenge in order to alert the authorities, management circles and public opinion to the need for action;

o   to provide data and indicate trends for the purpose of planning and allocating resources for management education and training, or increasing the intake of students in programmes of management studies.

Quantitative data ought to be produced and interpreted with great caution, keeping in mind the following factors:

o   the different definitions of "manager" and "management training and development" used in various organisations;

o   the different career paths to management positions in particular organisations and/or countries;

o   the different national models of education and training for managerial occupations.

These factors reflect the fact that management has not been recognised and structured as a profession in the same way as medicine, law, or, in some countries, accountancy. It is a sort of "superimposed" informal profession, to which an individual may accede in many different ways. For example, two managers of the same age and at the same level within one organisation may have the following career backgrounds: manager A has specialised education, undergraduate and postgraduate (7 years) in business administration, plus 10 years of experience; while manager B has a first degree in engineering (4 years), plus 13 years of experience, including two short management courses (one of 3 months and one of 2 weeks). Both managers are regarded as equally competent although they acquired their competence in different ways.

To identify patterns and establish standards that would have a practical meaning in various corporate, sectoral and national settings is therefore extremely difficult.

The basic approach

In the absence of national or sectoral standards for the professional education and training of managers, the basic approach used in national studies consists of:

o   collecting data on educational background, career paths and in-service training of the managers;

o   producing global and average data characteristic of managers of various categories (by level, size of organisation, sector, etc.) in order to identify prevailing patterns;

o   analysing these data using comparisons with other countries, sectors and companies regarded as models of best experience;

o   analysing major environmental trends and developments (new technology, growing competition, global markets, etc.) likely to require changes in the volume of management education and training;

o   defining standards of management training and development as targets to be attained in the future;

o   drawing other conclusions concerning conditions and resources needed to attain the future standards.

Some ratios

A frequently quoted figure is the average number of days per year spent by a manager in off-the-job training. For example, recent studies of the management scene in the United Kingdom have shown that managers, on average, receive at most one day's formal training per year. Senior managers receive the least: less than 10 per cent of senior managers in companies employing over 1,000 people receive any training. These figures can be compared with standards achieved by progressive international companies, which are reported to provide five, and in some cases even ten, days' off-the-job training per year for every manager (see section 7.7). The British studies conclude that five days per year of off-the-job training/education for every manager is a figure that could be adopted as a target.[22]

Managerial manpower planning

Despite the difficulties faced in defining the term "manager", the qualifications required by a manager and the managers' characteristic career paths, there are situations where it may be useful to undertake a degree of manpower planning for managers at the national level.[23] This would include estimates of current stocks and flows and projections of demand and supply.

This might be the case in a developing country which is planning to replace expatriate managers or increase the supply of managers to meet the requirements of an expanding national economy. The purpose would be to establish new management education and training facilities or expand the existing ones, to provide some basis for planning fellowships for study abroad in management-related technical areas (business administration, marketing, accounting, etc.) and to make recommendations to companies on the desirable volume of in-service training.

However, similar consideration may apply in an industrialised country under certain circumstances. For example, the above-mentioned studies completed in 1987 in the United Kingdom arrived at important conclusions concerning the necessity to expand facilities for management education. The number of people entering management roles each year in the United Kingdom was estimated at 90,000. In 1985, the supply from formal management education (various forms and levels) was 12,300. It was suggested that this figure should be increased by establishing a new type of diploma in business administration with a target annual intake of up to 35,000 to be attained within ten years, and by raising the output of undergraduate studies (business and management degrees) from the current 4,500 to 7,000 per year. The number of managers promoted annually to senior positions was estimated at 17,500, assuming that some 350,000 managers held such positions and that the average managerial life-span at that level was 20 years. These figures were compared with the current output of 3,100 and a recommendation was made to increase the annual output of MBA degrees to 10,000 by the end of the century.

It is important to notice that rather than assuming a major expansion of the economy, these figures reflect thinking concerning needed changes in the educational patterns and career paths of future British managers. The basic assumption is that the currently prevailing pattern, i.e. learning management on the job, without any formal management education and training, or with very limited formal training, has become outdated and is hampering the modernisation of the British economy. Hence there is a need to promote a new pattern, without, however, making an unrealistic assumption that the old one would completely disappear.

Needs and demand

In any national study aimed at this sort of recommendation, it is essential to make a realistic assessment of the relationship between needs and demand. If employers have a free choice in deciding whom to recruit or promote to a managerial job, we have to assess the factors that will be influencing this choice. The number of graduates available is one factor, and the quality of these graduates is another. Established practices, company traditions and the ways in which the current decision-makers arrived at their senior positions have to be considered. For example, in 1987 in the United States about 240,000 persons completed undergraduate studies (BA) and 70,000 graduate studies (MBA) of management and business administration.[24] The ratio of BA and MBA graduates to the total population was 0.00124 per capita. The ratio of graduates to the number of new recruits to management and similar positions (about 360,000 a year) was 0.86. These are unique ratios, reflecting not only the size and structure of the American economy, but also the established position of education for business and management and the prevailing recruitment and career patterns.

Similar considerations are relevant in working with figures concerning the volume of training and retraining of practising managers. The British objective of moving from an average figure of one day to five days per year is a tremendous task, although the target does not appear to be high. In several studies carried out in developing countries, an assessment of real demand was omitted and factors affecting demand were not fully appreciated. As a result, target figures reflecting established needs could not be attained.

8.5 Survey reports

Every special study or survey produces a report. In some studies several interim reports are submitted and examined before drafting the final one. The principal criterion for structuring and writing these reports is that of their final use. The main questions are: For whom is the report intended? How will it be distributed and who is likely to read it? How will its conclusions and recommendations be used? What follow-up is required? These questions may look self-evident, but they are not. Too many survey reports are poorly structured and drafted, ignoring the fact that what will be seen and judged is not the course of the survey itself, but the report. The readers have no alternative – the survey is over, the report is what is left, and all the important messages are in the report; or else the authors failed to make the right points, thus losing their main opportunity to communicate with those for whom the report was intended.

Whom is the report for?

It is difficult to serve many different clients by one report. An "executive summary" has become common practice of most reports, but does not always solve the problem. It may be better to consider the differences between information on which senior decision-makers in business and government can act, and that addressed to directors of institutions or individual management trainers and researchers. This can lead to the decision to produce two or three different reports on the same study, or one report with distinct parts addressed to different readers.

The methodology and the findings

Of course, it is not unimportant to describe methodology, showing that the approach taken was not pseudo-scientific and that the authors knew their subject. However, the description of methodology in the body of the report must be concise, leaving the details to appendices. Reports whose body is overloaded with issues of research methodology tend to be boring and ineffective.

Findings (facts, conclusions, recommendations) are the key feature of every report. The problems faced are:

o   structuring the findings in a logical and systematic way (e.g. by management functions, by major trends in the external environment, by problems that need to be resolved);

o   identifying key findings and showing them separately from less important findings;

o   drawing significant new conclusions (rather than repeating known facts) from facts that were collected – this is perhaps the main difficulty, with which many authors of reports are unable to cope.

The report and the appendices

Deciding what will be in the body of the report and what in appendices is extremely important. Key information, including short summary tables and diagrams, must be in the report, not in the appendices. A busy person should be able to read the report and get all the important facts and opinions without perusing the appendices. Also, the number and the degree of detail of the appendices should be in reasonable proportion to the report (a 20-page report would not normally have 30 appendices on 200 pages).

In any event, it is useful to show the draft report to colleagues and friends from among the intended readers. Thus the author will find out about issues of substance and style that may be improved, and points that risk being misunderstood by the readers.

The report outline

o   Executive summary of purpose, approach taken, findings, conclusions and recommendations.

o   Introduction.

o   Aim, context and background of the survey.

o   Methodology and techniques used, survey planning and organisation.

o   One or more chapters describing specific existing situations, characteristics of industries and/or enterprises, scale of the problem, existing managerial profiles and patterns in management development, ethnic balance, institutional management development and educational mechanism, obstacles to management development, etc.

o   One or more chapters describing management training and development needs.

o   Survey conclusions and recommendations, follow-up.

o   Appendixes (tables, details of information collected, supplementary information on methodology, sources used).

8.6   Utilisation of results

No author of a report on management training and development needs would regard the report as an aim in itself – the fact that such a report is to stimulate and orient action is generally recognised. Yet many reports do not receive the desired attention and in some cases the projects have ended with the publication of the report, without any significant follow-up. We can discard the instances of poor studies and reports, which do not lend themselves to any meaningful follow-up. However, even reports that are the result of solid professional work are often poorly utilised. Why is this so?

No follow-up foreseen

When designing and planning the whole project, it is important to consider the action to follow the completion and submission of the report. This involves:

o   the distribution of the report (to whom, with what covering message, in how many copies, for what price, if any, who is responsible for distribution);

o   in-depth examination of the report and decision on action;

o   the definition of responsibility and resources for action;

o   further conceptual and detailed technical work required.

Inadequate resources

In several instances, major national studies of needs were launched without giving due consideration to the commitment required and considerable resources to be mobilised for implementing recommendations. The discrepancy between the ambitions of the study team and the resources that could be realistically expected to be found was quite considerable. Yet the scope of the study was not modified.

Unfinished job

If a study suggests further studies and no action, the policy-makers may lose interest and decide to withdraw their support from a project that is turning into a very lengthy and expensive undertaking.

Who will take the lead?

The implementation of the report's conclusions and recommendations will depend eventually on the interest and motivation of organisations and individuals who play important roles in management training and development, and in dealing with the "non-training" factors. The many actors involved need a leader and co-ordinator whom they respect and who enjoys their confidence. He or she must be perceived as a leader who can and wants to undertake action on recommendations and enlist the support of government and business circles. For example, a chairman of a federation of industrialists, or a minister of

industry and commerce can play this role. Finding such a leading personality –
a "champion" – and providing him or her with technical backstopping, may be
as necessary as submitting a good report with feasible proposals.

---

[1] EFMD: *Enquête sur les besoins de formation au management en Europe* (Bruxelles, 1972).

[2] Office of the Prime Minister, Management Development and Advisory Service: *Final report of the Zambia managerial manpower and training needs survey of the private and parastatal sectors* (Lusaka, 1977).

[3] See E.A. Powers: "Enhancing managerial competence: The American Management Association Competency Programme", in *Journal of Management Development* (Bradford, West Yorkshire), Vol. 6, No. 4, 1987; and R.E. Boyatzis: *The competent manager: A model for effective performance* (New York, Wiley, 1982). The description of the AMA programme is taken, with acknowledgement of the origin, from the article by E.A. Powers. The programmes described are now sponsored by the consulting firm Powers, Wayno and Associates.

[4] World Bank: *Indonesia: Management development*, 3 vols. (Washington, DC, 1985; report 4965-IND).

[5] NASPAA: *Improving management in Southern Africa* (Washington, DC, 1985).

[6] See H. Mintzberg: *The nature of managerial work* (New York, Harper and Row, 1979).

[7] See J. Prokopenko and J.H. White (eds.): *Modular programme for supervisory development*, 5 vols. (Geneva, ILO, 1981); and J. Prokopenko and L.R. Bittel: "A modular course format for supervisory development", in *Training and Development Journal* (Washington, DC), Feb. 1981.

[8] R.A. Gordon and J.E. Howell: *Higher education for business* (New York, Columbia University Press, 1959).

[9] F.C. Pierson: *The education of American businessmen* (New York, McGraw-Hill, 1959).

[10] AACSB and EFMD: *Management for the XXI century* (Boston and The Hague, Kluwer-Nijhoff, 1982).

[11] L.W. Porter and L.E. McKibbin: *Management education and development: Drift or thrust into the 21st century?* (New York, McGraw-Hill, 1988).

[12] ibid., p.10.

[13] ibid., p.298.

[14] ibid., p.44.

[15] ibid., pp.316-325.

[16] ibid., pp.333-334.

[17] ibid., p.307.

[18] ibid., p.18.

[19] A part of the material on sampling is taken from A.R. Smith: *Techniques for managerial manpower planning* (Geneva, ILO, 1988; technical paper Man.Dev/47).

[20] See, for example, J. Ashford: *Statistics for management* (London, Institute of Personnel Management, 1977), or J.J. Clark and M.T. Clark: *A statistical primer for managers* (London, The Free Press, 1983).

[21] Adapted from Ashford, op. cit., p.307.

[22] See J. Constable and R. McCormick: *The making of British managers* (London, British Institute of Management and Confederation of British Industry, 1987), and C. Handy: *The making of managers* (London, Manpower Services Commission, National Economic Development Council and British Institute of Management, 1987).

[23] See Smith, op. cit.

[24] See Handy, op. cit., p.29.

NEEDS ASSESSMENT BY MANAGEMENT DEVELOPMENT INSTITUTIONS

9

This chapter is addressed to management development institutions. These institutions face particular problems in assessing management training and development needs. To them, correct information on current needs, and a visionary but realistic assessment of future needs, constitute the foundations on which all their work must be built. As service institutions, the very purpose of their work consists of satisfying their clients' needs. In addition, they can be, and many of them aim to be, the principal promoters of more effective needs assessment practices. Some institutions have made great efforts in this field in close collaboration with business enterprises and other client organisations. Many institutions in both industrialised and developing countries have worked at national studies of management education and training needs. Thus, management institutions have accumulated considerable experience in needs assessment, and in making use of this assessment for their own strategic planning and programme design. However, the differences between needs assessment practices applied by the leading institutions, and those used by the less dynamic and proficient ones, are still quite important.

9.1 Five behavioural models

No training and development institution would pretend that it is not important to know and respect the clients' real needs. Statements about the primacy of the clients' needs and the necessity to focus all programmes on these needs are increasingly becoming the profession of faith of management institutions. Yet different kinds of behaviour can be observed in practice, as demonstrated by the five patterns described below.

We teach what we know!

Many institutions start by teaching what their staff is able to teach. The staff members may be rather inexperienced and their contacts with business practice limited. They may even be afraid that practitioners would not take them seriously if asked about training needs. Often these trainers do not know how to talk to managers. Therefore, they choose the only available alternative

---

– teaching what they learned from their own professors. Clearly, some faculty members will have had better professors than others and will be alert to the need to understand the course participants' specific needs. However, they will not dare to modify the curriculum they know and to delve into unfamiliar problems.

This approach can easily turn into intellectual arrogance. Instead of seeking information and inspiration in business and management practice, some faculty members continue to "teach the body of knowledge" even when they become more senior and experienced. This happens even to some graduates of Ph.D. programmes if their advanced studies overrate intellectual capabilities and theoretical knowledge and underrate application and the unity of practice and theory.

We know what the managers need!

The second posture is the logical and inevitable consequence of the previous one. The construction of an "ivory tower" has been completed. The teacher is up to date in all relevant management theories and techniques – therefore who else could be better placed to decide what should be covered in a course? If a manager does not really see the usefulness of a theory or technique, that is his or her problem, not the teacher's. The manager has been taught about the techniques and must now find out how to use them.

We do what the leaders in our profession do!

The third attitude is justified to some extent. After all, it is based on comparison with a model and we have made it clear in this book that referring to models and learning from others can be most useful in assessing training and development needs. Therefore most institutions tend to watch what the leading institutions in the management development profession do. The approach is particularly attractive if another institution has clearly had success with some programmes and is being praised in business circles. Why not try the same things? We may learn how to do it by inviting visiting lecturers, by seeing how the "leader" works, by asking for a twinning arrangement with an excellent school, and so on. Unfortunately, the different conditions, and different needs of the clients served, are often overlooked, or the importance of existing differences is not correctly appreciated. What works in one environment may turn into a disaster in another.

We do what our clients want!

The fourth approach is a negation of the three previous ones. The institution has no preconceived ideas, no models copied from the "leaders", and is genuine in its endeavour to be useful to the practitioners. Instead of being told to take what is on offer, the manager is asked what he wants, and the institution makes every effort to satisfy and to please him. The requests are collected through questionnaires, by visiting personnel and training managers, by interviewing course participants, and so on. This is an important step towards a productive relationship between the institution and its client base. The training is demand driven. The "service ethos" starts emerging and the criteria for judging institutional effectiveness begin to be sought in business and management practice.

There are problems, however. For example, who was interviewed and was he (or she) in a position to speak on behalf of the whole organisation? On what basis did he formulate demands? Did he reply off the cuff or did he himself analyse the organisation's needs? What standards were used? What about "training" and "non-training" needs? And there are still other questions.

A variant of this approach is focusing on top management's perception of needs. Top and senior managers are asked not only about their needs, but also about the needs of their subordinates. There is logic behind this – top managers are responsible for running organisations, and therefore no one can be better placed for knowing and expressing the organisations' training and development needs. However, even in this instance the above-mentioned questions may remain unanswered and the institution may be unable to determine the difference between the managers' perception of needs, and the real needs.

This fourth pattern of behaviour can be found in institutions that have decided to be "reactive". One more step is to be made if the institution chooses to be "pro-active".

We aim to provide what our clients need!

The difference between needs and demand was explained in chapter 1. This difference can be subtle, but is significant. A pro-active institution is aware of this difference, and makes its clients aware of it. This may be necessary if enterprise managers ask for courses they do not need, or get unduly impressed by techniques that are nothing more than passing fads. The institution has to be frank with clients in discussing needs, and try to separate real needs from those that are fictitious. Listening to the clients does not mean being a passive listener. A pro-active institution tries to take a broad view of the managerial, business and social environment and consider future trends in addition to immediate needs and demands identified in individual organisations.

Of course, it is not possible to offer training programmes that the clients do not understand and do not ask for. Therefore the identification of needs is an interactive process. It is undertaken in close contact with the clients, as well as with other public and private organisations that can help to throw light on training and development needs reflecting changes in the environment. These changes can be short term, such as the introduction of severe import restrictions requiring immediate adjustments in business policy, or long term, such as an anticipated scarcity of labour in an area where labour is abundant at the present time, or the emergence of new social attitudes that will require major changes in personnel policies. A pro-active institution helps its clients to become aware of these trends and developments, and assess whether and in what way they generate new training and development needs. This requires vision, a great amount of information on what is going on in business society, courage to raise unusual and unpopular issues, and a strong sense of responsibility to the clients and to society.

To assume the role of a pro-active institution is difficult and there are many temptations to drift back and be merely reactive, in particular if the current demand for services is high. Also, a pro-active institution must not only be *determined*, but also be *able*, to play such a role. Therefore this chapter focuses on needs assessment approaches that can be used to increase this ability.

9.2 Needs assessment as a feature of current interventions

A pro-active institution is forward looking. It tries to apply some form of strategic planning in order to anticipate future management training and development needs, and prepare itself for helping clients to meet these needs. However, the key to a pro-active approach is in current activities. To be in a position to adopt a strategic posture and play the role of a change agent in the future, an institution should be fully embedded in current practice, be a part of it, and be perceived as such by the users of the institution's services.

This last point cannot be overstressed. If an institution lives in an ivory tower, in isolation from the everyday concerns of managers in business and government, teaching what it can teach or wants to teach without really knowing what is going on within the enterprises, it will find it difficult to develop a meaningful future strategy. If may not even know what questions to raise in order to come to grips with new needs, and its strategic decisions may be as remote from the real course of events as its current activities are.

Therefore, future-oriented strategic management, in anticipation of clients' future needs, is based on lessons learned from current interventions and activities. The principal decision on how to handle needs assessment is made when the institution chooses the basic intervention methods to be applied in working with a particular group of clients.

As a rule, institutions that have developed close linkages with their client base do not run a separate activity called "needs identification", or "needs assessment". Occasionally they may organise an ad hoc survey or special study

---

for this purpose, but this would be an exception. As expressed in the title of this section, needs assessment is treated as a "feature of current interventions".

What does this mean from a methodological and organisational point of view? Some examples of approaches taken by institutions are given below.

Courses, seminars and workshops

Preparing and delivering courses, seminars and workshops is the main activity of management training and development institutions and offers a wide range of opportunities for assessing the managers' training and development needs. During training, the institution is in direct contact with its clients who have decided to allocate time to training and will be keen to maximise the benefits they can draw from this opportunity. Therefore they will be particularly prone to reveal information on their training needs, thus helping the institution to make the training programme more relevant. Some participants even come to the course with a strong determination to influence the programme in order to maximise the benefits of learning.

The training staff, must likewise be keen and able to use this opportunity. In the worst case, managers will come to the institute, politely listen to lectures, and leave without providing any information and feedback on training and development needs. However, participative training methods, and engaging managers in active discussion or group work on specific problems and projects, create many situations in which knowledge gaps, skill shortages and behavioural problems come to the surface. In addition, managers readily provide a great deal of information on training needs of other categories and groups of personnel, such as the staff of a supervising ministry, credit officers in banks or the management of supplier enterprises. Some findings about training and development needs will be of immediate use, in particular if the institution practices flexible training programme design and is able to adjust both the content and the method before the current course is completed. Other findings will be useful to future sessions of the same programmes, and for designing and marketing new programmes.

It is essential to pursue needs assessment during training as a matter of policy. The training staff must know what is expected from them in terms of needs assessment. Periodic review sessions with the programme director and the management of the institution allow the categorisation of findings on which immediate action can be taken (e.g. include in a current course a new topic originally not foreseen), and those to be used for future programmes.

Consulting activities

Management development institutions become involved in consulting for various reasons.[1] They increasingly appreciate that the relationship between training and consulting is very close. They do consulting in order to help clients in dealing with practical issues that cannot be solved by training only. Very often, such interventions develop as a follow-up of training courses and seminars, where problems are identified and discussed. The participating managers then invite the faculty members to their enterprises to give a short practical consultation, or to undertake a fully-fledged consulting project. Many institutions also seek opportunities for consulting assignments in parallel with training, or in preparing for training programmes. This makes it possible to deal both with "training" and "non-training" issues and solutions faced by the clients. The role played by management institutions in changing the management practices and performance of client organisations is thus considerably enhanced.

While management centres and institutes have expanded their consulting activities, consulting firms do more and more training. In most cases this training is a component of consulting assignments, e.g. seminars on communication techniques or on new developments in marketing or another functional area covered by the assignment. Extensive training of a client's personnel can be part of the implementation phase. In addition, many consulting firms also run regular and ad hoc training courses, conferences, round-tables and briefing seminars for a wide clientèle in a similar way as management centres and institutions do.

Thus, management consultants use consulting methods and interventions as their main means of action, and supplement and support them by training interventions. In management institutions this relationship is reversed. However, the problems faced in relating training to consulting, and in diagnosing training and development needs, are similar. There are, too, many opportunities for trainers to learn from consultants, and vice versa.

If an institution works with one client on a major management consulting or OD project, the issues of training and development needs assessment are essentially those described in chapters 6 and 7. Each step in the assignment normally has a training needs assessment dimension. The needs identified can then be met by tailor-made training within the framework of the same project, or the client organisation will be advised to use various external programmes.

A more complex question is how to use consulting for the planning and design of standard (scheduled) courses and seminars offered by training and development institutions. The experience of many leading institutions seems to confirm that consulting generally helps management trainers and teachers not only to learn what is going on in the world of practice but also to acquire practical skills and a sense of achievement that is often missing among the academics. This increases the trainers' and the teachers' ability to conduct a dialogue with the practitioners and perceive their real training needs. Thus, consulting can be used as a general competency development tool for more professional needs assessment.

Turning to needs assessment required for planning and designing specific institutional programmes, there is no automatic guarantee that all consulting work will produce the desired results. On the contrary, faculty members may do a lot of consulting which has little impact on the relevance and quality of teaching. This occurs if consulting assignments are chosen and accepted in a haphazard way without thinking of the potential contribution to the improvement of training and teaching programmes. For example, the problem tackled may be new to a client, but not to the institution. Or the problem may be in an area where the institution is not planning to provide any training programmes.

There is, then, the question of transfer of expertise from consulting to training. If certain training needs are identified in the course of one or several consulting assignments, it would be risky to generalise and conclude that the same needs exist in other organisations, and, therefore, justify the design of a new training programme. In such cases it may be advisable to regard information obtained from consulting as signals whose meaning and importance ought to be verified by a sectoral survey, compared with information gathered by other institutions, and so on.

It should be stressed that the transfer of information and know-how between consulting and training requires careful organisation and management within the training institution. This includes:

o   seeking assignments that will provide information and know-how needed for planning and designing training;

o   systematically evaluating the results of all assignments and examining their findings about training needs;

o   sharing the findings from consulting with other faculty members or consultants who were not directly involved in the assignments;

o   proper recording, filing and classification of consulting reports to make them available and usable in preparing training;

o   pursuing the objective of preparing training materials (such as case studies and practical examples) as a by-product of consulting assignments.

The Swedish Management Group (SMG), owned by the Swedish Employers' Confederation, defines itself as a management training company first and foremost.[2] However, every professional employed by the group must be able to work as both trainer and consultant. In addition to meeting clients' direct needs, consulting work aims at (i) keeping abreast of practical developments and the changing needs of managers, in order to keep the training programmes up to date, and (ii) preparing specific training programmes for individual companies tailored to their needs. These technical objectives have important financial implications. On average, one "training day" (sold to a client company or delivered through open training programmes available at the Group's training centres) generates income that is three times higher than income from one "consulting day". Hence it is necessary to monitor carefully the balance between training days and consulting days, and use consulting for preparing training technically.

Research projects

Management research is another area of institutional activity that can be most useful in identifying training and development needs. Research that looks into wider issues common to a number of organisations (e.g. in the whole sector) can complete the job started, but not finished, in individual consulting assignments. For example, it can verify the occurrence and significance of a problem identified by several consulting assignments, and try to establish general causes and trends of that problem. However, as in consulting, there is no automatic guarantee that every research project will produce information on training needs, or other conclusions and materials suitable for use in training. Research can even be quite irrelevant to training. This happens, for example, if research projects:

o   are regarded mainly as a source of income;

o   pursue the achievement of an advanced degree (Ph.D. or similar) or the writing of a publication as their only objective;

o   are fully subordinated to the interests and methodological approaches of an external body, e.g. of a co-operating institution in another country, or of an organisation providing funding for the project.

It is essential to start by asking what research projects should be undertaken, and for what purpose. Discussing the potential practical usefulness of a project helps to define its potential to contribute to diagnosing training and development needs and determine whether the project will:

o   pursue the definition of these needs as its major objective;

o   generate information on needs as a by-product;

o   help to orient further studies of needs;

o   be of no immediate interest to assessing needs.

The prevailing current trend in management development institutions is to do research that is useful for both theory and practice.[3] Therefore research projects tend to be chosen and structured with needs assessment as their main or secondary purpose. This is a key factor in the institution's research policy. It is equally important to co-ordinate various research projects so as to avoid fragmented reports that highlight separate elements of business and managerial reality, but do not provide a comprehensive and reliable explanation of events, relationships and trends.

A growing sector of research undertaken by management centres and institutes is the study of organisational change. The study is usually undertaken as *action research*. Action (e.g. the solution of a problem regarding some aspects of organisational change and development) is both the subject of the research study and a part of the research process. As the research progresses, practical changes are introduced based on the findings made at the previous stage. For example, the researcher may provide feedback, based on his or her observation of the process, to a team in the client organisation. The team will be able to use this feedback in deciding on the next step to take (e.g. trying to change behaviour in dealing with another team in the organisation). Action research does not develop general knowledge. However, through its direct involvement in organisational change action research produces a great deal of very specific information on training needs in organisations, information that can be immediately verified and corrected since the training provided as part of the change process is also studied.

External faculty members

External faculty members, drawn from businesses and government organisations, are an invaluable source of information on training and development needs. Here again, it is important that the institution is able to work with external trainers to tap their know-how. It is not enough to ask a practitioner to give an occasional lecture or conduct a workshop. External faculty members have to be more involved in the life of the institution, including discussions on course design, consulting work and the planning and evaluation of research. They must share the institution's philosophy or doctrine on how to go about implementing change and improving performance in organisations, and how to train and educate managers. Only then will it be possible to get their maximum help in determining training and development needs.

Membership of boards and committees

Membership of, and active involvement in, boards of directors, supervisory boards, and various advisory or review committees, private or governmental, provides access to important information on management development needs and enables a very productive dialogue with senior decision-makers. Only heads of institutions and senior faculty members can expect to be offered such membership. However, other opportunities are available even to less senior staff – for example, working with junior chambers of commerce or management associations.

Business associates

The system of business associates, which has been launched by some institutions, links the latter in a structured way with a group of business firms. On the one hand, these firms are offered certain services and privileges, such as special information services or reduced course fees. On the other hand, a business associate that knows the management institution from a variety of working contacts is usually more open than any other firm in helping diagnose needs and in sharing information that can be exploited in needs assessment.

Former participants (alumni)

Relations with former participants can be maintained in an institutionalised way, through an association of alumni, or through informal individual contacts and ad hoc events to which they are invited (conferences, workshops, social events). Not many institutions can afford to establish and sustain an active association of alumni. However, every institution should be able to find some way of tapping the expertise and interest of its former participants for assessing training and development needs.

Some well-established institutions have been quite successful in developing an "institutional culture" that also embraces their relations with their former students. The alumni enjoy this relationship and the prestige of having learned and graduated from a leading business school or management institute. The institution, on the other hand, has easy access to its alumni even when these reach top positions in business and government.

Tracer studies

Tracer studies look back at the effectiveness of institutionalised training by examining the experience of former trainees in the labour market. These studies are often used for evaluating the impact of vocational training and assessing the relevance of existing training programmes to the participants' needs and to labour market requirements. In management training and development, the use of tracer studies has been limited. However, business and management schools in several countries have done tracer studies of former graduates, focusing on questions such as:

o   the initial job in which employment was found;

o   progress in the career;

o   the initial and further salary levels;

o   the knowledge and skills that the graduate missed in his or her job(s).

Tracer studies would be less useful for assessing short-term and higher-level management programmes, where the focus is on solving specific management problems rather than on preparing individuals for future careers.

9.3 Needs assessment for strategic decisions

Strategic decisions of management development institutions concern issues such as the purpose, goals and objectives of the institution, target sectors and populations, means of action, resource allocation and organisation, and patterns of institutional behaviour in interacting with the environment. Strategy can also be defined as the institution's response to environmental opportunities, challenges and threats, consistent with its competence and resources.[4]

Not all institutions practise strategic management in the same way. Some have adopted a highly structured approach, which includes a strategic plan for three to five years or more, a statement of strategy and a periodic review of strategy, e.g. a strategic audit, whereby current strategy is reassessed and new decisions taken that reflect new opportunities and react to new constraints. Other institutions have no structured system of strategic management. However, even this latter group faces strategic choices from time to time and makes decisions with considerable long-term implications for the basic orientation of the institution and the use of its resources.

It would be risky to take decisions of strategic importance without trying to know as precisely as possible what the needs are, or are likely to be. Observation and analysis of environmental trends are essential for anticipating the clients' future concerns and needs, and getting ready to take future opportunities. This has to be coupled with periodic reassessment of current concerns and problems, and with an effort to develop a balanced view of developments occurring in management practice and theory.

Strategic signals from current activities

In the previous section we showed that the foundations for effective strategic management are laid down in current activities, by establishing and maintaining close linkages with clients (both individual managers and organisations) and by following as closely as possible changes that occur in the environment. Most of the information thus gathered can then be reflected in immediate adjustments of current training programmes and other services. However, this information also includes signals that may require strategic decisions. It is important to watch these signals, and make sure that they are not overlooked and misinterpreted.

For example, managers express their concern about the ability of their organisations to adjust personnel practices to the changing educational level and cultural values of new young recruits for technical and functional staff positions. This signal may come from several management courses, as well as from consulting assignments. Discussing it at staff meetings might establish whether, merely by coincidence, a few participants experienced a problem that was not seen as a problem by other managers, or whether the observed change is starting to be perceived as a significant trend that will affect many organisations. If the institution is not sure about the scope and nature of this problem, it may decide to explore it further by a special study, or by talking about it to other client organisatio s and other management institutions. This may lead to a conclusion that there is a growing need for a new type of personnel management programme both for general managers and for personnel specialists.

Another quite common signal is falling demand for certain courses. This may have various causes. The course may be poorly run, existing needs may have been well covered, a competitor has started a better course on the same topic, or a major change in the client's needs has made the original course design obsolete. Falling demand ought to be examined carefully to make sure that the institution receives the right signal. It is possible that the course continues to be quite relevant but demand has fallen because the quality of the training is low, or that the level of teaching is satisfactory but the clients' needs have changed.

In summary, to be able to receive and exploit strategic signals from current activities, an institution:

o   has to obtain first-hand information on what the clients do and think, and how they react to its services;

o   has to be able to take a detached view, looking beyond the clients' and its own current activities and concerns, to detect events and views that may be indicative of important environmental and structural changes.

Strategic audit

A strategic audit is a structured exercise whereby the institution evaluates its current position, achievements and strategy, and defines new strategy to respond to changed needs and opportunities. Such an audit can take many different forms and may be called by different names. It can be an ad hoc exercise triggered by an external demand or by an internal management decision, or a periodic exercise that becomes a regular feature of the institution's management.[5]

Irrespective of these different approaches, a strategic audit normally includes an assessment (or reassessment) of:

o   the client base (to whom to offer and provide services);

o   the clients' changing needs;

o   the potential future demand for new services.

The assessment of the client base can reveal that the institution has potential for offering services and meeting needs in sectors, technical areas or countries that have been outside the scope of its interest and mandate. This is particularly important in connection with structural changes occurring in many countries and with the growing internationalisation of the world economy. For example, many institutions in developing countries have started training and advisory programmes for entrepreneurship development and new enterprise creation, thus reacting to the perceived need to foster the development of small, private enterprises started and operated by local entrepreneurs.

As regards the changes in the clients' needs, the strategic audit is essentially future oriented, looking beyond the current needs and demand for services. The objective is to prepare the institution for helping clients with new needs, including those of which they may be unaware at the present time. A dialogue with management in client organisations is therefore essential, but would not suffice. Environmental analysis focusing on future trends, and their most probable impact on management and business, is the main technique used.

Here again, the rather complex relationship between needs and demand will be kept in mind. Demand will depend not only on the existence of certain needs that ought to be met, but also on the clients' perception of these needs and on the institution's image, technical competence, links with clients and marketing capabilities. In addition, other institutions may be undertaking the same sort of strategic audit and planning and may be deciding to enter the same market. Thus, demand will also be influenced by the services offered by competitors, the performance of individual competitors and by the clients' decisions to internalise certain new types of training services rather than using external training facilities.

Therefore, the assessment of quantitative demand for new types of services may be very difficult even if considerable needs have been identified. Institutions tend to take a cautious approach in assessing their future share of the market and allocating resources (teaching staff, marketing, facilities) accordingly. Or they decide to test demand, and their own ability to meet it, by running a limited number of experimental programmes, before deciding to increase the programmes on offer.

Special considerations in establishing a new institution

If a new management institution is being established, an assessment of the training and development needs of the potential target organisations is normally regarded as a prerequisite. It should justify the decision to create a new institution, or show that such an intention ought to be abandoned.

Furthermore, needs assessment would provide information required for decisions on sectoral focus, size, types of programmes, intervention methods, sources of funding and similar strategic issues.

Two cases are most common. In the first case, the institution is being established because certain needs (and demand) are not being met. In the second case, needs (and demand) are being met, but there is a feeling that a new institution could do it better.

·The first case is common in developing countries. Most of their management and productivity centres and institutes were established on this basis – following a more or less structured survey of management training and development needs. As a rule, these surveys focused on the modern segments of the industrial and commercial sectors, and on public administration. However, instances of training and development needs that are not being met are not confined to the developing countries. Recent developments have demonstrated that new training and development needs continue to emerge as a corollary of new technologies, transfers of technology, growing internationalisation of business or changing relationships between industrialised and developing countries. New institutions, or new programmes in existing training institutions and consulting firms, continue to be established to meet these new needs.

In the second case a new institution, if established, would enter a market that is already being serviced by one or more institutions. Therefore such a decision would make sense if a new institution were to offer a better service – "better" meaning higher quality, lower cost, a more appropriate learning environment, shorter distances from the clients' premises, or other features that may be missing in the services currently available. In this case an assessment of needs ought to be supplemented by a thorough analysis of current services on offer, keeping in mind the differences between the quantitative and qualitative aspects of such services.

In both cases needs assessment faces a common problem. A new institution will be an organisation that has not been "embedded" in the current economic, administrative and social system. If established, it will be a new element in this system. Therefore it has no links with clients and no experience from current work with them, although some individuals involved in planning a new institution are likely to have such experience. There is a case for a thorough and cautious assessment of needs, both qualitative and quantitative, of the potential clients. This means combining a variety of needs assessment techniques to obtain a picture that can be regarded as relatively complete and objective. Study of demand will be as important as study of needs since a lack of demand, and a lack of belief that training could bring about improvements in competence and performance, may be the main problem to tackle.

9.4 Case: Strategic self-assessment of the IMI

The Geneva-based International Management Institute (IMI) undertook its first strategic planning exercise, entitled "The CEI in the year 2000", during the academic year 1978-79.[6] Several years later, in 1985, the IMI went through the "second round" of strategic audit. The Foundation Board of the IMI established a "Commission for the year 2000", consisting of Board members, senior faculty members, and external experts drawn from top management and business school circles in various countries. The Commission's mandate was to "re-examine all aspects of IMI to enable it to be relevant and appropriate in the light of expected changes in the business environment of the 1990s". Put another way, the question was how to make an international management institution with the IMI profile most useful to its stakeholders in meeting their future needs and detecting and taking future opportunities. The Commission's work methods included individual papers submitted by the external members and extensive discussions at a number of the Commission's meetings. The results were summarised in a short report.[7]

The report takes the stakeholders' future needs as a starting-point for required changes in programme and methodology to be pursued by the IMI. It stresses that:

o   speedier changes will occur in the environment in which management functions;

o   most of these changes will be unpredictable exogeneous shocks;

o   therefore the IMI should focus on developing managers capable of making the most of an unpredictable future.

These summary conclusions are based on a more detailed assessment of future trends concerning the overall process of management, areas of concern to managers and the ways in which managers will need to learn.

Future management processes are likely to be highly unstructured and impossible to force into neat categories. Hence what will be mainly required from managers is vision (the ability to apply a holistic view and ask the right questions), the creation and selection of options, and the ability to ensure implementation. The areas of concern will include the categories of environment, sector and company, and their interaction in various situations. The increasingly important ways in which the managers learn will emphasise integrative (interfunctional and interdisciplinary) and participative approaches, enhanced forward orientation, more action learning, and the use of advanced instructional technologies and teaching tools.

In addition, the Commission agreed to present its own conception of the "profile of the effective manager of the future" (a sort of competency model), stressing a number of characteristics. These reflect the perception of managers' future needs by the members of the Commission and not the results of any research project. They are as follows:

o flexibility (openness to new ideas and concepts);

o breadth plus depth (combination of functional depth with managerial breadth);

o leadership (leading people in response to change and to unpredictable systemic shocks);

o ethics (extreme sensibility to issues of ethics and morality, value systems and social codes);

o global orientation (keen interest in all regions and all areas of activity);

o decision-making under uncertainty (speedy decisions, risk management needs);

o communication skills (both within and outside the company);

o ability to discriminate (between significant and marginally important events and changes);

o technological literacy (including the impact of technology on various areas of management);

o emotional and physical fitness (for coping with rapid changes and inevitable stress);

o adaptability (not only in action but also in careers, in changing sectors etc.).

Furthermore, the Commission's report outlines the basic elements of the IMI's required response, stressing:

o integrative management education (including integration of functions as well as of various environments);

o helping managers to handle complexity and innovation and be responsive to an ever-changing environment;

o new ways of learning from individual and collective experience.

Finally, the Commission recommended that the actual adaptation of the IMI's programmes (concept, context, method, organisation) should be treated as an ongoing evolutionary process, for which the Commission provided broad orientation rather than a blueprint.

9.5 Inter-institutional co-operation in needs assessment

We have shown that institutions differ in the levels of needs-assessment proficiency and in their ability to make full use of existing information on management training and development needs. It is also fair to say that, to an independent management centre or institute, an intimate knowledge of the clients' needs, and the ability to translate this knowledge into new services, provides a competitive advantage over other institutions. It is one of the main reasons why some institutions are highly thought of by the practitioners, and their programmes are overbooked, while others are regarded as less relevant.

Learning about needs assessment practices of the leading institutions enhances the overall level of the management training and education profession. In addition, the small size of faculty, and the limited resources for research and consulting, prevent many institutions from directly undertaking comprehensive needs assessment in all technical areas where they have to run courses. Therefore co-operation among institutions can be of great help. Some useful forms of co-operation are mentioned below.

Co-operation through associations

National, regional and global networks of institutions, established as associations or foundations, can help member institutions assess needs by organising co-operative studies and research projects, and by sharing information and exchange of experience concerning environmental trends, new developments in management technologies, needs assessment methods, or innovative types of organisation development and performance improvement programmes.

In 1978, for example, the AACSB and the EFMD agreed on a joint three-year project to examine important economic and socio-political changes likely to occur in future years, the impact of these changes on management patterns and practices, and implications for management education and development programmes and institutions. The main purpose was to make management educationalists and trainers (both in-company and in external institutions) aware of significant trends, and stimulate thinking on changes to be foreseen in educational and training programmes. The focus was on preparing managers for the 21st century. Therefore a 30-year time-frame (1980-2010) was chosen.

The project organised a number of national and regional meetings on the topics of "The changing expectations of society" and "Management in the XXI century". The final event was a major conference held in Paris in 1980 which undertook to synthesise the conclusions from previous events and discuss the main trends and demands concerning management education and development for the 21st century. No attempt was made to induce delegates to vote on any item, or to ratify or reject a proposition or suggestion. The purpose was "to explore but not to conclude, to analyse but not to prescribe, to survey the terrain but not to assert ownership". Over 1,000 management education and training specialists, as well as practising managers from 35 countries, participated in the project. This provided an international perspective, but with a predominance of North American and Western European experience and perceptions.[8]

Joint training programmes

If two or more institutions agree to design and implement a joint training programme, they can share their know-how and experience in assessing needs. This approach has been used in a number of cases, e.g. in trainers' training courses, programmes on managing new technology or seminars on public policy or public enterprise management. As a rule, institutions are interested in this sort of co-operation if they perceive the advantages of working together in a new area, where one institution by itself would be short of resources and experience for assessing the needs of, and developing and delivering, the programme.

Assistance by more advanced institutions

Many institutions in developing countries enjoy various types of co-operative relationships with a sister institution in more developed countries. Often this relationship is established and financially sponsored by a technical assistance project. This assistance should also help the institutions in learning how to diagnose needs. However, the more advanced partner institution must be cautious not to impose its approach and methodology rather than helping the assisted institution to develop its own approach.

9.6 Training faculty in needs assessment

Given the significance of needs assessment, and the complexity of issues to be covered, the ability to assess the managers' training and development needs belongs to the basic skills of every faculty member. Every individual has to make a contribution and new faculty members need to learn this right from their appointment. This will help them escape the pitfalls of mechanistic transfer of curricula and teaching materials, and make them alert to signals indicative of existing or emerging training needs.

As in other areas, the skill of needs identification and assessment is best acquired by identifying and assessing needs. Therefore, it is useful to involve young faculty members in various exercises and techniques of needs assessment described in this book. In doing this, it may be necessary to overcome certain biases. The most widespread one is a simplistic approach that confines needs assessment to questionnaires and interviews. Indeed, inexperienced institutions often present information from questionnaires and interviews as an exhaustive and objective picture of needs.

Furthermore, faculty members should learn how to keep training and development needs in mind when doing consulting and research. This is best achieved by involving them in in-plant organisational development, performance improvement and action research projects assisting organisational change, and by making sure that research projects looking into wider issues also aim at clarifying training and development needs if possible.

Training courses for trainers should include sessions on conceptual and policy issues of needs assessment, as well as sessions where the main techniques are explained and practised. However, here again needs assessment is best learned if it is focused on particular issues of environmental and organisational change, shown as part of the training cycle rather than a separate activity, and studied in the total context of training, consulting and research.

----

[1] See also M. Kubr (ed.): *Management consulting: A guide to the profession* (Geneva, ILO, second (revised) edition, 1986), Ch. 1.

[2] See S. Friberg: *Designing and delivering effective services to clients: Experience of the Swedish Management Group* (Geneva, ILO, 1986; doc. Man Dev/41).

[3] These questions are discussed in detail in R. Bennett: *Management research: Guide for institutions and professionals* (Geneva, ILO, 1983), and E.E. Lawler et al.: *Doing research that is useful for theory and practice* (San Francisco, Jossey-Bass, 1985).

[4] See also M. Kubr (ed.): *Managing a management development institution* (Geneva, ILO, 1982).

[5] See ibid., Ch. 2 and appendix 1.

[6] See ibid., Ch. 2, p. 81 and Ch. 7, pp. 187-210. The original name of the IMI was CEI *(Centre d'Etudes industrielles)*.

[7] IMI: *Report of the Commission for the year 2000* (Geneva, 1986).

[8] See AACSB and EFMD: *Management for the XXI century* (Boston and The Hague, Kluwer and Nijhoff, 1982).

DIAGNOSING NEEDS IN THE SMALL ENTERPRISE SECTOR

10

A separate chapter on diagnosing training and development needs in the small enterprise sector was included in our book for three reasons:

o   the importance of the sector, and the current emphasis on its promotion in both industrialised and developing countries;

o   the specific characteristics of small-scale entrepreneurs and the owners and managers of small firms, and of the environment within which small enterprises operate;

o   the rapid expansion of enterprise creation and small business development projects and programmes, which calls for more exchange of experience on various approaches to designing training and other assistance.

The chapter starts by looking into training needs assessment related to the selection and development of new entrepreneurs and to small business creation (10.1). This is followed by a review of experiences and problems involved in training the owners and managers of existing small businesses (10.2). Finally, some guide-lines are provided on how to apply the various needs assessment techniques in this sector (10.3).

10.1   Training needs in new enterprise creation

There has been a long but inconclusive debate on whether entrepreneurs are born and create business opportunities, or whether opportunities generate entrepreneurship. However, as Malcolm Harper points out, policy-makers and programme managers need not concern themselves unduly with this debate. Increasingly, training is regarded and used as "one way of releasing and revealing latent entrepreneurial potential to the entrepreneur himself and ... a useful contribution to the supply of opportunities".[1] Indeed, there is little risk that training could inhibit entrepreneurship. What sometimes occurs is that unnecessary training is provided, resources are wasted and the cost of training becomes excessive. For example, extensive training may be provided in order to develop attitudes and skills that are not needed or would be acquired more easily by actually starting and operating a business. Or training is given to individuals or groups whose real chances to succeed in business are minimal. To avoid these pitfalls and maximise the results obtained with limited resources, some sort of selection of potential entrepreneurs and some training needs assessment is usually applied. However, the issues involved in this needs assessment tend to be more complex and controversial than in training for performance improvement in existing organisations, whether large or small.

The following issues have to be faced:

o   Potential entrepreneurs and founders of new small businesses come from various social environments, which may lack business experience and enterprise culture.

o   The persons concerned may have very different individual backgrounds as regards education, practical experience, family circumstances, etc.

o   The standards to be achieved are very difficult to establish since they depend on a number of factors and forces influencing the development of business in the given country environment.

o   In addition, many different views exist on whether and how training can help the potential and new entrepreneur; the different conceptual approaches to training and non-training assistance have considerable influence on all stages of training programme design and delivery.

Selection or training needs assessment?

It is important to understand both the differences and the common points between selecting entrepreneurs and assessing their training needs. In selection, the purpose is to identify those persons who will be accepted for an entrepreneurship or small enterprise development programme (whatever its concept) and those who will be rejected. Selection does not imply that the persons rejected cannot or must not become entrepreneurs. The purpose is not to assign social roles. Selection is a tool of a particular entrepreneurship development programme, reflecting the programme's philosophy and resources. Field research in several Asian countries has revealed that the figures for "valid acceptances" (i.e. individuals who have been rightly selected) are in most cases considerably higher than those for "false rejections" (i.e. individuals who were rejected although they demonstrated subsequently that they should have been accepted).[2]

Training and development needs assessment concerns those persons who will be served by a particular entrepreneurship training or development programme. The purpose is to optimise the design of the programme: its contents, methodology, sequence of topics, the participants' active involvement, and so on. If a standard programme is provided, needs assessment is not repeated each time the programme is offered. If the programme is totally or partially tailor-made, needs assessment is carried out separately for each group and possibly even for each individual participant.

Selection and needs assessment can be effectively combined. We shall see, for example, that interviews, questionnaires and tests are applied both in selection and in determining training and development needs. They can be used simultaneously to collect information for selection, and facts and opinions on training needs to be met by the programme.

It should be noted, however, that formal selection procedures tend to be used only in those developing countries that have opted for special entrepreneurship encouragement and development programmes which can be offered to limited numbers of participants or specific target groups. In other cases, such as training courses or seminars on how to establish a new business, organised in many industrialised countries, the policy tends to be to accept all or most applicants without prior selection.

The basic framework

If it is accepted as a starting premise that training can play a positive role in stimulating and facilitating business creation, a basic conceptual framework will need to be defined within which the trainers will operate at both the programme design and delivery stages. The current practice uses a wide spectrum of training and development programmes for entrepreneurs and enterprise creation, ranging from short briefing seminars on financial and legal aspects to comprehensive programmes lasting one year or more and providing information, project identification and development, counselling, credit and further assistance in addition to training.

As regards the training proper, all programme design starts by asking three basic questions:

(1) What training will help the participant to establish a viable new (small) enterprise?

(2) How will this training be related to other factors, forces and instruments that either inhibit or stimulate enterprise creation and growth?

(3) What type and amount of training will adequately reflect the purpose and set-up of the given entrepreneurship development programme (i.e. its size, economic and social objectives, target groups, resources available to the individuals and to the programme, time horizon, and so on)?

The first question helps to direct work concerning programme content, methodology and sequencing. Observers of small enterprise creation processes in various countries tend to agree that the training needs are to be sought in the following areas:

o   technical and technological (the object of the business, i.e. specific product or service, and the technology involved in its design, production, delivery, servicing and maintenance);

o   knowledge and skills needed for establishing a business (business idea and its feasibility, potential market, sources of information, sources of finance, sources of technical assistance, legal and fiscal aspects, assembling the various resources required, business plan, etc.);

o   small enterprise management (knowledge and skills needed once the new business starts operating);

o   attitudinal and behavioural (attitudes and behavioural skills exhibited by individuals who have been successful in establishing and running a business).

The second question helps keep the unity and relationship of training and non-training needs in mind, and helps reflect it in programme design. For example, training in financing a new enterprise will be related to existing local habits, traditions and practices concerning personal and family savings, methods of formal and informal credit and financial assistance, loan guarantees, the traditional forms of individual, family and community ownership and income, and profit-sharing, debt repayment, and so on. If appropriate, training will be used to explain what social habits and practices will need to be changed, or what modern business practices will be best suited to the habits and traditions that persist in the given community.

The third question helps to keep training needs assessment in line with the overall set-up and other elements of the given programme. For example, if the aim of the programme is socio-political, such as increasing the role of particular ethnic or social groups in the economy of the country, this will be reflected not only in the selection of participants, but also in criteria used for allocating resources, deciding on the scope and depth of needs assessment, and evaluating the programme's cost-effectiveness. Different social groups tend to have different training needs as regards business creation. These target groups may be known in advance (when the whole programme is intended for a particular group, such as graduates of faculties of engineering or returning migrant workers), or the definition of target groups may be one of the outcomes of needs assessment (when the original group is mixed and heterogeneous, but needs assessment finds out that the group can be divided into subgroups with substantially different needs, and recommends their being treated separately). In any event, a key aim of training will be to make good use of the financial, infrastructural and technical facilities that can be mobilised by the given programme.

Training needs and the business creation process

Some training programmes for new business creation have taken a maximalistic but static approach. The programme aims to impart the maximum possible knowledge and skills before the business (enterprise) creation process starts. As a result, the amount of knowledge provided exceeds the knowledge actually needed and the instruction remains essentially theoretical. Motivation and reinforcement through practical applications are missing. In contrast, the programme graduates will inevitably encounter numerous problems which were ignored in a generalised course.

To avoid these pitfalls, Allan Gibb and other practitioners of entrepreneurship development suggest that "the key to the answer to the design issue is understanding of the process which is being assisted by the training or counselling effort ... Training is thus related to learning needs as and when they occur during the start-up process".[3] Different needs arise at each stage of the process, as summarised in figure 10.1. This approach makes it possible to discriminate effectively between common training needs of all programme participants, which can be met through courses, workshops, group discussions and briefing sessions before and during the programme, and individual needs, which can be met successively in many different ways (courses, reading, counselling, discussion with another entrepreneur, action learning, etc.) at the appropriate points of the enterprise creation cycle. Training can be paced to fit individual learning needs and the pace of learning which a participant is able to follow. Furthermore, training can be better focused not only on the profile of a particular individual, but simultaneously on needs related to his or her specific business idea and project. Flexibility and motivation for learning can be enhanced quite considerably.

However, before adopting this pattern of tailor-made and action-oriented training, it is necessary to ascertain its feasibility from the viewpoint of time, cost, and the competence and flexibility requirements of trainers and counsellors. Generally speaking, the trainers' experience and competence is a very important factor affecting the design of a training and assistance programme. In many cases it will be a limiting factor: a programme that is too demanding on methodology, and on the trainers' time and experience, will have to be simplified to be realistic.

Linking training needs assessment with the business creation and growth process increases the efficiency of training. In one particular case, an ILO design of a business creation programme assumes that out of 100 potential entrepreneurs involved in the first programme module focused on general information and creating awareness and interest, 10 entrepreneurs will actually pass through all programme modules, receive more extensive training and create enterprises. Thus not only will consulting and training focus increasingly on the partipants' specific needs, but the more time-consuming and costly

Figure 10.1. Key tasks and learning needs at each stage of development of the new business

Key tasks	Key learning and development needs

Stage 1: From idea and motivation acquisition to raw idea

● find an idea	● the process of idea generation and evaluation
● generate an idea	● knowledge of source of ideas
● explore personal capability and motivation for self-employment	● understanding of the ways in which existing personal skills/knowledge might be used in self-employment
	● understanding of what self-employment means
	● personal insight into self-employment
	● positive role image/exploration/feedback
	● self-evaluation

Stage 2: From raw idea to valid idea

● clarify idea	● what constitutes a valid idea
● clarify what needs it meets	● understanding the process of making/doing it
● make it	● technical skill to make or do it
● see it work	● customer needs analysis
● see it work in operating conditions	● customer identification
● ensure it can be done to satisfactory quality	● who else does or makes it
● explore customer acceptability — enough customers at the price	● idea protection
● explore legality	● pricing and rough costing
● ensure entry into business (no insurmountable barriers)	● ways of getting into a market
● identify and learn from competition	● quality standards
	● competition analysis

Stage 3: From valid idea to scale of operation and resource identification

● identify market as number, location, type of customers	● market research
● clarify how market will be reached (promotional)	● marketing mix (promotion, etc.)
● identify minimum desirable scale to "make a living"	● pricing
● identify physical resource requirements at that scale	● production-forecasting and process-planning to set standards for utilisation, efficiency, etc.
● estimate additional physical resource requirements	● distribution systems
● estimate financial requirements	● materials — estimating and wastage
● identify any additional finance needed	● estimating labour, material, capital requirements
	● profit/loss and cash-flow forecasting

Stage 4: From "scale" to business plan and negotiation

● develop business plan and proposal	● business plan development
● negotiate with customers, labour, suppliers of materials, premises, capital suppliers, land, etc., to ensure orders and physical supply capability	● negotiation and presentation skills
● negotiate with banks and financiers for resources	● knowledge of suppliers of land, etc.
	● contracts and forms of agreement
	● knowledge of different ways of paying
	● understanding bankers, and other sources of finance
	● understanding forms of assistance available

Stage 5: From negotiation to birth

● complete all legal requirements for business incorporation	● business incorporation
● meet all statutory requirements to set up basic business systems	● statutory obligations (tax, legal)
	● business production, marketing, financial systems and control
	● what advisers can do
	● understanding how to manage people

Stage 6: From birth to survival

● consolidate business systems for processing	● management control systems
● ensure adequate financial control (debtors, creditors, bank, etc.)	● cash planning
● develop market, attract and retain customers	● debtor/creditor control
● meet all legal obligations	● marketing
● monitor and anticipate change	● selling skills
● maintain good relations with banks, customers, suppliers and all environment contacts	● environmental scanning and market research
● provide effective leadership development for staff	● leadership skills
	● delegation, time planning

Source: A. Gibb: "Stimulating new business development", in Technonet Asia: *Making small enterprises more competitive through more innovative entrepreneurship development programmes* (Singapore, 1987), p. 62.

training will be offered to a reduced number of participants. Different programmes achieve different ratios, but the share of those who actually create businesses tends to be between 7-15 per cent of those who expressed interest.

Motivation and behavioural training needs

Many programmes of assistance to new small-scale entrepreneurs are based on the theory that achievement in business is influenced by the individual's motivation which in turn can be not only tested (and the results of tests used in selection), but enhanced by specially designed training exercises. The best-known and most frequently mentioned programme, that of the Indian Entrepreneurship Development Institute in Ahmedabad, starts by intensive achievement motivation training provided in a five-day residential programme, which develops entrepreneurial traits such as the need to achieve, risk taking and initiative. Motivation is intended to help participants to increase their need for achievement, to define their goals realistically and work towards their achievement, and to heighten their self-awareness.[4]

Achievement motivation training is usually provided as a standard training package, in some cases with minor adaptations to the local culture. It is based on the original research and experimental work of David McClelland and his collaborators.

Some entrepreneurship development experts consider such generalised use of a standard achievement motivation package as unnecessary in many cases, pointing to the existence of alternative techniques, and to the fact that appropriate entrepreneurial behaviour can be better learned by practising it in direct contact with other entrepreneurs, business partners, community leaders and potential clients. It would seem that growing emphasis is being placed on the direct development of the behavioural skills of emerging entrepreneurs rather than on trying to change their motivation or other personality traits in the hope that this will bring about a change in behaviour.[5] This has led to recommendations to enhance elements of training and development programmes which develop competencies in negotiating, gaining confidence, gathering information, selling, advertising, requesting advice, presenting new business ideas, explaining the need for change within the community, and so on.

However, there is also the pragmatic view that although the need for standard achievement motivation training has not been established in every single case, the training packages are available, the experience with their use is positive, and the cost of using them is moderate. Ken Loucks points out that "little is to be gained by excluding achievement motivation training from entrepreneur development programmes".[6]

10.2 Training needs of owners and managers in existing small businesses

Training and development needs of owners and managers of existing small businesses are normally examined in every small enterprise development programme or project. This is justified by the findings of many surveys and programmes that better training can help small business practitioners to overcome many problems faced by their firms and make these firms more viable and profitable. After all, it would be of little use to select and train new entrepreneurs if existing small enterprises remained vulnerable and their failure rate high.

However, the approach taken will be affected by the specific characteristics of this target population. In particular:

o   Many owners and managers will be unaware of possibilities offered by training and will not know what to ask for.

o   A rapport will have to be established and confidence gained first, so that the client does not mistake training needs assessment for an attempt to elicit information that he or she does not want to reveal.

o   Training may not be the best point of entry in an effort to upgrade existing small businesses and increase their viability and performance; the analyst will have to consider at what point and in what way to start talking about training issues and needs.

o   The hand-to-mouth financial existence of the enterprise and the intensive occupation of the manager with ongoing operational problems make it difficult to think of the future of the business and of training that may require time and absence from the business.

o   In some cases training is considered as a remedy when it is too late or when the adverse policy environment and business climate condemns any training effort to failure.

o   A small business may pursue different objectives and use different criteria from a larger firm in making basic financial and commercial decisions and allocating resources (for example, cash flow will be very important, but the notions of cost and profit may be less important in certain situations, or capital budgeting decisions may be affected more by family considerations than by conventional criteria of business strategy and efficiency).

o   Training and needs assessment techniques applied in larger businesses and sophisticated management institutions are often not suited for use in small businesses, but many techniques can be simplified and adapted to this sector.[7]

Self-diagnosis

An ideal situation is encountered if the owner or manager of a small business asks for training and has an idea of what he or she wants, which probably will be based on some sort of self-diagnosis. This happens in some business communities whose members have become aware of the benefits to be drawn from well-chosen training programmes. It may be that certain programmes (e.g. on how to improve marketing or how to use computers in small businesses) are even overbooked, thus demonstrating what the small business people regard as their priority needs. Although many of these programmes are not free, the applicants do not hesitate to pay. However, this situation is not common among small businesses in industrialised countries, and even less so in developing countries.

Self-assessment can be encouraged in various ways (for example, at meetings, through trade associations' publications, or through public information media, such as television programmes on successful entrepreneurs who have made good use of training). If a small-scale entrepreneur decides to look into training needs but is uncertain about making a correct assessment, assistance could be offered by a trade association, or a training and advisory centre – on condition that the person asks for it and does not feel that someone else is going to take control. It is useful to provide small business managers with information that permits comparison – for example, with data on performance of comparable businesses operating in other countries or communities.

Another approach to assisting self-diagnosis is provided by various workbooks and checklists. There is a wide range of them. The underlying idea is that by following the suggested routine step by step, filling in the information asked for, and giving thought to a range of logically connected issues, the small-enterprise owner or manager will become aware of problems and needs ignored hitherto. Or the difficulties encountered in trying to answer certain questions will show that there are gaps in his or her knowledge and experience.

For example, the ILO programme *Improve your business* provides a workbook which guides the owner or manager through sets of questions covering all key aspects of a small business. In addition, there are simple exercises simulating business practice. A small-scale entrepreneur can attempt to answer the questions and do the exercises alone, or with assistance from a trainer. He or she can then turn to the handbook provided in the same package, ask for explanations, apply for a course or consider another form of training and advice.[8]

Assisting small businesses by identifying training needs

In the practice of most small business development programmes and projects, the clients' training needs are assessed by trainers, counsellors, extension officers or other "helpers" responsible for defining and delivering the training component of the programme. This implies that there is a third person, or team, assessing training needs, and business owners and managers whose needs are being assessed. This relationship and the problems involved were described in chapter 1.

The objective is not only to establish the training needs more or less correctly, but to make the client aware of them and of the practical benefits to be obtained from training and self-development. If this can be achieved, the client will become more interested in carrying out the needs assessment properly and objectively. This calls for the client's active participation even when he or she knows little about training and about the programmes and facilities that are available. From a strictly technical viewpoint the results of this participation may be modest, but there will be an important psychological benefit: curiosity will have been awakened and a sense of "ownership" of the needs will have been created.

An adviser on small businesses may work with the client on a certain business problem that has "a training dimension". In other words, it may be useful, or even necessary, to do some training to solve the problem and achieve better business results. The context provides an excellent opportunity for defining very specific individual training needs and selecting the most adequate way of coping with them. In defining training needs the adviser will be able to choose from among the different approaches and techniques (see section 10.3).

There will be problems, however. Some small business advisers may have received only elementary training in intervention and training methodology and may miss this opportunity. Or even if the need is properly defined, the relevant training infrastructure and materials may not be available or easily accessible. Finally, the approach is time-consuming and costly and the advisory and extension services can seldom cover more than 5-10 per cent of potential clients who could benefit from their help.

A feasible alternative has been sought (but not always found) in group techniques, some of which will also be described in the next section. Their advantage lies not only in reduced cost per client but in interaction among the owners and managers of small businesses, who can help each other to define training needs, provided a competitive relationship does not prevent them from open discussion and collaboration. However, group approaches to small business counselling and problem-solving are not sufficiently widespread, and experience with their effective use is still limited.

Sector surveys

Finally, there are sector surveys of training needs undertaken for the purpose of planning and designing courses and seminars, preparing training materials and dealing with other policy and operational issues of training in the sector. General characteristics and methodological problems of sector surveys were reviewed in detail in chapter 8. As regards the small business sector, the following specific comments can be offered:

o   Effective targeting is essential. This is because the training needs of various groups and subsectors tend to be very different and a general survey will produce only general conclusions. Examples of target groups are: urban or rural enterprises; women entrepreneurs; industry subsectors (e.g. woodworking, car maintenance and repair, shoemaking); export-oriented artistic handicrafts. Each survey will have to determine its particular target or client groups.

o   The clients' participation is equally essential for reasons already explained. Even if the study cannot be totally individualised owing to the size of the target population and cost considerations, a convenient way of associating selected individuals and recognised representatives of the client groups can be found.

o   In developing the sector it may be difficult and even inappropriate to study the training needs separately from the non-training needs. Most surveys try therefore to identify sectoral problems and development prospects and needs, and treat training issues within this broader framework, keeping in mind the relationships between training and changes in the policy environment, creating better technical, information and advisory services, improving access to credit, and so on.

o   Also, in many surveys it has been found more appropriate not to separate the study of management training and development needs from the study of technical training needs for improved product design and quality, the use of more effective technologies, equipment and materials, improved maintenance, energy savings, and so on. Here too, the reasons are both technical (technical training needs may be as important as, or more important than, management training needs, and changes in technology will create new management training needs) and psychological (many clients will perceive management training needs more easily if they have become aware of technical problems in their small businesses).

10.3   How to use needs assessment techniques

In planning for needs assessment, a small business trainer or adviser will be able to choose from the wide portfolio of techniques presented in part II of this book. However, it will be useful to keep in mind the specific characteristics of small-scale entrepreneurs, the nature of the new business creation process and the particular socio-cultural environment.

Environmental analysis

Environmental analysis, or future trends and opportunities analysis (see also section 6.2), is a basic component of any assessment of training needs in the small enterprise sector. Its purpose is to relate training to the actual constraints and opportunities that characterise a particular business environment. If a standard training package is used, environmental analysis helps to adapt it to local needs.

The issues covered include:

o   political climate as regards private enterprise and business creation;

o   established ways of doing business;

o   cultural values and traditions related to business and entrepreneurship;

o   existing and potential markets (including competition) and forecast of demand;

o   resources that are available or can be mobilised;

o   infrastructure and technical services;

o   availability and forms of credit;

o   information, training and advisory services;

o   legislation.

Training will have to take these issues into consideration both at the stage of new enterprise creation and in strengthening existing small businesses. A proper time perspective is important: the analysis not only has to identify the factors and forces that operate in the current period, but should also aim to reveal or predict future developments.

Assessment of the entrepreneurs' personal history and background

This assessment reveals a great deal of information on probable training needs. It can be retrieved from various information sources and records on the persons concerned, through questionnaires, by interviewing the individuals and by collecting information from other persons who have had business and social contacts with them. For example, an ILO project which assists refugees in setting up small businesses in Kenya, examines the personal history of every applicant as completely as possible in order to estimate the chances of success, make proper selection and identify in what way to assist each candidate accepted.

The main issues to be covered include:

o   family and ethnic background (with focus on business experience and value system);

o   previous education and training;

- o   personal experience (trade, handicrafts, skilled worker in industry, migrant worker, civil service, liberation movement, army, etc.);

- o   social activities and connections (knows other business people, knows many people in the community, is active in social, religious, sporting or other organisations);

- o   interests, inclinations and hobbies.

Records and reports analysis

As compared with larger businesses, the study of records and reports for the purpose of training needs assessment (see section 6.1) is more difficult to apply in dealing with small businesses. It is a well-known fact that the quality of accounting and other records kept by small businesses is often less than desirable, and there may be no usable records whatsoever. This very fact is quoted by some analysts of the small business scene as obvious evidence of training needs: the owner or manager ought to be trained to become aware of the importance of good records and to learn the basics of bookkeeping and record keeping. Such a conclusion, however, should not be made hastily. There is little point in keeping records for their own sake, or suggesting complex records if simple ones suffice. Thus, the need for training in better record keeping can be considered as real when it can be established what records are actually necessary for improving the performance and viability of the business.

Observing

Observing (see section 4.5) is a very useful technique that is insufficiently used in the small enterprise sector. Observing successful entrepreneurs helps to identify skills and behavioural patterns that bring about good business results in a given environment. The findings can be used in training in numerous ways: in choosing subjects to be covered and training techniques, in case studies based on role models of selected entrepreneurs and managers of small businesses, or by inviting successful practitioners to meetings and workshops with the trainees.

Observing at work the individuals who are clients or potential clients of an assistance programme reveals behavioural problems and knowledge and skill gaps, including gaps that were not bridged by training and where further help is required. This observing is normally combined with counselling.

Counselling

Counselling includes a dialogue between the small business adviser, consultant, extension officer or counsellor and the client. During this dialogue, the adviser aims to develop an unbiased opinion of the health and prospects of the client's business. He or she can then provide a solution to the client's problem, suggest a feasible way of implementing it, indicate sources of information and training, assist a client who appears to be able to find his own solution, and so on. Encouraging clients to develop and justify their own approaches can be of immediate help in improving their skills, and also in identifying training needs. The adviser can consider whether to deal with the needs thus uncovered individually, which may be most desirable from the client's viewpoint, but time-consuming and costly. An alternative can be found in organising group seminars involving several entrepreneurs, or indicating standard courses which can provide answers.

Generalised feedback from counselling services helps to identify practical problems most frequently encountered by new and existing small businesses, as well as the most common gaps in knowledge and skill.

Group approaches

As mentioned, group approaches have not been sufficiently explored in the small business sector, and experience with their use is limited. However, the following four examples may be of interest.

The first case concerns *action learning* (see also section 4.9 describing action learning used as an individual technique). In action learning, needs assessment is directly coupled with problem identification and with individual or collective work on finding and implementing a practical solution to the problem. Our example shows how the technique can be applied by groups of small-scale entrepreneurs.

Owners of small enterprises in four countries in the Central American region (Costa Rica, Honduras, Guatemala and Panama) participated in an ILO/Federal Republic of Germany technical co-operation project built on the action-learning approach. Small groups of entrepreneurs (10-15 in one group) are organised and an effort is made to include individuals whose enterprises (namely very small ones) face similar practical problems, and who have compatible (technical and business) backgrounds and personalities. The approach has been applied with small-scale entrepreneurs in both urban and rural areas.

Every participant presents one or more practical problems to the group (this can be to do with management, infrastructure and resources, labour, a product or technology, etc.). After a final discussion, the group determines those problems which are of interest to most participants and should be examined collectively. The problems selected are analysed in greater depth by the whole group or its subgroups. Then the group comes up with one or more possible solutions. The groups would meet once a week for 3-4 hours and would continue for some 12-16 seminars. However, some groups decide to pursue their exchange of experience in a less structured and more informal way.

The assessment of training needs is integrated with the collective processes of problem identification, analysis and resolution. Training can even be indicated and dealt with as a problem. However, even in dealing with other problems, the very group process of problem identification, screening and solving is simultaneously a process of identification of training and learning needs. All participants in the group share the roles of "training needs analysts" and also of training resource persons by contributing the relevant experience that is of interest to others. If the group's own knowledge and experience is not enough, the group defines information and training requirements that are met by the group facilitator or another external expert, case by case, dealing with issues that will help the group to proceed with its work (e.g. with issues concerning credit facilities, production costs calculation or labour legislation). This training need may be perceived as collective or individual. Individual needs would be covered by individually arranged consultations.

The urban entrepreneurs identified various management areas in which their technical knowledge was deficient (and for which appropriate training was organised), and formed working groups to address other problems such as quality of raw materials. The farmers identified problems of soil diseases and insect pests and made contact with the appropriate phyto-sanitary and public health agencies (positive results are already being obtained). They also discovered gaps in their knowledge of planting and cultivation techniques, for which appropriate training is now in progress. Various community-level problems were identified and collectively resolved, particularly those to do with medical services and road communications. More important, if less visible, than achievements such as roads or bridges built, is the fact that the people in these communities now realise that through their own efforts they can bring about significant improvements in their circumstances, and know how to define their needs and mobilise collective efforts.

The second group technique is *inter-firm comparison* (see also section 6.3). It is a procedure whereby key performance figures for a group of enterprises engaged in similar (comparable) activities are presented in a way that allows any one enterprise to compare its own performance with other enterprises in the group, and with group averages. Such a group can be organised within a trade association or employers' organisation, by a small enterprise development agency or centre, or the like. The members of the group can compare performance figures individually or in group seminars. Differences in performance indicators (ratios) are analysed, causes identified and suitable remedies, including training, considered. For example, in a small transport enterprise, higher costs of fuel, lubricating oil and tyres per 100 km may point to training needs of drivers, maintenance staff and the owner/manager. However, the process of inter-firm comparison constitutes in itself a self-development exercise, in which the participants' learning needs are identified and met, although the term "training needs" may not even be pronounced.[9]

The third group technique is *the business clinic*. It is an arrangement whereby a group of small enterprise owners/managers meets to get advice and exchange experience on how to deal with the same or similar problems faced by all of them. It can be a one-off exercise (e.g. a one-day session) or a set of 4-8 meetings similar to those run in action learning. A business clinic can be combined with inter-firm comparison when the members of the group decide to collaborate in order to find solutions to their business performance problems.[10] In other cases, a business clinic can be arranged to deal collectively with problems previously identified by small business advisers or chosen by the small business owners themselves (how to identify product costs, how to control and reduce energy consumption, etc.).

The fourth group approach became known as *the solidarity group*.[11] It has been used in technical assistance programmes in several Latin American countries. This approach uses self-selected solidarity groups of 5-8 micro-entrepreneurs as the centre of all programme activity. Credit and training are the two major components of the programme.

The solidarity group is eligible to receive small-scale credit (primarily for working capital) for each member's needs. The programme disburses one loan to each group, this loan then being divided among the members. No collateral is required. The group is responsible for collecting the payment on time, with members acting as guarantors for each other. When the loan is repaid, the group becomes eligible for a second, larger loan.

Training is provided in short sessions (3-6 hours per month) to small groups of 15-25 individuals coming from several solidarity groups. It addresses personal and group development needs in two areas defined to be of priority to all groups: economic and social. Economic modules relate to enterprise production and focus on buying and selling, managing credit and record keeping. Social modules focus on co-operation and solidarity, leadership, commitment to the programme, communication and public relations, and the identification and understanding of individual and common needs.

The common training modules have developed gradually, on the basis of experience with the solidarity group approach. In some programmes, the supporting institutions provide training in selected areas specifically requested by the beneficiaries, even if these areas do not relate to micro-enterprise activity in certain cases. Individual training needs in micro-enterprise development and management, which are not met by the standard modules, can be met in one-to-one technical (counselling) sessions. In addition, group discussions help the groups to share experience in areas where individual members have different training and development needs.

Interviewing

Interviewing (see also section 4.4 and chapter 8) is probably the most popular technique used for identifying training needs in the small enterprise sector. It is practised in many ways, ranging from brief informal conversations to systematic application of structured interviews in sectoral surveys and in screening applicants to entrepreneurship development programmes.

It is quite common to interview individuals who are regarded as experts knowledgeable about the small business environment, traditions, problems and development prospects in a particular community. These may be officers of employers' organisations and chambers of commerce and industry, central and local government officials, bank managers and credit officers, lawyers, accountants, university teachers and researchers, community leaders and other personalities likely to provide information on "how things are normally done" and "what can and needs to be changed" in the community, and what chances an envisaged approach to small business promotion may have. This interviewing is of the sort that was described as "using expert opinion" (section 3.3).

When interviewing existing or would-be small-scale entrepreneurs, it is useful to keep in mind that informal and "indirect" interviewing, combined with providing immediate advice and help, tends to produce better results than lengthy and highly structured interviews organised as a separate exercise. It is important for people running small businesses to understand the purpose and implications of the interview and to be assured that they have no reason to be suspicious about the use of information provided to the interviewer. This can be achieved, for example, by asking appropriate questions that can reveal training needs while discussing a new business idea or credit application.

The profile and attitude of the interviewer have a considerable impact on the course and outcome of interviewing. Small-scale entrepreneurs are pragmatic people and realise that the interviewer may not be the most experienced business consultant – the services of such a person would be far too expensive for most small enterprise development programmes. They will co-operate and share information even with a less experienced interviewer if the latter exhibits frankness and genuine interest in being helpful to the client. However, their common sense and life experience help them quickly to recognise an interviewer whose knowledge of business is bookish and interest merely academic.

Questionnaires

An obvious factor in deciding whether and how to use a questionnaire (see section 4.3) requiring written answers (even a closed-ended one with "yes/no" responses) is the literacy level and language proficiency of the target group surveyed and the particular individuals. When this is ignored, the answers tend to be affected more by the person's reading and writing proficiency and knowledge of vocabulary than by actual business knowledge and experience.

Generally speaking, written questionnaires on training needs appear to be the least effective and least suitable technique in the small enterprise sector. There are, perhaps, certain exceptions. For example, specially designed questionnaires are frequently used in entrepreneurship development and business creation programmes.

The usual approach is as follows. At some point of the business creation cycle, as a rule after having expressed interest, attended an introductory briefing session and undergone a short interview, the participant is asked to fill in a fairly comprehensive questionnaire (application form) intended to throw light on his or her personality, background motives, general intentions, specific ideas, capabilities, resources and chances of succeeding. In addition, the individual is asked if he or she had to call on another person's help in preparing the answers. As mentioned above (section 10.1), the primary purpose of such a questionnaire may not be the identification of training needs. Nevertheless, careful analysis by an experienced small business adviser will provide a great amount of information on the sort of training needed by the applicant.[12]

Psychological and other tests

The use of tests (see also section 4.2) in selecting entrepreneurs has become quite popular and certain tests, particularly some achievement motivation tests, tend to be regarded as "classic" instruments for making better selection. As mentioned above, selection and needs assessment can be combined and this is what has been done in some programmes. A particular test may even be used for the triple purpose of:

o   participant selection;

o   identifying training needs;

o   training.

For example, in the "ring-toss game" participants toss a certain number of rings into a target object (rod) from a distance they choose freely. The smaller the distance, the smaller the risk of missing the target. However, the reward (points) gained without taking any risk is very small. And vice versa. This exercise has been used in selection to identify two characteristics of people with high achievement motivation, namely taking calculated risks and using feedback to improve performance. The exercise can also indicate the training needs of participants who take too much risk by choosing a unrealistically large distance, or no risk by choosing a small distance despite the minimal reward. If used as a training exercise, the ring-toss game includes feedback sessions and discussions on the distance chosen, and changing the distance until each participant finds the distance at which he or she feels comfortable and achieves optimal results.[13]

If paper-and-pencil tests are used, the comments made in the previous paragraphs on the influence of literacy levels ought to be kept in mind. In tests where people can choose among several answers, there may be a tendency to choose those answers that are likely to show the person in a positive light. For example, if asked how they would react to a particular event, candidates may try to choose an answer that, in their opinion, will please the evaluator, and not one showing how they would actually act. Also, some tests may meet resistance in certain cultural environments and may therefore be quite inappropriate.

Generally speaking, tests, in particular psychological and behavioural tests, ought to be chosen and used cautiously. Their design, selection and adaptation require professional background and experience in behavioural sciences, and even if the tests are adapted for being administered by trainers with other backgrounds, these trainers need to be thoroughly briefed and the actual use of the tests carefully monitored. The value of the results of tests must not be overestimated. As Malcolm Harper points out, "tests based on behavioural science research have some validity, but can easily be misapplied when the user has not been properly trained, and more subjective indicators are more subject to cheating and personal prejudice. Since the subject of analysis, namely human personality, is essentially unquantifiable and unpredictable, it is unlikely that a perfect test will ever be developed".[14]

---

[1] M. Harper: *Selection and training for entrepreneurship development* (Geneva, ILO, 1983; technical paper SED/8/E), p. 9.

[2] See conclusions from the VASE (Validation of selection schemes for entrepreneurial development in Asia) study reported in Technonet Asia: *Selecting entrepreneurs: Is it worthwhile?* (Singapore, no date).

[3] A. Gibb: "Stimulating new business development", in Technonet Asia: *Making small enterprises more competitive through more innovative entrepreneurship development programmes* (Singapore, 1987), p.62.

[4] See V.G. Patel: "Developing indigenous entrepreneurship: The Gujarat model", in P. Neck and R. Nelson (eds.): *Small enterprise development: Policies and programmes* (Geneva, ILO, second (revised) ed., 1987), pp. 107-123.

[5] Cf. Gibb, op.cit., p.67. See also W. Fonviella: "Behaviour vs. attitude: Which comes first in organisational change?", in *Management Review* (New York, American Management Association), Aug. 1984, p.14.

[6] K. Loucks: *Training entrepreneurs for small business creation: Lessons from experience* (Geneva, ILO, 1988), p.68.

[7] See also Ch. 17, "Consulting in small enterprise management", in M. Kubr (ed.): *Management consulting: A guide to the profession* (Geneva, ILO, second (revised) edition, 1986).

[8] See D. Dickson (ed.): *Improve your business*, Workbook and Handbook (Geneva, ILO, 1986).

[9] For a detailed description and examples see C. Guthrie: *Interfirm comparison for improving performance: How employers' organisations can help the business community* (Geneva, ILO, 1986; technical paper SED/12/E).

[10] ibid., p.25.

[11] See M. Otero: *The solidarity group concept: Its characteristics and significance for urban informal sector activities* (New York, PACT, 1986).

---

[12] On request, the ILO Management Development Branch can provide examples of questionnaires used in various programmes. Examples can also be found in Technonet Asia: *Achievement motivation training: Trainer's guide and handbook of exercises* (Singapore, 1984).

[13] The use of various tests and exercises is described in Technonet Asia: *Achievement motivation training*, op. cit.

[14] Harper, op. cit., pp. 7-8.

APPENDICES

RATING TECHNIQUES

There are two general classes of rating techniques used in needs assessment, as shown in figure 1: comparative and absolute.

Figure 1. Rating techniques

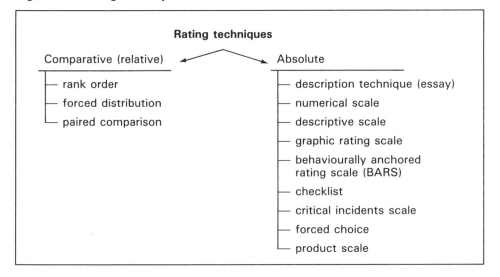

1. Comparative rating techniques

Comparative (or relative) techniques are used to compare the performance of two or more managers with one another.

Rank order

The rank order (or ranking) technique involves the comparison of each member within a group, for example, from the highest to the lowest. This ranking can be improved by alternative ranking, when evaluators choose the top and bottom employees first, then select the next highest and next lowest, and move towards the middle (figure 2).

Figure 2. Example of a ranking record

Manager		Rank
Albert	▲	1 - Highest
Bob		2 - Next highest
Carl		3 - Next highest
Dan		4 - Next highest
Frances		5 - Next highest
Phil		6 - Next highest
Fred		6 - Next lowest
Mary		5 - Next lowest
John		4 - Next lowest
Walter		3 - Next lowest
George		2 - Next lowest
Rose	▼	1 - Lowest

However, there are limitations in this method as it is difficult to define the magnitude of differences between group members and rank the members of a large group. Also, ranking within one group cannot be meaningfully compared with that of another group.

Forced distribution

Forced distribution begins by setting up categories from poor to good with the restriction that only a certain percentage of the managers concerned can be assigned to each category. This forces the rater to distribute the managers according to a pre-scaled scheme (or curve). An example (figure 3.) shows the results of forced-distribution evaluation of 18 managers by job performance.

A variation of the forced-distribution technique is the so-called equal-interval technique, which assumes that managers with similar abilities or traits can be placed in the same group. However, qualitative intervals or gaps between each nearest group (as determined by expert assessment) should be equal.

The point-allocation technique (PAT) is another alternative of forced distribution. Here each rater is given a number of points per manager in a group, and the total points for all managers actually rated must not exceed the number of points allocated to the rater. The points are allocated according to a criterion (e.g. planning, decision-making authority).

Forced distribution helps to avoid inflated rating and a central tendency in the graphic rating scale. A disadvantage of this technique is that it assumes

Figure 3. Forced-distribution evaluation

High 10%	Next 20%	Middle 40%	Next 20%	Low 10%
Moore	Lanyon	Coggins	Willis	Allison
Little	Feltman	Holmes	Salter	Gruber
	Dorsey	Jimenex	Booth	
	Dyer	Amendale	Smith	
		Gaillard		
		Harrington		

either normal or at least a comparable distribution of proficiency or performance in each rating group.

Paired comparison

Paired comparison makes the ranking easier and more reliable. Each manager is compared with all other managers in the group and an explicit judgement is made as to who is a better performer according to a certain criterion. For example, six managers are to be rated on leadership. Their names are placed on a matrix as shown in figure 4.

The analyst begins by comparing Moore and Feltman on leadership ability. He decides that Feltman is a better leader than Moore, so he places a plus sign in Feltman's column next to Moore's name. Then the analyst goes on to compare Moore and Smith, Moore and Gruber, and so on. The process is continued until all comparisons have been made, and all blocks of the matrix have been filled in. The person with the highest number of pluses (Gruber) ranks first.

One of the advantages of paired comparison is that it reduces the influence of personal biases in subjective judgements, thus increasing objectivity, reliability, and validity. In addition, this rating can be easily computerised.

In summary, the main advantages of all comparative rating techniques are simplicity and clarity. The main limitations are the following:

o these techniques permit rank ordering of individuals without indicating the exact degree of difference between them;

Figure 4. Paired-comparison matrix

	Managers rated					
Compared with	Moore	Feltman	Smith	Gruber	Wallas	Allison
Moore		+	+	+	+	–
Feltman	–		+	+	–	–
Smith	–	–		+	–	–
Gruber	–	–	–		–	–
Wallas	–	+	+	+		–
Allison	+	+	+	+	+	
Total	1	3	4	5	2	0

o   the managers are usually compared only in terms of a single criterion or overall impressionistic assessment;

o   it is difficult to rate larger numbers of managers (more than ten at a time).

2. Absolute rating techniques

These techniques assign absolute values to the characteristics or performance levels on a fixed scale without any reference or comparison to other persons.

Description technique

This technique consists of a description, in writing, of a manager's strengths, weaknesses and potential in the evaluator's own words. Clearly, the rater must be knowledgeable about the manager's performance and an expert in a specific field (or criterion) of evaluation.

The advantage of narrative description is that it can provide detailed specific feedback to managers regarding their performance.

The limitations include the subjectivity of evaluation first of all. In addition, comparison among different managers is impossible. A manager's rating may depend as much on the drafting skills of the evaluator as on the manager's actual performance. For these reasons, it is usually preferable to use quantitative absolute techniques aimed at measuring behavioural aspects (see BARS, below).

Numerical rating

The simplest technique is the numerical one. An odd number of points is usually selected so that the middle number may represent the average. The number of points on the scale depends upon the number of observable differences in performance or competence that are to be rated, and on the ability of the raters to discriminate accurately.

Most people can make at least 5 differentiations. Few evaluators – even highly trained – can use a 9-11 point scale. For this reason most rating scales contain 5-9 points (example A in figure 5.).

Descriptive scale

Descriptive scales are adjectives or phrases to rate levels of ability or performance. For example, planning ability could be rated as shown in example B in figure 5.

Descriptive scales are more versatile than numerical scales because the adjectives or phrases can be varied to suit the situation.

Graphic rating scale

This is one of the oldest quantitative performance-appraisal techniques. It usually contains a number of job performance qualities and characteristics to be evaluated. It also combines the numerical and descriptive scales. For example, a manager's appearance could be rated as shown in example C in figure 5.

The length of the line represents the full range of the ability, performance or trait to be rated. The analyst should consider both the numerical scale and the descriptive phrases. A graphic rating scale normally requires the evaluator to rate managers on each of the characteristics listed in the rating scale. The number of characteristics rated varies from a few to several tens. An example of a graphic rating scale form is given in figure 6. After each description the rater places a check mark in the appropriate box (the manager fits the description).

Among the advantages of this technique are the following:

o   As with questionnaires, the technique may be used with many respondents, with rapid response.

o   The findings lend themselves readily to quantitative analysis.

Figure 5. Examples of absolute rating scales

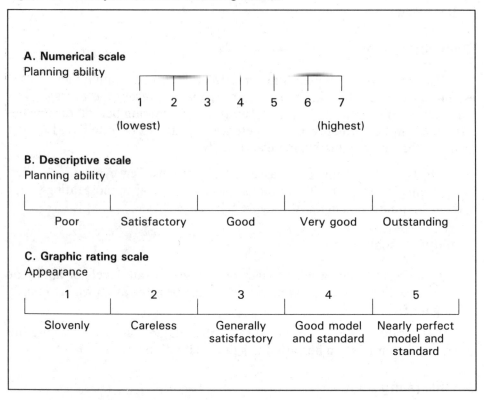

A. Numerical scale
Planning ability

1　2　3　4　5　6　7

(lowest)　　　　　(highest)

B. Descriptive scale
Planning ability

Poor　　Satisfactory　　Good　　Very good　　Outstanding

C. Graphic rating scale
Appearance

1　　　2　　　3　　　4　　　5

Slovenly　Careless　Generally　Good model　Nearly perfect
　　　　　　　　　satisfactory　and standard　model and
　　　　　　　　　　　　　　　　　　　　　standard

o   It is easy to plot scores and feed them back to respondents, or include them in reports.

The limitations of graphic rating scales include:

o   The dependence on a framework or model for designing the items.

o   The danger of falling into the trap of spurious and unjustified statistical analysis.

o   The difficulty of designing a valid and reliable scale.

Behaviourally anchored rating scales

Behaviourally anchored rating scales (BARS), sometimes called "behavioural expectation scales" (BES), are based on the critical incident approach. Here the descriptions of actually good and bad performance, supported by incidents, are grouped into 5 to 10 dimensions. An example of BARS is given in figure 7.

Figure 6.   Example of a typical graphic rating scale

	Out-standing	Good	Satis-factory	Fair	Unsatis-factory
Quantity of work Volume of acceptable work under normal conditions Comments:	☐	☐	☐	☐	☐
Quality of work Thoroughness, neatness and accuracy of work Comments:	☐	☐	☐	☐	☐
Knowledge of job Clear understanding of the facts or factors pertinent to the job Comments:	☐	☐	☐	☐	☐
Personal qualities Personality, appearance, socia- bility, leadership, integrity Comments:	☐	☐	☐	☐	☐
Cooperation Ability and willingness to work with associates, supervisors, and subordinates toward com- mon goals Comments:	☐	☐	☐	☐	☐
Dependability Conscientious, thorough, accu- rate, reliable with respect to attendance, lunch periods, reliefs, etc. Comments:	☐	☐	☐	☐	☐
Initiative Earnestness in seeking increa- sed responsibilities. Self- starting, unafraid to proceed alone? Comments:	☐	☐	☐	☐	☐

Source: W.F. Glueck: *Personnel: A diagnostic approach* (Dallas, Texas, Business Publications, 1978), p. 302.

Figure 7. Example of behaviourally anchored rating scale for a checker (BARS)

Extremely good performance	7 -	By knowing the price of the item, this checker would be expected to look for mismarked and unmarked items
Good performance	6 -	You can expect this checker to be aware of items that constantly fluctuate in price
	-	You can expect this checker to know the various sizes of cans
Slightly good performance	5 -	When in doubt, this checker would ask another checker if the item is taxable
	-	This checker can be expected to verify with another checker a discrepancy between the shelf and the marked price before ringing up that item
Neither poor nor good performance	4 -	When operating the quick check, while the lights are flashing, this checker can be expected to check out a customer with 15 items
Slightly poor performance	3 -	You can expect this checker to ask the customer the price of an item that he does not know
	-	In the daily course of personal relationships, this checker may be expected to linger in long conversations with a customer or another checker
Poor performance	2 -	In order to take a break, this checker can be expected to block off the checkout with people waiting
Extremely poor performance	1 -	This checker is unable to cope with basic requirements of the function

Source: Adapted from Glueck, *op. cit.*, p. 308.

An advantage of BARS is that it concentrates on the behaviour of the manager rather than his personality. It can be very useful for developmental purposes and training needs analysis. However, BARS requires a great amount of time and effort to be designed and properly used.

Checklist

A checklist is a set of adjectives or descriptive statements. It is actually marked on a two-point rating scale – "yes" or "no". The rater marks the item with a tick only when the manager possesses the trait listed. A rating score from the checklist is given by the number of ticks (e.g. six positive checks out of ten possible).

An advanced variation of the checklist is a weighted checklist. This lists various types and levels of skills for a particular job or group of jobs. Weights are assigned to each item by a group of experts based on how significant it is to successful performance. The rater indicates the extent to which each statement describes the manager being evaluated. The marks awarded and their corresponding weights are summed up for each manager. An example is shown in figure 8.

Figure 8. Example of use of weighted checklist of the supervisor Mr. Smith

Skills	Skill level (max. 10) (1)	Importance of particular skills for job (O-1) (2)	Weighted marks (1×2)
Leadership	2.5	0.8	2.00
Communication	3.6	0.7	2.52
Planning	7.1	0.3	2.13
Organisation	6.2	0.7	4.34
Motivating	5.3	0.9	4.77
Controlling	4.8	0.5	2.40

The reliability of checklists is usually quite high because the range of choices is reduced to two. However, only a limited amount of information can thus be obtained since there is no more specific indication of how successful the manager is in performing particular tasks.

Critical incidents scale

This scale is a sort of behaviourally oriented checklist. Critical requirements here include those which have been demonstrated to have made the difference between success and failure in carrying out an important part of the job assigned in a significant number of instances.

The advantages of this technique are that managers rated will receive meaningful feedback and that real incidents are discussed with them.

Product scale

A product scale (or direct index) is used when a product (or other output) is to be rated as an indication of performance, since products are usually tangible and measurable things. The technique focuses attention on the specific accomplishments or results achieved by the manager. With this approach managers are evaluated solely on the basis of the results actually achieved.

For each managerial job, several measures of output or results are identified and combined to form a numerical index. It could be, for example, product output, sales volume, market share, productivity or profit. Such a direct index avoids errors of perception and biases on the part of the ratee. However, changes in the index may not always represent changes in the manager's performance.

Forced choice

Forced choice is a method of rating which uses two to five descriptions of behaviour in each section; both favourable and unfavourable statements may be used in the same section. For example, one of the manager's characteristics could be as shown in figure 9.

Figure 9. Forced-choice technique

Statement	Most characteristic	Least characteristic
1. Reluctant to make decisions	✓	
2. Possesses a strong personality		✓

The rater has to select the statement that is most characteristic and the one that is least characteristic. As a rule, in using this technique sets of four statements, known as tetrads, are so constructed that each one contains two favourable and two unfavourable characteristics. Only one of the favourable statements in each tetrad will yield a point on the report if it is chosen as "most characteristic" of the person rated. Similarly, only one of the unfavourable statements will yield a point if it is selected as "least characteristic". In other words, although the favourable items in each pair appear equally favourable to the rater (and the unfavourable items equally unfavourable), only one item in each pair has been demonstrated to discriminate between good and poor performers. Since the rater reports behaviour without being permitted to judge the quality of the behaviour, reliability is greatly increased. An example of the technique is given in figure 10.

Figure 10. Example of a forced-choice performance report

a.	Always criticises, never praises	M	L
b.	Carries out orders by "passing the buck"	M	L
c.	Knows the job and performs it well	M	L
d.	Has no favorites	M	L
a.	Commands respect by his or her actions	M	L
b.	Cool-headed	M	L
c.	Indifferent	M	L
d.	Overbearing	M	L

Which is most (M) and least (L) characteristic of the manager? Please circle.

Source: L.R. Bittel (ed): *Encyclopedia of professional management* (New York, McGraw-Hill, 1978), p. 50.

3. How to select rating techniques

The effective use of techniques depends not only upon the skills of the evaluator but also on the right choice of technique. Figures 11-13 can assist the practitioner in choosing the right set of rating techniques depending upon the tasks and the dimensions of needs analysis.

Figure 11. Rating techniques: The needs assessment cycle

		Dimension of needs assessment				
Rating technique		Spotting organisational problems (1)	Tracing problem areas and causes (2)	Recognising individual (group) performance problems (3)	Determining management development needs (4)	Separating training from non-training needs (5)
Comparative	Rank order		X	XX	X	
	Forced distribution		X	XX		
	Paired comparisons		X	XX		
Absolute	Essay (description)		X	X		
	Numerical scale		X	XX	XX	X
	Descriptive scale		X	X	XX	X
	Graphic rating scale		X	XX	XX	X
	BARS		X	X	XX	
	Checklist		X	X	XX	XX
	Critical incidents	X	X	XX	XXX	XX
	Product scale	X	X	X	XX	
	Forced choice		X	X	XX	

Key: X - good; XX - very good; XXX - excellent.

Figure 12. Rating techniques: Type of development needs

Rating technique		Dimension of needs assessment			
		Knowledge (1)	Skills (2)	Attitude (3)	Actual behaviour (4)
Comparative	Rank order	X	XX	X	X
	Forced distribution	X	XX	X	X
	Paired comparisons	X	XX	X	X
Absolute	Essay (description)	XX	XX	X	X
	Numerical scale	X	XX	X	XXX
	Descriptive scale	X	X	XX	XXX
	Graphic rating scale	XX	XX	X	X
	BARS	XX	X	XX	XXX
	Checklist	XX	X	X	X
	Critical incidents	X	XX	XX	XX
	Product scale	X	XX	X	X
	Forced choice	X	XX	X	X

Key: X - good; XX - very good; XXX - excellent.

Figure 13. Rating techniques: Cost-effectiveness

Rating technique		Dimension of needs assessment		
		Develop-mental cost (1)	Use cost (2)	How easy to use (3)
Comparative	Rank order	L	L	E
	Forced distribution	L	L	E
	Paired comparisons	L	L	E
Absolute	Essay (description)	L	H	D
	Numerical scale	L	L	E
	Descriptive scale	L	L	E
	Graphic rating scale	M	L	E
	BARS	H	L	E
	Checklist	M	L	E
	Critical incidents	M	H	M
	Product scale	M	L	E
	Forced choice	H	L	M

Key: H - high; L - low; M - moderate; D - difficult; E - easy.

CHECKLISTS FOR SELECTING NEEDS ASSESSMENT TECHNIQUES

A wide range of techniques is available for assessing management training and development needs. More than 40 techniques are described in various parts of this book, but many techniques have several variants and we have refrained from giving marginal, little-used and purely experimental techniques.

We have stressed, too, that several techniques have to be combined in most cases and that it would be risky to draw conclusions from information collected and analysed through only one technique. However, one should not expend so much time and effort in assessing needs that no energy and other resources are left to take action once the assessment is completed.

To facilitate the choice of techniques appropriate to different situations, it is useful to classify (or categorise) by several criteria. As no formally agreed categorisation is available, we present below some figures (1-3) in which certain criteria are applied to all techniques covered, thus pointing out some of their common features and differences. However, this appendix is intended to supplement, not to replace, the technical comments made when describing the techniques in the various chapters of the book.

1. General selection criteria

A useful general checklist for selection criteria was provided by S.V. Steadham.[1] It is as follows:

(1) What resources are required and available for the needs assessment?

    1.1 Time involved for both client system and the consultant in the needs assessment effort:

        – in developing the data collection process;

        – in administering or implementing the process.

    1.2 Money needed for the effort:

        – direct costs for processing a computerised survey;

        – indirect costs for excusing staff from regular duties for interviews.

(2) To what degree will the needs assessment consultant and the client system be involved in the design and administration of the data collection effort? What is to be gained by having the client system share responsibility for data collection:

  – In terms of increased awareness?

  – In terms of immediate problem-solving simply as a result of surfacing the needs data?

  – In terms of commitment to take action on basic findings?

(3) How "healthy" is the client system? Are there massive communication blocks that would preclude using certain collection methods such as group discussion? (For example: It would be inappropriate to use a method that could produce a mountain of needs data if there was already a low limit on budget expenditure for a programme response).

(4) Who is to be involved in the data collection?

  (What are the reasons certain people were excluded or included?)

(5) What does the client system intend to do with the assessment?

  (What are the limits or plans for using the assessment results?)

(6) Do the client system's decision-makers have a preference for one data collection method over another?

(7) To what extent does the client system already know the needs?

  (How clearly is the need already being articulated?)

(8) How much time-lag can there be between collecting the data and taking action?

(9) What types of "needs" are to be uncovered:

  – Needs felt by the actual or potential programme participant?

  – Needs which others (staff, for example) either observe or presume the programme participant has or should have?

(10) What degree of reliability or validity is needed by the client system to act on the data?

  (To what extent must programme participants agree with or accept the results of data collection?)

(11) How confidential or anonymous are the data to be?

(12) What is the level of trust between the client system and the consultant in the needs assessment effort?

  (How good is the relationship?)

(13) How comfortable is the needs assessment consultant with a particular method?

2. Needs assessment cycle

Figure 1 shows how the various needs assessment techniques are suitable for:

(1)	spotting organisational problems;

(2)	tracing problem areas and causes;

(3)	recognising individual (or group) performance problems;

(4)	determining management development needs;

(5)	separating training from non-training needs.

The nature of needs assessment purposes and activities for each element of the cycle requires only those techniques which are best suited to these purposes. For example, among the best techniques to spot organisational problems – the very first step in results-oriented assessment of management development needs – are such techniques as reports and records analysis, inter-firm comparisons, creativity techniques (brainstorming), etc. Using this table, the management development practitioner could first select the best set of needs assessment techniques for particular steps and then choose among selected techniques those which are simpler to practise and which correspond better to specific purposes of needs analysis.

3. Type of training and development needs

In figure 2, the techniques are assessed from the viewpoint of their suitability of finding out about:

(1)	knowledge;

(2)	skills;

(3)	attitudes;

(4)	managerial behaviour.

4. Cost-effectiveness

Cost-effectiveness is important since needs assessment could easily turn into a costly research project of limited practical use. Costs must be justified by results. Therefore the more complex (more difficult to use) and costly techniques must be chosen cautiously, if this is justified by the complexity of the situation and the expected results, and if resources are available both for the needs assessment and for subsequent action. Some indications on cost-effectiveness are given in figure 3.

Figure 1. Needs assessment techniques: The needs assessment cycle

Needs assessment technique	Dimension of needs assessment	Spotting organisational problems (1)	Tracing problem areas and causes (2)	Recognising individual (group) performance problems (3)	Determining management development needs (4)	Separating training from non-training needs (5)
Generic approaches	Problem analysis	XXX	XXX	XX	X	X
	Comparison		X	XX	XX	
	Expert opinion	XXX	XX	XX	XXX	XXX
Individual techniques	Job analysis			XXX	XXX	XX
	Job description			XXX	XX	XX
	Tests and examinations			X	XX	XXX
	Questionnaires	X	X	XX	XXX	XX
	Interviews	X	X	XX	XX	X
	Observations	X	XX	XX	XX	X
	Critical incidents	XX	XX	XX	X	XX
	Diary method	X	XX	XX	X	X
	Management by objectives	XX	XX	XX	XX	X
	Action learning	XXX	XXX	XXX	XX	XXX
	Performance appraisal			XXX	XXX	XXX
	Self-assessment			XX	XX	XXX
	Career planning			XX	XX	XXX
	Assessment centres			X	XX	XXX
Group techniques	Meetings of management teams	XX	XXX	XX	X	X
	Group meetings and discussions	X	X	XX	X	X
	Syndicates	XX	XX	XX	X	X
	Nominal group technique	X	XXX	XX	X	
	Group projects	XX	XX	XX	X	
	Group creativity techniques	XXX	XXX	XX	X	
	Simulation training techniques	X	X	XXX	XX	
	Sociograms	XX	XXX	X	XX	XX
	Behaviour modelling (analysis)	XX	XX	XX	X	
Organisational techniques	Records and reports analysis	XXX	XX	XX	XX	X
	Future trends and opportunities	XXX	X			
	Inter-firm comparison	XX	XX	X		
	Management (diagnostic) surveys	XX	XX	X	XX	
	Management development audits				XXX	XX
	Attitude surveys	XXX	X	XX		
	Management climate surveys	XX	XXX	XX	XX	
	Organisation development	XXX	XXX	XX	XX	X
	Structured PIP	XXX	XXX	XX	XX	X

Key: X - good; XX - very good; XXX - excellent.

Figure 2.   Needs assessment techniques: Type of training and development needs

Needs assessment technique		Dimension of needs assessment			
		Knowledge (1)	Skills (2)	Attitude (3)	Managerial behaviour (4)
Generic approaches	Problem analysis	X	XX	XX	XXX
	Comparison		XX		XX
	Expert opinion	XXX	XXX	XX	XX
Individual techniques	Job analysis	X	XX	X	
	Job description	X	XX	X	
	Tests and examinations	XXX	XXX	X	
	Questionnaires	XX	XX	XXX	X
	Interviews	XX	X	XXX	X
	Observations		XX	XXX	XXX
	Critical incidents	X	XX	XX	XX
	Diary method	X	X	XX	XXX
	Management by objectives	X	XX	X	
	Action learning	X	XX	XX	XX
	Performance appraisal	XXX	XXX	X	XX
	Self-assessment	XX	XX	XXX	XX
	Career planning	X	XX	XX	X
	Assessment centres	XX	XX	XX	X
Group techniques	Meetings of management teams	X	XX	XX	X
	Group meetings and discussions	X	X	XXX	X
	Syndicates	X	XX	XX	X
	Nominal group technique	X	XX	XX	
	Group projects	X	XX	XX	XX
	Group creativity techniques	XX	XXX	XXX	XX
	Simulation training techniques	X	XXX	XX	X
	Sociograms			XX	XXX
	Behaviour modelling (analysis)			XXX	XXX
Organisational techniques	Records and reports analysis		XXX	XX	XXX
	Future trends and opportunities	XX	X	X	
	Inter-firm comparison		XX		XX
	Management (diagnostic) surveys		X	XX	X
	Management development audits	XX	XXX	X	X
	Attitude surveys			XXX	X
	Management climate surveys		XX	XX	X
	Organisation development		XX	XXX	XX
	Structured PIP	X	XX	XX	XX

Key: X - good; XX - very good; XXX - excellent.

Figure 3. Needs assessment techniques: Cost-effectiveness

Needs assessment technique		Dimension of needs assessment		
		Developmental cost (1)	Cost of use (2)	How easy to use (3)
Generic approaches	Problem analysis	H	H	D
	Comparison	M	H	M
	Expert opinion	L	H	M
Individual techniques	Job analysis	H	H	M
	Job description	H	H	E
	Tests and examinations	H	H	M
	Questionnaires	H	M	M
	Interviews	H	H	M
	Observations	L	H	E
	Critical incidents	M	H	D
	Diary method	L	M	E
	Management by objectives	M	H	M
	Action learning	H	H	D
	Performance appraisal	H	H	M
	Self-assessment	M	L	E
	Career planning	H	H	D
	Assessment centres	H	H	D
Group techniques	Meetings of management teams	L	L	M
	Group meetings and discussions	L	L	E
	Syndicates	M	M	M
	Nominal group technique	H	M	M
	Group projects	H	H	D
	Group creativity techniques	H	H	D
	Simulation training techniques	H	H	D
	Sociograms	M	M	D
	Behaviour modelling (analysis)	M	M	M
Organisational techniques	Records and reports analysis	M	M	M
	Future trends and opportunities	M	H	D
	Inter-firm comparison	M	M	M
	Management (diagnostic) surveys	L	L	M
	Management development audits	H	H	D
	Attitude surveys	H	H	M
	Management climate surveys	M	H	M
	Organisation development	H	H	D
	Structured PIP	H	H	D

Key: H - high; M - moderate; L - low; D - difficult; E - easy.

5.   Personal and organisational preferences

In using any of these checklists, and any general rating of techniques concerning their suitability for dealing with one or another dimension of the problem at hand, personal and organisational preferences will play an important role. In particular, the user has to feel comfortable with the technique – he or she must regard it as a good and practical one, and be able to use it without difficulty. The clients (the managers whose needs are assessed) must not resent the technique (e.g. because it is too intrusive) or regard it as trivial and unproductive. Practical experience and common sense are your best advisers in choosing techniques.

---

[1] S.V. Steadham: "Learning to select a needs assessment strategy", in *Training and Development Journal* (Washington, DC), Jan. 1980, p. 57.